HUGH MCLEOD is Professor of Church History at the University of Birmingham. His previous publications include *Piety and Poverty* (1996) and *Religion and the People of Western Europe* (1997). He is president of the British branch of the international Church History organisation.

WERNER USTORF is Professor of Mission at the University of Birmingham. His first book was on the Kimbanguists in Zaire. He has also published books on missionaries in Togo and Ghana, and on the relationship between German missions and the Nazis.

The Decline of Christendom in Western Europe, 1750–2000

Christendom lasted for over a thousand years in western Europe, and we are still living in its shadow. For over two centuries this social and religious order has been in decline. Enforced religious unity has given way to increasing pluralism, and since 1960 this process has spectacularly accelerated. In this book, historians, sociologists and theologians from six countries answer two central questions: what is the religious condition of western Europe at the start of the twenty-first century? And how and why did Christendom decline? Beginning by overviewing the present situation, the authors then go back into the past, tracing the course of events in England, Ireland, France, Germany and the Netherlands, and showing how the fate of Christendom is reflected in changing attitudes to death and to technology, and in the evolution of religious language. They reveal a pattern more complex and ambiguous than any of the conventional narratives will admit.

HUGH McLEOD is Professor of Church History at the University of Birmingham. His previous publications include *Piety and Poverty* (1996) and *Religion and the People of Western Europe 1789–1989* (1997). He is president of the British branch of the International Church History Organisation.

WERNER USTORF is Professor of Mission at the University of Birmingham. His first book was on the Kimbanguists in Zaire. He has also published books on missionaries in Togo and Ghana, and on the relationship between German missions and the Nazis.

The Decline of Christendom in Western Europe, 1750–2000

edited by Hugh McLeod and Werner Ustorf

CAMBRIDGE
UNIVERSITY PRESS

PUBLISHED BY THE PRESS SYNDICATE OF THE UNIVERSITY OF CAMBRIDGE
The Pitt Building, Trumpington Street, Cambridge CB2 1RP, United Kingdom

CAMBRIDGE UNIVERSITY PRESS
The Edinburgh Building, Cambridge, CB2 2RU, UK
40 West 20th Street, New York, NY 10011-4211, USA
477 Williamstown Road, Port Melbourne, VIC 3207, Australia
Ruiz de Alarcón 13, 28014 Madrid, Spain
Dock House, The Waterfront, Cape Town 8001, South Africa

http://www.cambridge.org

First published 2003
Reprinted 2004

Printed in the United Kingdom at the University Press, Cambridge

Typeface Times 10/13 pt   *System* LATEX 2_ε [TB]

A catalogue record for this book is available from the British Library

Library of Congress Cataloguing in Publication data

ISBN 0 521 81493 6 hardback

Contents

Contributors

CALLUM G. BROWN is Professor of Religious and Cultural History, University of Strathclyde.

JEFFREY COX is Professor of History, University of Iowa.

SHERIDAN GILLEY is Reader in Theology, University of Durham.

MARTIN GRESCHAT is Emeritus Professor of Church History, University of Giessen.

EVA M. HAMBERG is Professor of Migration Studies, University of Lund.

DAVID HEMPTON is Professor of Church History, Boston University.

LUCIAN HÖLSCHER is Professor of Contemporary History, Ruhr University, Bochum.

THOMAS KSELMAN is Professor of History, University of Notre Dame.

MICHEL LAGRÉE was Professor of Modern History, University of Rennes. He died in 2001.

YVES LAMBERT is a member of the Groupe de Sociologie des Religions et de la Laïcité in the Centre National de la Recherche Scientifique, Paris.

HUGH McLEOD is Professor of Church History, University of Birmingham.

WERNER USTORF is Professor of Mission, University of Birmingham.

PETER VAN ROODEN is Reader in the Research Centre Religion and Society, University of Amsterdam.

Preface

This volume has grown out of a conference held in Paris in April 1997. It was the last of a series of three on the theme of 'The Rise and Decline of Christendom in Western Europe', organised by the History Group of the Missiology of Western Culture Project. The Group comprised Dr Neal Blough (Paris), Dr Alan Kreider (then Oxford), Prof. Hugh McLeod, and Prof. Werner Ustorf (both Birmingham). A. Kreider (ed.), *The Origins of Christendom in the West* (Edinburgh and New York: T&T Clark, 2001) was the result of the first of these conferences. The second focused on the period of the Reformation and Counter-Reformation.

The Missiology of Western Culture Project (1992–1997) was an ecumenical attempt by western missiologists to mobilise the thinking of specialists in a variety of disciplines about the interplay of the Christian message and churches with the culture of the contemporary west. Subsidised by substantial grants, notably from the Pew Charitable Trust (Philadelphia), the project sponsored study groups in seven areas (the arts, ecclesiology, epistemology, social structures and systems, history, the individual, and health and healing), and each group organised its own study processes and colloquia. The Project ended with the groups sharing their findings with each other in September 1997 in a major international consultation at the Bon Secours Center, Marriottsville, Maryland, USA. Their learnings are gradually appearing in print. The first direct fruits came from the Epistemology Group: J. A. Kirk and K. J. Vanhoozer (eds.), *To Stake a Claim: Mission and the Western Crisis of Knowledge* (Maryknoll: Orbis Books, 1999).

The editors of the present volume would like to thank Grace Davie and Loek Halman for their generous help.

1   Introduction

Hugh McLeod

In 312 the Emperor Constantine declared Christianity the religion of the Roman Empire. Thus began the 'Constantinian' or 'Christendom' era in the history of Christianity. After nearly three centuries of intermittent, but sometimes very severe, persecution by the civil authorities, Christianity was now in alliance with the powers that be. By the end of the fourth century a large part of the Roman elite had converted to Christianity and other forms of religious worship were prohibited. The process by which the mass of the population became fully integrated into the Christian church was much more long drawn out. Equally, a variety of rival religions continued to be privately practised long after they were officially proscribed. But a pattern of relations between church and state and between church and society had been established.[1] It would be repeated as Christianity spread to northern and eastern Europe and, much later, to the Americas. For the next 1500 years most Christians learnt and practised their faith in the context of 'Christendom'. That is, they lived in a society where there were close ties between the leaders of the church and those in positions of secular power, where the laws purported to be based on Christian principles, and where, apart from certain clearly defined outsider communities, every member of the society was assumed to be a Christian.

Naturally 'Christendom' has been challenged by non-Christians, whether in fourth-century Rome or in modern Europe. But it has also been a subject of intense debate between Christians. At most points of Christian history there have been those who have opposed the identity between church and society or over-close links between church and state, or between the church and social elites. From the fourth century onwards there have been Christians who saw these associations as damaging to the church: 'Christendom' meant that the church was subjected to state interference, that it was forced to admit into membership those who were not true Christians, and that it was under pressure to condone contemporary customs and values which were unchristian. Since the radical Reformation of the sixteenth century there have always been Christians in western Europe who have insisted, as a matter of principle, that the church should remain independent of the state and that Christians must not use coercion to enforce their beliefs. From the later seventeenth century, religious toleration was being advocated both for pragmatic reasons, and on the grounds of the rights of the individual conscience. With the rise of Liberalism in the nineteenth century the virtues of pluralism, voluntaryism and the free market in ideas began to be argued by many Christians, as well as by religious sceptics. At the same time, members of established churches often remained loyal to the ideal of 'Christendom', even if they accepted that political realities might require some dilution of the ideal. So throughout the nineteenth century, and well into the twentieth, the relations between church and state and church and society were central political issues, and even today the debate has not ended, though for most people it is no longer of such burning concern.

'Christianity' and 'Christendom' can be separated. There was Christianity for three centuries before Christendom. There are parts of the world, for instance China, where there has never been a Christendom, but where there are many millions of Christians. Christendom is no more than a phase in the history of Christianity, and it represents only one out of many possible relationships between church and society. Yet in western Europe this phase lasted for more than a thousand years, and we are still living in its shadow. There are few people who can contemplate the end of this particular era with detachment. There are some who mourn the decline of Christendom, and some who see it as a cause for celebration, while most, probably, have more mixed emotions. Members of all three groups are to be found among the contributors to this book.

I

In 1999 a substantial majority of west Europeans claimed to be Christians. According to the figures presented by Yves Lambert in this volume, the proportion of the population describing themselves as either Catholic or Protestant was as high as 89 per cent in Ireland, 88 per cent in Denmark and 85 per cent in Portugal. Only in the Netherlands and in the territory of the former East Germany[2] did the figure fall below 50 per cent, and France was the only other country where it fell below 60 per cent. Relatively impressive as these figures are, they should be compared with the overwhelmingly high levels of nominal Christian affiliation in the early 1960s. Even in East Germany 65 per cent of the population were then Protestant or Catholic, in the Netherlands around 80 per cent. In Britain the figure was 95 per cent, and in Denmark, Switzerland and the Irish Republic it was 99 per cent.[3] Up to the 1960s this general recognition of some kind of Christian identity was also reflected in very high rates of participation in the Christian rites of passage, though the popularity of the various rites varied between countries and religious traditions. For instance, the frequency of infant baptism was especially high in Catholic countries, and confirmation was especially widespread in Lutheran countries. Christian funeral rites predominated almost everywhere. In the 1990s the great majority of west Europeans continued to be buried or cremated with Christian rites. But the popularity of the other rites had declined, sometimes quite substantially. In France, for instance, between 1958 and 1990 the proportion of babies receiving Catholic baptism fell from 91 per cent to 51 per cent and the proportion of weddings with a Catholic ceremony fell from 79 per cent to 51 per cent.[4] This reflected the emergence of a substantial section of the population rejecting any kind of Christian identity, however tenuous, whether because they belonged to another faith or, more often, because they had no religion.

While levels of nominal Christian affiliation and participation in the rites of passage were still very high in 1960, levels of participation in Sunday worship or in communion varied greatly. At one extreme, over 90 per cent of the population were regular church-goers in the Irish Republic, and very high levels of attendance at mass were also found among the rural populations of Brittany, the Basque Country, the Veneto, and other traditionally pious Catholic regions. At the other extreme, weekly attendance fell below 5 per cent in many parts of Scandinavia, as well as in the 'dechristianised' regions of central France. In the 1990s, the highest levels of church-going were still found in Ireland and in some rural regions of Italy and Portugal, but there had been a general levelling down. Quite large drops have been seen in some areas previously known for their piety, whereas there has been a more modest decline in other areas where attendance was already low.[5]

The signs were that belief in various Christian tenets and doctrines declined between the 1960s and the 1990s, though there is insufficient evidence to say whether the figures for the 1960s represent a decline from a higher level at some earlier point.[6] Admittedly, questionnaires may be too blunt a tool to elucidate some of the complexities and ambiguities of individual belief. For instance, while about two-thirds of west Europeans will say when asked that they believe in God, this does not tell us very much, as conceptions of God vary so greatly. This is even more true of beliefs concerning the after-life, where the findings of surveys often appear to be contradictory. For instance, in a number of countries the proportion of respondents claiming to believe in heaven exceeds the proportion claiming to believe in a life after death.[7]

The area of most evident conflict between established Christian teaching and contemporary practice is that of sexual ethics. Before the 1960s there had often been a wide divergence between the generally recognised rules of sexual morality and what people actually did. But the rules were those laid down by the churches. The 'sexual revolution' of the 1960s opened up all aspects of sex for discussion and debate, and for explicit description in books and films, leading to widespread rejection of the churches' teaching that sex was only morally right within heterosexual marriage. The 1960s and 1970s also mark a turning-point in the relationship between Christianity and the laws relating to sex, marriage and the family. Britain set the trend with the liberalisation of the laws on obscenity (1959), abortion (1967) and divorce (1969), legalisation of homosexual acts between consenting adults (1967), abolition of theatre censorship (1968), and provision of contraceptives to unmarried couples through the National Health Service (1967). In Britain, Christian opinion on all of these issues was divided. While many of the leaders in the movements for change were themselves secularists, there was also a significant degree of support for these reforms from within the churches. So the forces for change were varied, including growing secularist influence, changes in Christian opinion, and also a realisation that in an increasingly pluralistic society some compromise was needed between the various and conflicting moral standards that were current. Thus the extension of the legally permitted grounds for abortion was opposed by Roman Catholics and by many evangelical Christians, committed to the 'right to life'. But it fell a long way short of granting the 'abortion on demand' for which feminists were campaigning. It was supported by many Christians on the pragmatic grounds that legal abortion was at least preferable to the widely prevalent 'backstreet' abortions. The legalisation of divorce in Italy and Ireland, and of abortion in France, Belgium and Italy, marked more unequivocally a defeat for the church in those countries.[8]

One may ask, therefore, what is left of Christendom in western Europe at the beginning of the twenty-first century.[9] A considerable proportion of west European countries retain links of one kind or another between church and state. In Germany and Scandinavia there is the church tax system, which has placed the churches in those countries in a uniquely favourable financial position. In Belgium the state pays the salaries of the clergy. In England twenty-six Anglican bishops have seats in the House of Lords. In Italy the church–state treaty of 1984 contained very favourable terms for the Catholic Church. Maybe there are four other areas in which the remains of Christendom are still visible. First there are the rites of passage. Even in those countries where marriage in church and the baptism of infants have seen a major decline, they remain quite widespread, and are asked for by many couples who seldom go to church at other times. In other countries participation in these rites remains the general practice. And in nearly all countries Christian funerals are heavily predominant – whether or not, as Callum Brown suggests, this is beginning to change. Second there is education. In some countries, such as England and the Netherlands, there are considerable numbers of church schools. In most countries (France being the major exception) religious education is provided in state schools. Though this education may no longer be exclusively Christian, and though there may be an increasing emphasis on 'balance', it inevitably includes a major element of teaching on Christianity, often by teachers who are trained in theology. In some countries, including Germany and Italy, this teaching has a strongly confessional character. A third area is that of welfare and charity.

In Germany, a major part of the public welfare system is church-based. In every country a large proportion of private charities have religious origins, and religious motivation continues to be important for many of those working for them. A fourth area is the role of 'public conscience' which churches may still perform even in apparently very secular societies. This is perhaps most evident in totalitarian societies, such as East Germany where the Protestant churches were among the very few bodies enjoying some limited degree of independence and where they accordingly became a major forum for the expression of dissent and played an important part in the protest movements culminating in the fall of the Communist regime in 1989–90.[10] But even in democratic and pluralist societies the churches may have a unique role, because of their ability to mount a moral, rather than purely political, critique of government. For instance in the 1980s the British churches mounted a sustained attack on the policies of Margaret Thatcher's administration, to which Thatcher herself felt obliged to respond, and in France the Catholic Church has played an important part in speaking up for the rights of immigrants and combating racism.[11]

II

The decline of Christendom has been a very long drawn out process, and the historian can distinguish between several distinct stages. First, there was the toleration by the state of a variety of forms of Christianity. Second, there was the open publication of anti-Christian ideas. Third was the separation of church and state. The fourth and the most complex phase has been the gradual loosening of the ties between church and society.

To begin with the rise of toleration:[12] in the wake of the Reformation, the principle was generally adopted that all subjects should follow the religion of their king, whether Catholic, Lutheran, Reformed or Anglican. But even in the sixteenth century there were some states where the application of this principle was not practicable. Several German cities, most notably Augsburg, adopted the principle of 'parity', whereby Catholics and Lutherans enjoyed equal rights. In Poland, the nobility, whose members acted as patrons to a variety of religious communities, agreed in 1573 to a regime of toleration, and this was accepted by successive monarchs.[13] During the French Wars of Religion in the second half of the sixteenth century, a *politique* party emerged which saw attempts to impose religious orthodoxy as a threat to the peace of the kingdom, and so tried to achieve a *modus vivendi* between Catholics and Calvinists. The wars ended with a Catholic victory, but the Edict of Nantes (1598) allowed partial toleration for the Protestants. During the seventeenth century, Catholicism became increasingly dominant in France and Poland. In France, especially, the rights of the Protestant minority were gradually whittled away, and then abolished entirely by the Revocation of the Edict of Nantes in 1685. But in various other parts of Europe the seventeenth century saw growing toleration, whether *de facto*, as in the Dutch Republic, or supported by law, as in Prussia (1685) or England and Wales (1689). Scotland followed in 1712. The reasons for this were mainly pragmatic. In Prussia, economic considerations were paramount. In the Dutch Republic, as it emerged from the long war against Spain, only the Reformed Church had the status of a 'public church', but with nearly half the population belonging to other religious communities, the imposition of uniformity would have been impossible. In England the chaotic conditions of civil war in the 1640s and 1650s had led to a huge growth in religious diversity, and subsequent attempts to restore religious unity were a failure. The kind of toleration that European states were prepared to allow in the seventeenth century remained limited. For instance both England and Prussia extended toleration only to certain specified groups, rather than laying down a general principle. And in England, as in the Dutch Republic, religious minorities continued to suffer political disabilities.

However, more radical experiments in toleration were taking place in some of the British colonies in North America. The Baptist founders of Rhode Island and the Quaker founders of Pennsylvania introduced freedom of religion as a matter of principle, and the Catholic founders of Maryland were required by the British crown to allow equal rights to Protestants. In the later seventeenth century important steps were also being taken in the intellectual case for toleration, notably in John Locke's *Letter on Toleration*. The eighteenth century saw the gradual emergence in most parts of Europe of a public opinion which favoured toleration as a matter of principle, though changes in the law were delayed until the 1770s and 1780s. In England and Ireland (1778) first steps were taken towards the abolition of the anti-Catholic Penal Laws. Toleration laws were also enacted in Catholic Austria and France (1781 and 1787) and Lutheran Hamburg (1785).

In a few west European countries, only one form of Christianity was legally recognised until the middle or later years of the nineteenth century. For instance, laws on religious freedom were enacted in Denmark in 1848, in Sweden in 1860 and in Spain in 1869. More generally, however, even those states which had long allowed religious minorities freedom of worship were often slow to grant them full civic equality. The process by which Christian minorities, Jews and unbelievers gained civic equality belongs to a later stage in the history of the dissolution of Christendom.[14]

Those countries, England and the Dutch Republic, where Christian minorities first gained the right to worship were also those where the open avowal of religious scepticism first became possible. In England, the abolition of censorship in 1694 was followed by the publication of a number of books advocating Deism. Deists believed in a creator God, knowledge of whom could be achieved by observation of nature and the use of reason, but they rejected all revealed religions, such as Judaism, Christianity and Islam. In the early eighteenth century, Deism was fashionable in England. In countries like France, where a stringent censorship continued at least until the 1740s, books attacking orthodox Christianity were smuggled in from the Dutch Republic, and there was also a growing underground literature. Indeed it was in France, the former stronghold of Catholic orthodoxy, that religious scepticism began to take a more radical turn. The first widely influential advocate of atheism in France was a country priest, Jean Meslier, who died in 1729, leaving a *Testament* which anticipated most of what would become the standard atheist arguments, and which enjoyed a cult status among religiously sceptical French intellectuals.[15]

By the second half of the eighteenth century, Deism had become one of the standard religious options for men of the aristocracy and the wealthy bourgeoisie; and atheism, though more daring, and indeed repugnant to many Deists as well as to devout Christians, was a recognised possibility. During this period there is considerable statistical evidence from France and Germany of a decline in various forms of religious observance, especially in the towns and among members of the middle class. For instance, in the first half of the eighteenth century it had been common for German Protestants, both in town and country, to receive communion three times in the year. But by the early nineteenth century this was rare, and there were many who did not go to communion at all. In the towns the fastest decline took place between 1750 and 1800. During that period the ratio of communions to Protestant population fell from 115 per cent to 20 per cent in Hanover, from 150 per cent to 40 per cent in Berlin, and from 100 per cent to 45 per cent in Hamburg.[16] In France, where religious statistics have been studied far more intensively than anywhere else, all the figures seem to have moved in a downward direction around 1750: recruitment to the priesthood and to religious orders, both male and female, was declining; religious books were declining as a proportion both of all books published and of those found in private libraries; the church's teachings on sex were being less widely obeyed; and fewer people wanted masses to be said for their souls after their death. Ralph Gibson, after summarising the French evidence, concludes: 'Each element taken separately is subject to major problems of interpretation, but taken together they form an impressive body of evidence. In nearly every case the middle of the eighteenth century seems to be a turning-point.'[17]

A turning to what, though? The most popular answer is that we are witnessing a process of 'secularisation' and 'dechristianisation'. This was the conclusion reached by Michel Vovelle in his pioneering study of wills in southern France, where he used this evidence to argue that major changes were taking place in attitudes to death.[18] Similar ideas have been presented by other historians, who have detected in roughly the same period the emergence of new forms of political, social and scientific thought independent of any religious reference. The best-known example would be the Utilitarianism of Beccaria and Bentham, which aimed to devise a science of law and morals based on the principle of 'the greatest happiness of the greatest number'. Attitudes to deviant behaviour were also changing under the impact of new scientific concepts: Michael MacDonald, in another statistical study, has identified a 'Secularization of Suicide' in England between 1660 and 1800, reflected in the increasing tendency of coroners' juries to decide that those who had killed themselves were suffering from mental illness, rather than acting at the instigation of the devil, as had been previously assumed.[19] On the other hand, as Thomas Kselman argues in this volume, it is equally possible to see these developments as examples of religious change rather than religious decline. By the 1770s the French clergy themselves were bequeathing less money for requiem masses; as Gibson suggests, the most likely explanation is not a massive loss of faith, but that 'the "baroque" attitude to death that expressed itself in rich ceremony was under attack from eighteenth-century taste, which preferred less extravagant treatment of death'.[20] Lucian Hölscher goes much further down this road, arguing that the eighteenth century brought not a decline of Christianity, but a reinterpretation – and one that was entirely beneficial. He claims that 'the period saw an heroic breakthrough in the development of modern piety'. He mentions, for instance, the shift towards a more personal piety, dependent on individual commitment rather than legal compulsion; the increasing association between Christianity and schemes of social amelioration; and a more tolerant mentality, reflected in better relations between the Lutheran, Reformed and Catholic confessions.[21]

In so far as Christendom depended on conformism and a degree of coercion, these developments were undermining Christendom, without necessarily undermining Christianity. In so far as they made it possible to think about various aspects of the world and various areas of life without having to presuppose the existence of supernatural powers, they potentially prepared the way for a more secular society, but they did not necessarily lead in that direction. In fact, as I shall suggest later, the nineteenth century was, from many points of view, a time of increased religious fervour, and one in which the social significance of the churches grew.

The eighteenth century ended with further important steps in the direction of the decline of Christendom. In 1791 the Separation of church and state was written into the Constitution of the United States, and laws of Separation were also enacted in France in 1795 and the Netherlands in 1796. However, in France church and state were reunited as early as 1801 – though in a novel form, since Protestants and Jews as well as Catholics were supported by and subjected to a measure of control by the state.[22] The defeat of Napoleon in 1815 meant that the alliance of throne, altar and château was in power again across most of Europe. But Separation returned to the political agenda in the second half of the nineteenth century, when it became a normal part of Radical and later Socialist programmes. It was enacted in Ireland in 1869, in France in 1905, in Geneva in 1907, in Germany in 1919, in Wales in 1920 and in Spain in 1931. In Sweden this happened as recently as 2000, and in several countries, including Belgium, Denmark, England and several Swiss cantons, no formal Separation has taken place. The question of the formal relationship between church and state has often had great symbolic significance. Secularists and members of religious minorities have seen the Separation as an act of cleansing, while members of established churches have often been passionately committed to retaining a formal connection with the state. But the practical significance of such laws, and the circumstances in which they have been enacted, have varied greatly. In France and Spain, for instance, the proponents of Separation were mainly militant anti-clericals who hoped by crippling the Catholic Church to weaken the forces of political conservatism.[23] In Germany on the other hand, most of the powers and privileges of the Protestant and Catholic Churches were left intact.[24] In general the formal relationship between church and state has been less significant than the role given to the churches or to religion in the schools, in the welfare system or in other public institutions. In France in the 1880s, church and state were formally united, but the government imposed a sweeping secularisation of the education system; on the other hand, in Ireland in the 1920s, 1930s and 1940s, where church and state were formally separated, the Catholic Church was allowed a dominant position in education and welfare, and when bishops intervened in politics, politicians felt obliged to take notice.[25]

In questions to do with church and state and the role of religion in public institutions, there is no single European pattern, but there have been wide differences from country to country. In a few cases the Separation of church and state has taken a violent form, with the state changing from protector to persecutor. The prototype here was the French revolutionary 'dechristianisation' of 1793–4. One could also mention the killing of thousands of Catholic priests and nuns by the Spanish republicans during the Civil War of 1936–9, and the less violent, but more sustained and comprehensive attack on Christianity in East Germany between 1949 and 1989. But forcible dechristianisation has been the exception in western Europe. Overall the trend has been a gradual movement away from 'Christendom' towards a society whose institutions and laws reflect a pluralism in which a wide variety of religious groups, as well as other people with a more secular orientation, each have their place. Other trends have been for the state to take over functions formerly performed by the church, and for trained professionals to take over roles that once belonged to priests, nuns, or others impelled by a sense of religious vocation. But these changes have often been slow, and are by no means completed even at the present day.[26]

Questions concerning the role of the church and of religious teaching in the education system were at the centre of political debate in the second half of the nineteenth century, and remained so throughout the twentieth. Although the state assumed control of education in Prussia as early as 1794, and in most other countries during the nineteenth century, this seldom meant that schooling was in any real sense secularised. Religious teaching was generally provided in state schools; in many countries there were also church schools, partly or wholly funded by the state; and the state in many cases funded Theology faculties in the universities. For much of the nineteenth and twentieth centuries there were large numbers of teachers who were clergymen or nuns. A striking example of the latter phenomenon was the English 'public schools' where most of the rulers of the British Empire were educated in the later nineteenth and early twentieth centuries, and which even today educate a large proportion of those who go on to leading positions in industry, commerce and the professions. In the nineteenth and early twentieth centuries the overwhelming majority of these schools were headed by an Anglican clergymen, and still today they have a full-time chaplain and pupils are required to attend regular services in the school chapel.

The classic attempt at introducing an entirely secular system of state education was made by the French in the 1880s. Not only was religious teaching stopped and priests excluded from teaching in state schools, but Catholic schools were refused any form of state funding. Moreover, teaching on ethics and citizenship was introduced to take the place of religion, and many of the teachers were convinced freethinkers. The remarkable point is how few imitators the French system has found. In so far as there has been a 'decline of Christendom' within the education system, it has generally happened in more subtle ways. One obvious change has been the recent switch from a religious education designed to strengthen Christian identity and to train future church-members to one intended to provide information about religion and to enable students to make an informed choice as to the kind of religion they might choose to adopt.[27] Here the pioneer seems to have been Sweden, where the change to a more 'objective' religious education reflected the frequent suspicion of the Lutheran Church among members of the dominant Social Democratic party. More recently the pressure for change has come mainly as a result of the large-scale immigration into western Europe in the 1950s, 1960s and 1970s of Muslims, Hindus and Sikhs from Turkey and from former colonies in Africa, Asia and the Caribbean. One can also argue that even where the state provides for, or even requires, religious teaching in the schools, the subject is often given a low priority. But there is no unilinear trend. For instance, in England and Wales religious education assumed a higher profile during World War II. It was the 1944 Education Act that for the first time made religious education compulsory and also decreed that the school day should begin with a collective act of worship.

The state has also generally continued to fund chaplaincies in the armed forces and in such institutions as hospitals and prisons. Here again, the main change has been that since the 1960s and 1970s, in addition to the longstanding presence of small numbers of Jewish rabbis, there has also been a growing number of chaplains of other non-Christian faiths. In the United Kingdom, which in 1969 became one of the last west European states to abolish capital punishment, a telling example of the continuing significance of such chaplaincies was the prominent part played by chaplains in ministering to condemned prisoners – often concluding by giving them communion on the morning of the execution.[28] Again France provides an exception to the general rule, in that the secularisation of municipal hospitals in the 1870s and 1880s included the abolition of chaplaincies.[29] Only a relatively small number of military chaplains were allowed, though in World War I, when priests were conscripted, many of them doubled the roles of combatant and unofficial chaplain.[30]

The most long-drawn-out and the most elusive process has been the gradual loosening of the ties between church and society. In Christendom, Christianity was a common language, shared by the devout, the lukewarm and even the secretly sceptical, through which a wide range of social needs could be met, and which provided generally accepted concepts and symbols. These could be drawn upon by more or less everyone, especially in times of collective crisis, or in situations of personal danger or tragedy. A good example, as Thomas Kselman shows, is the general use, at least in traditionally Catholic countries, of the cross to mark the place of burial. In 'Christendom', to be baptised not only marked entry into the church: it also meant entry into society. In England, before the introduction of civil registration in 1836, the Anglican baptismal registers provided the only official record that a person had been born. Until the nineteenth century this linking of civil and ecclesiastical requirements was commonplace. In Sweden, for instance, those wishing to marry needed to provide a confirmation certificate. While Liberal legislation often removed such formal requirements, the social pressures towards religious conformity remained considerable.

The decline of Christendom has meant that Christianity has been gradually losing its status as a lingua franca, and has tended to become a local language used by those who are professing Christians, but not understood by others. This process began as early as the 1790s, with the short-lived but extremely intensive campaign to 'dechristianise' France. New rituals were created to replace those of the churches, and 'masquerades' were performed with the aim of discrediting Catholic ceremonies through ridicule. A new calendar was produced which had no Sundays or saints' days.[31] In the short run the dechristianisation was a failure. Indeed it helped to spark off a Catholic revival in France during the later 1790s.[32] But many of those on the French Left cherished the dream of devising a new sacred language, rooted in the ideals of 1789, which would take the place of Catholicism. In the later nineteenth and twentieth centuries, the dream reached partial realisation as the Socialist and later the Communist movements built up a vast militant subculture, with its own rituals, symbols and celebrations, its own 'saints' and its own esoteric jargon. By the 1920s and 1930s, Paris was surrounded by a 'Red Belt', in which Socialism and Communism had become a way of life for a large part of the working-class population,[33] and one aspect of this for many people was a thorough detachment from Catholicism. The most visible symbol of detachment was the secular funeral, with red flags taking the place of the cross, and singing of the *Internationale* instead of Christian hymns.[34] Although relations with traditional religion varied considerably from country to country, Socialist or Communist politics had a similarly central role in working-class communities in many parts of Europe, and frequently took on the character of a new faith.[35]

Yet this new faith had its limits. Except in a relatively few places, it did not entirely succeed in dislodging the old faith. As a mainly working-class phenomenon, it was vulnerable to rising levels of social mobility in the later part of the twentieth century. It was also much more successful in appealing to men than to women. There were many households where the men talked about atheism in the pub or in public meetings while the women were passing on Christianity to the younger generation.[36] Furthermore, while priests and cadres might agree that church and party were incompatible, the rank and file often thought otherwise: adoption of the new faith did not necessarily mean a rejection of the old. In the working-class suburbs of Berlin, for instance, which were Communist and Social Democratic strongholds during the Weimar Republic, the overwhelming majority of infants continued to be baptised and adolescents to be confirmed.[37]

Socialism and Communism as an alternative faith and a way of life have certainly been in decline since the 1980s, and in many respects the decline started earlier.[38] At the end of the twentieth century the signs were that a new pluralism was emerging, with many attempts being made to devise new sacred languages, but with none yet achieving widespread acceptance. In Britain the marriage ceremony has become a major field for experimentation and, as Callum Brown suggests, funeral rites may become so. The possibility of an explicitly Humanist funeral has long existed, but so far has remained relatively uncommon. It is more likely that experimentation will take the form of the mixing of language and symbolism drawn from a variety of sources, including the Christian and the more broadly 'spiritual' – reflecting eclecticism, and indeed a recognition of the different beliefs and needs of different mourners, rather than any self-conscious secularism.[39]

In the nineteenth century the distancing from the church of certain social groups was reflected in declining attendance at Sunday church services. In France during the first half of the nineteenth century the most conspicuous absentees were middle-class men. There was a 'return to the church' by many of the middle class after the revolution of 1848, and the fears unleashed by the working-class uprising in Paris in the summer of that year. In the second half of the nineteenth century, however, large sections of the working class and the peasantry were giving up going to church.[40] While each country had its own distinctive patterns of church-going, the tendency for the working class to go to church less than those in other classes was common to most parts of Europe.[41] Not that absence from church necessarily meant a lack of religious belief. The phenomenon of 'believing without belonging' identified by Grace Davie in Britain in the 1990s[42] was already widespread in the nineteenth and early twentieth centuries. As Sarah Williams and others have shown, those who seldom went to church often insisted that they were believing and practising Christians, and many of them continued to take part in pilgrimages or processions, or to pray, sing hymns or read the Bible at home.[43] But their Christianity was likely to be significantly different from that of the regular church-goer. It was certainly likely to be distant from the church as an institution, and maybe also from some of the official doctrines and ethical teachings of the church.

The existence of 'Christendom' did not preclude considerable tensions between clergy and laity or between religious and secular values. Widespread anti-clericalism is to be expected in any society where the church is wealthy and influential, and is quite compatible with high levels of devotion. But the morality taught by the church was often in competition with other moral values. Among the aristocracies of eighteenth-century Europe, loyalty to family and an overriding concern with family and personal honour were powerful alternatives to religiously based morality, and found expression in feuds, duels and marriages based entirely on considerations of money or status. Equally contrary to any Christian ethic was the double standard of sexual morality, widely accepted and practised by upper-class men. Among the poor the overriding concern was with survival, and this sometimes led to infanticide, as well as to theft and prostitution.[44] All of this continued in the nineteenth century. The novelty of the situation in the later nineteenth and twentieth centuries, and more especially in the period after 1960, lay not so much in the fact that the precepts of Christian morality were being widely ignored in practice, but more in the fact that alternative principles were being openly advocated. For instance, from about 1890 there was a growing literature advocating sexual liberation through rejection of the limits imposed by monogamous heterosexual marriage. Again it was only in the 1960s that these ideas became generally popularised, and underpinned by ideals of individual self-fulfilment and rejection of formal moral codes.

III

As for why Christendom has declined in western Europe, the theories are many and varied. The most widely popular of these is the secularisation thesis, according to which the decline of Christendom is just one example of a general decline of religious belief and a marginalisation of religious institutions in modern societies. This idea goes back to Emile Durkheim and Max Weber at the end of the nineteenth century, and beyond them to Auguste Comte, whose *Cours de philosophie positive* was published between 1830 and 1842.[45] The principle that secularisation and modernisation go hand in hand was systematically developed in the 1960s and 1970s by such sociologists as Bryan Wilson and Peter Berger,[46] and in more recent times this thesis has been defended against all comers in numerous publications by Steve Bruce. Wilson defines secularisation as 'the process by which religion loses social significance',[47] and argues that this has happened in every modern society, including those like the United States where religious institutions appear to be flourishing. Bruce, whose *magnum opus* on *Religion in the Modern World* is subtitled 'From Cathedrals to Cults', argues that, whereas religion once acted as a binding force, the 'irreversible' trend towards individualism in modern societies has caused religion to fragment, leading ultimately to a pick 'n' mix approach, where each individual buys a packet suited to her or his own tastes, and the resulting chaos neutralises religion as a social force.[48] Elsewhere, Bruce has defined the social processes which have promoted secularisation.[49] First there is 'social differentiation', as a result of which a variety of specialised institutions and professions have arisen to take the place of functions which, in earlier societies, were the preserve of the church and the clergy. Second, there is 'societalization', meaning the growing power of the state, of bureaucracies and of large corporations. According to Bruce, religion flourishes best in small communities, marked by face-to-face relationships, and bound together by shared beliefs. Third, there is 'the growth of technical rationality, which gradually displaced supernatural influences and moral considerations from ever-wider areas of public life, replacing them by considerations of objective performance and practical expedience'.

But while those historians who deal with religion only in passing have often accepted the 'secularisation thesis' as a proven fact, specialists have tended to be more sceptical. Some have argued that secularisation is a useful description of the main trends in European religion over the last two or three centuries, but that the secularisation thesis is inadequate as an explanation. Some have argued for a 'European exceptionalism', according to which secularisation describes the way in which modernisation has happened in western Europe, but the relationship between religion and modernity has taken other forms in other parts of the world.[50] Some have argued that the decline of Christendom should not be equated with a decline of religion in general: Christianity has adapted and will continue to do so, and a whole range of new religious options has emerged.[51] Others have gone much further in their rejection of the traditional wisdom. Their objections have been both empirical and theoretical. The empirical objections have been presented particularly strongly by Callum Brown and Peter van Rooden. Here and elsewhere they have argued that Christianity remained central to Scottish and Dutch society respectively until the 1950s, and that the kind of drastic erosion of Christian influence which secularisation theory predicts happened only from the 1960s. Thus they accept the reality of contemporary secularisation, but they deny that it has happened in the way that the various theories of secularisation would lead one to expect.[52] The theoretical objections have been presented by Sarah Williams and Lucian Hölscher. Both claim that theories of secularisation depend on a narrowly institutional definition of religion, and tend to overlook both popular religion (the area highlighted by Williams) and the wider diffusion through society of religious identities, symbols and values (the area emphasised by Hölscher).[53]

Two overlapping alternatives to the secularisation thesis are those which focus on pluralism and on competition as defining characteristics of the modern world. According to the first view, all overarching institutions and systems of belief are vulnerable in the modern world, but religious beliefs and institutions are no more so than others. Similarly, the nature of social change in the nineteenth century meant that no institution or social group could play such a central role as the churches had done in the sixteenth and seventeenth centuries. Thus Anthony Steinhoff, after emphasising the importance of religion and the churches in Europe between about 1830 and 1960, goes on to argue:

during the modern period *no single force* drives the processes of social and cultural evolution. Rather, change emerges out of a bumpy, constantly shifting interplay of factors, among which are religion and confession . . . Indeed, the advent of modernity complicates considerably our ability to make sense of religious change, for greater room for individual autonomy emerges and the new modes for social interaction develop.[54]

While many historians and sociologists have depicted modern Christianity as battling with social forces beyond its control, others have insisted that the fate of a church lies in its own hands. A second way of challenging the secularisation thesis is the 'supply-side' approach to understanding religious change, focusing on the kinds of religion that are available and the ways that these are being marketed. This approach is especially popular in the United States, and is associated with sociologists such as Stark, Iannaccone and Finke.[55] They argue that the decline of religion in any given country is due to factors specific to that country or to the kinds of religion which happen to be available in that country, and should not be attributed to the nature of modern societies in general. Members of this latter school of thought tend to be especially enthusiastic about the virtues of pluralism and competition, and they often attribute the problems faced by Christianity in Europe to the undue prominence of inflexible, monopolistic state churches, offering the consumer little choice. Eva Hamberg is sympathetic to this line of argument which, she feels, offers some clues towards interpreting the religious situation in Sweden. Writers in this school tend to take the United States as the best example of the alliance between religion and modernity, though they also tend to highlight developments in

East Asia, especially Korea, where impressive economic growth has gone hand in hand with religious growth.

There are also many more pragmatic historians who have contented themselves with showing how the decline of Christendom happened in a particular country, city, region or even village, without relating this particular story to any general theory of modern religious development – except perhaps in a negative way, by showing that the general theories are oversimplified.[56]

Even highly theoretical accounts usually include at least an implied chronology, and for more pragmatic historians chronology is of fundamental importance. Historians using the same concepts may have radically different ideas as to when and why the decisive changes took place. For instance, a broad distinction can be drawn between those who locate the key developments in the seventeenth and eighteenth centuries – or even earlier; those who highlight developments in the period between the French Revolution and the Second World War; and those who argue that the most significant changes have taken place since World War II, or maybe since 1960.

Those who see the decisive changes as taking place in the seventeenth and eighteenth centuries, or earlier, are likely to highlight changes in ideas and especially changes in the thinking of an educated elite. They emphasise the importance of the Enlightenment, especially in its non-Christian or anti-Christian phases. They also stress the many-sidedness of Enlightenment influence in such fields as politics, law and morals. This line of argument has a long history, and it has been especially influential in France, where it relates to the question of the 'intellectual origins of the French Revolution', and where, in any case, the Enlightenment took an anti-Christian form more often than elsewhere in Europe. On the other hand, it has always been vulnerable to the objection that the impact of the Enlightenment on the mass of the population was very limited, and that to focus on a few aristocratic and bourgeois sceptics is to overlook the massive social influence of the church and clergy and the strength of popular piety. Furthermore, the trend of recent scholarship has been to stress that a rational Christianity was more typical of the eighteenth-century elites than scepticism or irreligion.[57] Those who seek to trace a continuous line from Voltaire to twenty-first-century atheists also tend to overlook the fact that the first half of the nineteenth century saw a revival of more conservative forms of Christianity both among intellectuals and among the aristocracy and bourgeoisie more widely.[58]

With the rise of social history in the 1960s and 1970s, historians began to focus more on industrialisation and urbanisation as key stages in the history of modern Christianity, and a lively debate has ensued as to the role that fundamental social changes have played in the decline of Christendom.[59] This has often been linked with the long-running debate as to whether, and if so why, the working class was 'dechristianised' in the nineteenth century. At least four reasons have been suggested as to why the rise of industry and of great cities may have played a key part in the decline of Christendom. The first, and least controversial, argument is that the dramatic demographic shifts of the nineteenth century presented the churches with logistical problems which they failed to solve, or which were exacerbated by being addressed in ways that proved counterproductive. Insufficient churches and schools were built, and insufficient numbers of new clergy were recruited to meet the needs of fast-growing cities and industrial regions; high rates of mobility within those regions meant that migrants to the cities found it difficult to establish links with any particular clergyman or congregation. Moreover, in order to raise the necessary funds, established churches often formed close links with employers and they protected themselves from attacks by anti-clerical Liberal politicians by forming alliances with conservative parties; the result of these links was the alienation from the church of many of the working class.[60] This argument is relatively uncontroversial and would probably be accepted by most historians as a broadly accurate account of the ways in which urbanisation and industrialisation contributed to secularisation in the specific circumstances of nineteenth-century Europe. However, some historians and sociologists have posited a more general relationship. A second argument is that great cities are by their nature pluralistic: they lend themselves to the formation of numerous discrete subcultures, as supervision of morals and religion by employers, magistrates or the church is no longer possible. This in turn leads to a relativistic outlook, in terms of which all religious and moral absolutes are called in question.[61] A third argument focuses on the major advances in living standards and life expectancy that have become possible in modern industrial societies. As a result of these advances, the range of situations in which purely human solutions to human problems are available has been greatly extended. The crises in which people feel the need to 'turn to' religion have become more infrequent. Religion consequently has become less salient to most people's lives.[62] The fourth and most ambitious argument proposes that industrialisation has brought about a mental revolution, as a result of which a rationalistic and mechanistic way of thinking has come to prevail, and all forms of supernaturalism have lost their credibility.[63] However, there is quite a lot of evidence that would call in question the last of these arguments – not least that collected by Yves Lambert, which suggests that the decline of Catholic beliefs in France has been closely paralleled by the rise of alternative forms of supernaturalism.[64]

While social changes in the nineteenth century were undermining the foundations of Christendom, political changes did this more directly. In so far as Christendom was sustained by social hierarchy and by the use of coercion, it was weakened by the emergence of new Liberal elites. With the shift towards democracy and the emergence of mass politics at the end of the nineteenth century, some of their ideas were taken much further by Radical and Socialist politicians. Another chronology of Christendom in decline, therefore, focuses on the legacy of 1789 and 1848.[65]

In the 1980s and especially the 1990s there was, however, a growing tendency for historians to emphasise the continuing vitality of Christendom in the nineteenth century and the first half of the twentieth. Olaf Blaschke, for instance, has called the period 1830–1960 'the second era of confessionalisation'.[66] This vitality partly reflected the fact that large parts of the European population still lived in a highly traditional rural environment. But it also arose from the durability of old beliefs and practices in a new environment and the ability of the Christian churches to adapt and innovate. In Scotland, one of the most highly urbanised and industrialised countries in the world, the influence of Christianity and the churches, according to Callum Brown, remained central until the middle of the twentieth century. This was reflected in, for instance, the huge audiences attending Billy Graham's evangelistic Crusades in the 1950s, the continuing role of sectarianism, the prominence of clergymen and devout laymen in local government, and especially the part played by the churches in defining the norms of morality, including thrift, temperance, sabbatarianism, respectability and sexual restraint.[67] Peter van Rooden, in his contribution to this volume, argues a similar case in respect of the Netherlands, emphasising the all-embracing role from the 1880s to the 1950s of confessional subcultures, and the dominant position of confessional political parties through most of the twentieth century. Even where the idea of Christendom had long been in decline it enjoyed a fresh lease of life in the 1940s and 1950s, as Martin Greschat shows in the case of Germany. The rise of Nazi Germany, and then the emergence of the Soviet Union as a postwar super-power, led many people to think that 'Christian Civilisation' had to be defended against the forces of evil. Especially in the years immediately after World War II it seemed that the way forward lay in re-establishing a Christian basis for European society. One aspect of this was the emergence of powerful Christian Democratic Parties, which dominated the political scene in many parts of Europe in those years.[68]

Attention has therefore been increasingly focusing on the 1960s – or perhaps on a 'long 1960s', extending from the late fifties to the mid-seventies.[69] Among the relatively few historians who have attempted an overview of religion in west European countries during this recent period, there are several major lines of division. A first difference concerns the relationship between the 1960s and preceding decades. Does the decline in church membership and attendance in the 1960s and the rise both of alternative spiritualities and of those rejecting all forms of religion represent a drastic break with the religious situation in the 1940s and 1950s, or was it a logical continuation of long-established trends? Callum Brown stands at one end of the spectrum. He believes that Christendom was very much alive and well in the Britain of the 1940s and 1950s, and he emphasises the radical character of the break around 1960. Gérard Cholvy and Yves-Marie Hilaire, doyens of French Catholic history, stand fairly closely to Brown on this, if on little else. They refer to the period 1930–60 as the 'thirty glorious years' in the history of French Catholicism, and though they do detect signs during the 1950s of the coming storm, they too see the 1960s as marking a radical break.[70] Brown also finds support from one of our other contributors, Peter van Rooden, who emphasises the lack of continuity in Dutch religious history, and identifies the 1960s as one of the periods of radical change. On the other hand, Eva Hamberg, while not addressing this issue explicitly, emphasises the continuities in Swedish religious history. At the opposite extreme to Brown would be Alan Gilbert, whose overview of modern British religion presents the 1960s simply as a time when long-established secularising trends speeded up a little.[71]

A second difference would be between those writers who stress the role of specific events in the religious history of the 1960s and the decades following, and those who focus on broader changes in economy and society, altering the relationships between men and women, young and old, or different social classes. Here Brown stands out as the most thoroughgoing exponent of the structural approach, whereas most other historians have adopted a mainly narrative approach, highlighting, for instance, the impact of the Second Vatican Council, the radicalisation of Protestant theology, the origins of the charismatic movement, and the controversies surrounding Pope Paul VI's encyclical on birth control, *Humanae Vitae*.[72]

This relates closely to a third kind of difference, namely in the selection of the specific individuals, social groups or impersonal forces who or which are to be praised or blamed for bringing about the events of the 1960s. For Gilbert, this is, in a sense, not really a problem, since he sees the developments in that period as the inevitable consequence of a long process of secularisation. However, in so far as this process speeded up at that time, he sees this arising partly from the influence of a 'dechristianised' working class, and partly from that of John Robinson's *Honest to God* and other works of radical theology, which he sees as undermining whatever religious faith still remained. The latter point would probably receive the approval of Cholvy and Hilaire, who see the crisis in French Catholicism in the later 1960s as being mainly due to overenthusiastic applications of the principles of Vatican II, misguided pastoral experiments, anti-papal feeling, and the love affair of many radical Catholics with Marxism, as well as the general crisis in French society exemplified by the events of 1968. Perhaps the most novel aspect of Brown's contribution is his central focus on gender. He is the first historian to suggest that the principal significance of the 1960s in religious history lies in 'the defeminisation of piety and the depietisation of femininity', and this is an idea that is likely to be debated for years to come.[73]

IV

The book is concerned with two basic questions. What was the state of Christendom in the latter part of the twentieth century? And, in so far as Christendom has declined, how and why has this come about? A third question is implicit in some of the contributions, though the answers will necessarily be more speculative, namely, what will western Europe's religious future be after the end of Christendom? In exploring these questions we have deliberately selected an international team of authors, with expertise on a range of different west European countries. There are contributions on England, Britain generally, Ireland, France, Germany, the Netherlands and Sweden. Each country has its own history, and many of the chapters emphasise these differences, but these countries also have a lot in common. An understanding of the present situation, and indeed of the history of the past two or three centuries, is better served by studying these countries together than by maintaining the isolationism that still remains so common. The advantages of our approach are particularly evident in looking at the 1960s, when, with a very few exceptions, such as Ireland, every country of western Europe experienced changes of the same kind at more or less the same time. But even in the eighteenth and nineteenth centuries, when change tended to be slower, and national differences were more pronounced, the Enlightenment, the French Revolution of 1789 and the Industrial Revolution were all international events, affecting in greater or lesser degree all of the countries under consideration.

In Part I we review the situation at the end of the twentieth century. The contributors comprise the sociologists Eva Hamberg and Yves Lambert, and the historian Callum Brown. All agree that Christendom is at an end, but they disagree as to what is taking its place. Brown offers the most clear-cut view: the secular society, which earlier generations imagined, is now a reality – and indeed one from which there can be no escape. Hamberg reaches similar conclusions, though presenting them more cautiously. On the other hand, Lambert puts more stress on the contradictions and complexities of the contemporary situation, of which secularisation is only one among several aspects.

In Parts II and III we take the story back in time. We ask how and why the decline of Christendom has taken place. The contributors to these sections are all historians, and most are covering relatively long periods, going back in some cases as far as the eighteenth century and coming forwards in some cases very close to the present day. In Part II, the emphasis is on narrative. In the first three contributions, David Hempton, Sheridan Gilley and Peter van Rooden analyse the patterns of long-term religious change in England, Ireland and the Netherlands, focusing especially on the relationship between religion and modernisation in the nineteenth century. The familiar view that modernisation was closely linked with secularisation is found to have some validity in the case of England, but to be highly questionable in the cases of Ireland and the Netherlands. By contrast, Martin Greschat uses a detailed examination of the debates between German Protestants after World War II to illustrate the continuing tension within Christianity between acceptance of and rejection of 'Christendom'.

In Part III, several key themes have been selected, namely technology, death and language. Advances in technology, extending human control over the environment, have often been proposed as a cause of declining faith in, or at least interest in, religion, and secularist polemic has sometimes claimed that religion stands in the way of new technology. The relationship between technology and French Catholicism, the subject of Michel Lagrée's chapter, provides therefore an important area in which to explore the relationship between religion and 'modernity'. Thomas Kselman's chapter on beliefs and practices relating to death and the after-life in France identifies another area which has been central both to Christianity and to the interaction between church and society, and which may offer particularly striking evidence of the decline of Christendom. Lucian Hölscher's chapter focuses on changes in the language through which religion or the rejection of religion have been conceptualised, another important arena for studying processes of religious change. The contributors to this section eschew clear-cut narratives, emphasising the complexity of their subject-matter and the difficulties of generalisation. Their tendency is not so much to provide new answers, as to demonstrate the inadequacy of most of the familiar orthodoxies, and the need for new lines of research.

Jeff Cox would certainly agree with the diagnosis, if not with the prescription. His aim is both to demolish the prevailing master narrative of modern religious history, based on the story of secularisation, and to lay the foundations for a rival master narrative. According to Cox, all historians depend on 'master narratives' – 'big' stories, into which their own smaller stories can be fitted, and in terms of which a multitude of trivial and apparently meaningless incidents can begin to make sense. Secularisation has dominated this particular field, because there is no other master narrative available. In Cox's view, therefore, the most urgent task is not for more detailed research but for a new 'big story'.

Having started in the present and then moved into the past, the book ends in the future. Werner Ustorf, who is both an historian and a missiologist, places the west European situation in a wider context, and asks how western Christianity should respond to the end of Christendom.

NOTES

1. For contrasting perspectives, see the essays in Alan Kreider (ed.), *The Origins of Christendom in the West* (Edinburgh, 2001).
2. John P. Burgess, *The East German Church and the End of Communism* (New York, 1997), 48–9.

3. Hugh McLeod, *Religion and the People of Western Europe 1789–1989* (Oxford, 1997), 174–5.

4. Yves-Marie Hilaire, 'La sociologie religieuse du catholicisme français au vingtième siècle', in Kay Chadwick (ed.), *Catholicism, Politics and Society in Twentieth-Century France* (Liverpool, 2000), 256.

5. For the 1950s and 1960s see the statistics provided in the country-by-country survey, Hans Mol (ed.), *Western Religion* (The Hague, 1972); for 1990, see Grace Davie, *Religion in Modern Europe: A Memory Mutates* (Oxford, 2000), 9. Hilaire, 'Sociologie religieuse', provides an overview of the extensive literature on patterns of religious practice in France.

6. See for instance the evidence relating to Britain in Steve Bruce, *Religion in Modern Britain* (Oxford, 1995).

7. See Yves Lambert's contribution to this volume.

8. Arthur Marwick, *The Sixties: Cultural Revolution in Britain, France, Italy and the United States, c.1958–c.1974* (Oxford, 1998), provides an overview of these developments. For the role of the churches, see René Rémond, *Religion and Society in Modern Europe* (Oxford, 1999), 198–205; G. I. T. Machin, *Churches and Social Issues in Twentieth Century Britain* (Oxford, 1995); Gerald Parsons, 'Between law and licence: Christianity, morality and "permissiveness" ', in Gerald Parsons and John Wolffe (eds.), *The Growth of Religious Diversity in Britain from 1945*, 3 vols. (Manchester, 1994), vol. II, 233–63.

9. This paragraph draws mainly on Davie, *Religion in Modern Europe*.

10. There is an extensive literature on this. See, e.g., Trutz Rendtorff (ed.), *Protestantische Revolution?* (Göttingen, 1993).

11. Henry Clark, *The Church under Thatcher* (London, 1993); Kay Chadwick, '*Accueillir l'étranger*: immigration, integration and the French Catholic Church', in Chadwick (ed.), *Catholicism, Politics and Society*, 175–96.

12. On this theme, see the excellent volumes, based on a series of conferences: Ole Peter Grell, Jonathan Israel and Nicholas Tyacke (eds.), *From Persecution to Toleration: The Glorious Revolution and Religion in England* (Cambridge, 1991); O. P. Grell and Bob Scribner (eds.), *Tolerance and Intolerance in the European Reformation* (Cambridge, 1996); Ole Peter Grell and Roy Porter (eds.), *Toleration in Enlightenment Europe* (Cambridge, 2000); see also Richard Helmstadter, *Freedom and Religion in the Nineteenth Century* (Stanford, CA), 1997. A detailed study on one state is Joachim Whaley, *Religious Toleration and Social Change in Hamburg, 1529–1819* (Cambridge, 1985).

13. Jerzy Kloczowski (ed.), *Histoire religieuse de la Pologne*, French translation (Paris, 1987), 193–4.

14. See Rainer Liedtke and Stephan Wendehorst (eds.), *The Emancipation of Catholics, Jews and Protestants* (Manchester, 1999).

15. John McManners, *Church and Society in Eighteenth-Century France*, 2 vols. (Oxford, 1998), vol. 2, 709–11.

16. Lucian Hölscher, 'Säkularisierungsprozesse im deutschen Protestantismus des 19. Jahrhunderts', in Hans-Jürgen Pühle (ed.), *Bürger in der Gesellschaft der Neuzeit* (Göttingen, 1991), 244.

17. Ralph Gibson, *A Social History of French Catholicism 1789–1914* (London, 1989), 8.

18. Michel Vovelle, *Piété baroque et déchristianisation en Provence au XVIIIe siècle* (Paris, 1973). Rudolf Schlögl, *Glaube und Religion in der Säkularisierung* (Munich, 1995), uses similar methods in a study of Rhineland Catholic cities *c.* 1770–1830 and reaches similar conclusions.
19. Michael MacDonald, 'The secularization of suicide in England 1660–1800', *Past & Present*, 111 (1986), 50–100.
20. Gibson, *French Catholicism*: 6.
21. Lucian Hölscher, 'Secularization and urbanization in the nineteenth century: an interpretative model', in Hugh McLeod (ed.), *European Religion in the Age of Great Cities 1830–1930* (London, 1995), 270–3.
22. For a useful summary, see C. T. McIntire, 'Changing religious establishments and religious liberty in France, 1787–1908', in Helmstadter (ed.), *Freedom and Religion*, 233–301.
23. For France, see Maurice Larkin, *Church and State in France after the Dreyfus Affair* (London, 1972), and Jacqueline Lalouette, *La Libre Pensée en France 1848–1940* (Paris, 1997). For Spain, Frances Lannon, *Privilege, Persecution and Prophecy: The Catholic Church in Spain 1875–1975* (London, 1987), and William J. Callahan, *The Catholic Church in Spain, 1875–1998* (Washington, DC, 2000).
24. Christoph Link, *Staat und Kirche in der neueren deutschen Geschichte* (Frankfurt am Main, 2000), 99–133.
25. J. H. Whyte, *Church and State in Ireland 1923–1979*, 2nd edition (Dublin, 1980).
26. This section is based mainly on Hugh McLeod, *Secularisation in Western Europe 1848–1914* (London, 2000), 52–85, 108–17.
27. Davie, *Religion in Modern Europe*, 82–97; Gerald Parsons, 'There and back again? Religion and the 1944 and 1988 Education Acts', in Parsons and Wolffe (eds.), *Religious Diversity*, vol. II, 161–98.
28. Harry Potter, *Hanging in Judgment: Religion and the Death Penalty in England from the Bloody Code to Abolition* (London, 1993), chapter 16.
29. Lalouette, *Libre Pensée*, 276–82.
30. Jacques Fontana, *Les Catholiques français pendant la Grande Guerre* (Paris, 1990), 296–300. For the more typical British situation, see Michael Snape and Stephen Parker, 'Keeping faith and coping: belief, popular religiosity and the British people in two World Wars', in John Bourne, Peter Liddle and Ian Whitehead (eds.), *The Great World War, 1914–45*, vol. I, *Lightning Strikes Twice* (London, 2000), 397–420.
31. Nigel Aston, *Religion and Revolution in France 1780–1804* (Washington, DC, 2000), 264–5.
32. Olwen Hufton, 'The reconstruction of a church 1796–1801', in Gwynne Lewis and Colin Lucas (eds.), *Beyond the Terror: Essays in French Regional and Social History* (Cambridge, 1983), 21–52.
33. Annie Fourcaut (ed.), *Banlieue rouge 1920–1960* (Paris, 1992).
34. Lalouette, *Libre Pensée*, 233–67; François-André Isambert, *Christianisme et classe ouvrière* (Tournai, 1961), 89–114.
35. As one example among many, see Vernon L. Lidtke, *The Alternative Culture* (New York, 1985), which is about the great prototype, Social Democracy in Imperial Germany.
36. Hugh McLeod, *Piety and Poverty: Working Class Religion in Berlin, London and New York* (New York, 1996), 167–9.

37. Jörg Kniffka, *Das kirchliche Leben in Berlin-Ost in der Mitte der zwanziger Jahre* (Münster, 1971).
38. Jean-Pierre A. Bernard, *Paris rouge: les communistes français dans la capitale 1944–64* (Seyssel, 1991), is written in the spirit of rediscovery of a lost world. (The terminal date chosen was the death of Thorez, though at other points the author suggests that an appropriate end-date might be 1968.)
39. See the discussion in Tony Walter, *Funerals and How to Improve Them* (London, 1990), chapter 20; and for a high-profile example of contemporary eclecticism, Tony Walter (ed.), *The Mourning for Diana* (Oxford, 1999).
40. Gérard Cholvy and Yves-Marie Hilaire, *Histoire religieuse de la France contemporaine 1800–1880*, 2nd edition (Toulouse, 1990), chapters 3, 6, 8, 9 (see note 56 below).
41. McLeod, *Piety and Poverty*, xxiii–xxv, 103–26, and *passim*.
42. See Grace Davie, *Religion in Britain since 1945: Believing without Belonging* (Oxford, 1994).
43. S. C. Williams, *Religious Belief and Popular Culture in Southwark c.1880–1939* (Oxford, 1999). Williams' findings are broadly confirmed, while being further developed in certain respects, in Richard Sykes, 'Popular religion in Dudley and the Gornals, c.1914–1965', PhD thesis, University of Wolverhampton, 1999. For studies of popular religion in a Catholic context, see Ellen Badone (ed.), *Religious Orthodoxy and Popular Faith in European Society* (Princeton, NJ), 1990; Ruth Harris, *Lourdes: Body and Spirit in the Secular Age* (London, 1999); and numerous studies by William A. Christian, e.g. 'Religious apparitions and the Cold War in southern Europe', in Eric R. Wolf (ed.), *Religion, Power and Protest in Local Communities: The Northern Shore of the Mediterranean* (Berlin, 1984), 239–66.
44. V. G. Kiernan, *The Duel in European History: Honour and the Reign of Aristocracy* (Oxford, 1988); Keith Thomas, 'The double standard', *Journal of the History of Ideas*, 20 (1959), 195–216; Olwen Hufton, *The Poor of Eighteenth-Century France 1750–1789* (Oxford, 1974), 245–83, 306–17, 349–51.
45. Olivier Tschannen, *Les théories de la sécularisation* (Geneva, 1992). Here I differ from Callum Brown. While he locates the origins of the concept of secularisation in the anxieties of early nineteenth-century Christians, I would trace it back to the hopes of nineteenth-century sceptics and secularists.
46. Peter Berger, *The Social Reality of Religion* (Harmondsworth, 1972); Bryan R. Wilson, *Religion in Secular Society* (London, 1966).
47. Wilson, *Religion in Secular Society*,
48. Steve Bruce, *Religion in the Modern World: From Cathedrals to Cults* (Oxford, 1995), 233 and *passim*.
49. Steve Bruce and Roy Wallis, 'Secularization: the orthodox model', in Steve Bruce (ed.), *Religion and Modernization: Sociologists and Historians Debate the Secularization Thesis* (Oxford, 1992), 8–30.
50. This is suggested tentatively by Jeffrey Cox in 'Secularization and other master narratives of religion in the modern world', *Kirchliche Zeitgeschichte*, 14 (2001), 34–5, but more forcefully by such sociologists as David Martin, Grace Davie and Peter Berger (the latter having substantially modified his earlier views). See Peter Berger (ed.), *The Desecularization of the World: Resurgent Religion and World Politics* (Grand Rapids, MI, 1999).

51. See, e.g., Adrian Hastings, *A History of English Christianity 1920–2000* (London, 2001), which stresses the beneficial effects for Christianity of recent crises, and Gérard Cholvy, *La Religion en France de la fin du XVIIIe à nos jours* (Paris, 1991), which presents the period since 1975 as a time of religious revival because of the range of new forms of spirituality that have emerged at the same time that the Catholic Church has declined.

52. As well as their contributions to this volume, see Callum Brown, *The Death of Christian Britain* (London, 2000); Peter van Rooden, *Religieuze regimes: over godsdienst en maatschappij in Nederland 1570–1990* (Amsterdam, 1996).

53. Williams, *Religious Belief*; Hölscher, 'Secularization and urbanization'.

54. Anthony Steinhoff, 'Ein zweites konfessionelles Zeitalter? Nachdenken über die Religion im langen 19. Jahrhundert', forthcoming in *Geschichte und Gesellschaft*.

55. E.g. Rodney Stark and Laurence R. Iannaccone, 'A supply-side reinterpretation of the "secularization" of Europe', *Journal for the Scientific Study of Religion*, 33 (1994), 230–52. Roger Finke and Rodney Stark, *The Churching of America 1776–1990: Winners and Losers in Our Religious Economy* (New Brunswick, NJ, 1992), apply similar ideas to the long-term trends in the religious history of the United States.

56. E.g. Gérard Cholvy and Yves-Marie Hilaire in their impressive three-volume *Histoire religieuse de la France contemporaine* (Toulouse, 1985–8), with its clear narrative and mastery of detail, and avoidance of any overarching theoretical framework.

57. For instance, many of the contributors to Roy Porter and M. Teich (eds.), *The Enlightenment in National Context* (Cambridge, 1981), stress that the anti-Christian dimension of the Enlightenment, conspicuous in France, was untypical elsewhere.

58. Mary Heimann, 'Christianity in Western Europe since the Enlightenment', in Adrian Hastings (ed.), *A World History of Christianity* (London, 1999), 478–85.

59. For overviews, see McLeod (ed.), *Age of Great Cities*, and McLeod, *Piety and Poverty*. See also reviews of the debate in S. J. D. Green, *Religion in the Age of Decline: Organisation and Experience in Industrial Yorkshire 1870–1920* (Cambridge, 1996), and Antonius Liedhegener, *Christentum und Urbanisierung: Katholiken und Protestanten in Münster und Bochum, 1830–1933* (Paderborn, 1997).

60. These points are made in many of the contributions to McLeod (ed.), *Age of Great Cities*, notably those by William J. Callahan on Spanish cities and by Hans Otte on Hanover. See also Kaspar Elm and Hans-Dietrich Loock, *Seelsorge und Diakonie in Berlin: Beiträge zum Verhältnis von Kirche und Großstadt im 19. und beginnenden 20. Jahrhundert* (Berlin, 1990).

61. This is argued in Gregory Singleton, *Religion in the City of Angels: Los Angeles 1850–1930* (n.p., 1979).

62. See A. D. Gilbert, *Religion and Society in Industrial England: Church, Chapel and Social Change 1740–1914* (London, 1976).

63. This is argued most clearly by the Chicago urban sociologist Louis Wirth in his famous essay 'Urbanism as a way of life' (1938), reprinted in Louis Wirth, *On Cities and Social Life* (Chicago, 1964), 60–83. A similar view is taken by Thomas Nipperdey in 'Religion und Gesellschaft in Deutschland um 1900', *Historische Zeitschrift*, 246 (1988), 591–615.

64. See also Williams, *Religious Belief*.

65. For instance, Rémond, *Religion and Society*, and McLeod, *Secularisation in Western Europe*, which start in 1789 and 1848 respectively, and both of which give considerable attention to political developments.

66. Olaf Blaschke, 'Das 19. Jahrhundert: ein Zweites Konfessionelles Zeitalter?', *Geschichte und Gesellschaft*, 26 (2000), 38–75.

67. Callum G. Brown, *Religion and Society in Scotland since 1707* (Edinburgh, 1997), chapters 5, 6, 7; Brown, *Death of Christian Britain*, 170–5 and *passim*.

68. David Hanley (ed.), *Christian Democracy in Europe: A Comparative Perspective* (London, 1994). See also Dianne Kirby (ed.), *The Churches and the Cold War* (Basingstoke, 2003).

69. Marwick, *Sixties*, defines the 'long Sixties' as extending from 1958 to 1974. In Brown, *Death of Christian Britain*, 188, they extend from 1956 to 1973. For a summary of the debates on the significance of this period, see Hugh McLeod, 'The sixties: writing the religious history of a crucial decade', *Kirchliche Zeitgeschichte*, 14 (2001), 36–48.

70. Gérard Cholvy and Yves-Marie Hilaire, *Histoire religieuse de la France contemporaine 1930–88* (Toulouse, 1988).

71. A. D. Gilbert, *The Making of Post-Christian Britain* (London, 1980).

72. As well as Cholvy and Hilaire, other historians who adopt a mainly narrative approach to the crisis of these years include Hastings, *English Christianity*, and Gerald Parsons, 'Contrasts and continuities: the traditional Christian Churches in Britain since 1945', in Parsons and Wolffe (eds.), *Religious Diversity*, vol. I, 25–94.

73. Gilbert, *Post-Christian Britain*: 86–94, 121–57; Cholvy and Hilaire, *Histoire religieuse 1930–1988*, 282–90, 311–12, 315–24, 328–30; Brown, *Death of Christian Britain*, 192.

Part I

2 The secularisation decade: what the 1960s have done to the study of religious history

Callum G. Brown

Introduction

I start this chapter with a series of presumptions about the state of existing knowledge in the social history of religion. (1) Britain in the 1960s experienced more secularisation than in all the preceding four centuries put together. Never before had all of the numerical indicators of popular religiosity fallen simultaneously, and never before had their declension been so steep. (2) It is clear now at the start of the twenty-first century that what commenced in the 1960s was a statistically secular (i.e. permanent) change, and not a cyclical (or temporary) one. There is currently no evidence, nor theory of human behaviour (outside of faith itself), that posits that recovery in those numerical indicators will ever take place. (3) Statistical evidence previously used to identify what was once supposed to be secularisation during previous periods of history (notably in the eighteenth, nineteenth and early twentieth centuries) can now be seen in a new context as showing nothing more than relatively minor, ambiguous, often contradictory, and short-term religious change which was, in any event, neither statistically fool-proof evidence even on its own terms, nor sufficiently broad in its coverage of what religiosity is as to offer a safe conclusion.

What happened in the late twentieth century has been unique and epoch-forming. Since around 1963, Britain has been in the brave new world of secular secularisation – that is, the permanent decline of religion. This decline takes two main observable forms. It is the terminal decline of virtually all of the large, organised conventional Christian churches in Britain; and it is the permanent decline of the common and pervasive Christian culture to which most Britons had adhered most of the time to greater or lesser extents for centuries (and arguably since the start of the second millennium CE). For the historian of religious decline, there is no period in history as important as the 1960s. What was different about the 1960s in the history of religion was not just the scale and suddenness of religious decline. The uniqueness of the sixties was, first, that for the first time Christian religiosity underwent a common and virtually simultaneous change within nearly all countries in western Europe. Previous change had been non-simultaneous, appearing staggered between different nations; this is certainly the conclusion from Hugh McLeod's unique international study which showed that in the period 1880–1930 secularisation took place in stages, with Berlin in advance of London, and London in advance of New York, and from some other cases.[1] Second, the change was not engineered or guided by governments, churches or elites, nor was it the product of any denominational rivalry, nor any specifically anti-religious political ideology. Third, the religious change that occurred was one of profound secularisation of – or decline in – 'conventional' religion which opened up British popular access to previously exotic, bohemian or socially circumscribed religious/spiritual movements, and allowed for the lowering, at the point of consumption, of barriers between religious and spiritual movements. Fourth, the cause of this secularisation was linked to a sweeping and spontaneously developed popular culture that became, for the first time, a dynamic for religious change in the western world as a whole. And fifth, and most contentiously, the 1960s was and remains unique because it marked the beginning in many countries of the collapse of religious culture as a whole: the religious value-system which, embedded through complex cultural formations in the family, community and state, had stewarded European civilisation for a millennium (under Christianity), and possibly longer (under pre-Christian religions).

The themes and arguments in this chapter complement a previous study of gender, evangelicalism and the secularisation of British culture between 1800 and 2000.[2] This chapter is not a restatement of that book. Instead, it focuses on the impact of the 1960s upon aspects of the academic study of the social history of religion. What it argues is that if the 1960s changed British religion, that culture-event has also changed the way in which religion and the religious past (before 1960) are comprehended in the British imagination. The 1960s have changed the ways in which contemporary culture constructs what religion 'is', what it 'was', and what the difference is between what it 'is' and what it 'was'. In short, the 1960s have changed the way in which British culture narratises religion.

This has created an injunction to historians of religion that we too must change the way we construct our 'official' (academic) narratives of religion. A major factor impacting on this will be the greatest structural trend towards the fusion of conceptual approaches and methodologies between social history of religion, ecclesiastical (church) history, religious studies and cultural history – a process that is already underway. We will in the future be examining with greater clarity of terminology than ever before terms like 'religion', 'religious', 'irreligious' and 'spirituality'. In this chapter I want to look at the narrative of 'religious decline' – commonly referred to as 'secularisation' – which developed in the nineteenth and early twentieth centuries, but which has now been irrevocably altered by the 1960s. How has the narrative of secularisation been affected by the swinging sixties? And how does this leave our academic discipline?

The data on religion

The 1960s represented the majority of the decline in virtually all indicators of the Christian religion's currently quantifiable social significance in mainland Britain. Here I will speak of a 'short 1960s' of 1963–70, and a 'long 1960s' of 1956–73.

It seems irrefutable that church-going declined in mainland Britain during the 1960s, but that this was merely a continuation of an existing trend which stretched back until at least the 1890s and possibly to the 1870s. It might be fair to estimate that the proportion of the population attending church and Sunday school in mainland Britain on a given Sunday stood at around 40–45 per cent in 1851, and fell thereafter to about 30 per cent by 1900, 15 per cent by 1950, 11.3 per cent in 1979–84, and to less than 10 per cent in the 1990s.[3] Moreover, the 1960s seem to have cemented the trend for zones of relatively low church-going in the mid-nineteenth century (industrial zones, and highland and island rural zones) to become, by the late twentieth century, zones of relatively high church-going (not by virtue of any growth in church-going, but by virtue of a much *lower rate of decline* in church attendance compared to metropolitan and lowland agricultural zones). Yet, it is fair to conclude that, viewed in isolation, the decline in church-going in the 1960s was not epoch-making for the Christian religion nationally.

After church-going, the most active form of church connection in the Christian religion is celebration of the rites of passage. Between 1900 and 1997, the proportion of marriages that were religiously solemnised fell for Scotland from 94 to 56 per cent, and for England and Wales from 85 to 39 per cent. There were three main periods of decline: the First World War, the Second World War and the period after 1963. In the main, the declines of the two world wars were reversed in peacetime, and though there was a decline over the course of twentieth-century peacetime, it was the 'short 1960s' which saw the greatest permanent fall. Of the 36-point fall in religious marriage in Scotland during 1900–87, 15.6 points occurred during 1961–73. Of the 33-point fall in religious marriage in England and Wales during 1900–87, 16.5 points occurred during 1962–73. In short, of the whole fall in the proportion of religious marriages between 1900 and 1987, 43 per cent in Scotland and 50 per cent in England and Wales occurred during the 'short 1960s' – a staggering decline.

Interestingly, the other rite of passage for which there are data – baptism – started its rapid decline earlier. Infant baptisms performed in the Church of England as a proportion of live births were still rising in the first three decades of the twentieth century, from 609 per thousand in 1900 to a peak of 668 in 1927. Despite a slight decline to 621 by 1938, this was a remarkably high density of baptism in the English and Welsh population; the addition of baptisms performed by other denominations would raise this figure significantly. But after a gap in the middle decades of the century (when I was unable to locate data), the figure in 1956 was still relatively high at 602 per thousand – a figure only 7/1000 points down on 1900. But decline was rapid thereafter: within two years it had attained the lowest level for the century, and then kept falling until 1970–73 (when a brief levelling-off at 465/6 occurred) and then resuming from 1976. Of the 303-point fall in the baptism rate during 1927–81,[5] 174 points occurred during 1956–76.

Data for the proportion of funerals celebrated by Christian rite are, to my knowledge, non-existent. However, anecdotal evidence suggests that there was a continuing recourse until very late in the twentieth century by more than 90 per cent (perhaps close to 100 per cent) of British families to religious celebration of lives at death (either in a place of worship, in a crematorium or at a graveside, or any two or even all three of these). A change towards secular (often Humanist) celebration of death seems to have become significant only in the 1980s and 1990s, and from anecdotal conversations with Humanist celebrants this demand grew exponentially in the late 1990s and early 2000s. In any event, it seems highly likely that there was no marked change during the 1960s.

Youth connection with religion is one of the key areas in statistical analysis of religious change in the twentieth and twenty-first centuries. Data from Scotland show that the peak of Sunday school enrolment was achieved in the 1890s, and there seems every reason to believe that there was a comparable peak for England and Wales. Enrolments in all British Protestant churches represented 77 per cent of children aged between 5 and 14 years inclusive at the start of the twentieth century (a figure probably inflated by multiple enrolment).[4] By the 1990s, the level of Sunday school enrolment is difficult to ascertain because of discontinued statistical series (itself a commentary on crisis), but was probably in the region of 5–8 per cent. The greatest decline before the late 1950s occurred in the Nonconformist churches – especially in Methodist Sunday schools, where the rolls fell by 58 per cent between 1910 and 1956 compared to only 46 per cent over the same period for the Church of England. But the real crisis of Sunday schools occurred after 1956. In that year a peak of enrolment per capita unseen since 1936 was reached, but then the figures for all churches plummeted. The Scottish data are the most complete and – in terms of trend – representative. In 1956, Presbyterian enrolments represented 39 per cent of Scottish children, but then fell to 19 per cent in 1973; 20 of the 32-point fall in Presbyterian enrolments during 1903–81 occurred in the 'long 1960s' of 1956–73. The crisis for Sunday schools did not diminish after 1973. In the Church of Scotland it has continued unabated with a steepening in the 1990s. In 1994, enrolments stood at 60,936 – compared with 167,733 in 1973. The decline is at the rate of 8–10 per cent per year in Scotland in the mid-1990s, which leads to the projection that Sunday schools will have practically ceased to exist by 2010.[5] From the available data, there seems to be little cause for thinking that the situation in the rest of British Protestantism is any different.

A second form of data on youth and religion is confirmation in the Church of England. Girls and young women made up 59 per cent of confirmations in the late 1950s. The density of female confirmation in the population was significant, standing fairly level at around 40 per cent until 1961. Male confirmations, on the other hand, were already in a slow decline. However, it was between 1961 and 1974 that the major decline occurred; female confirmation more than halved from 39.3 to 19.6 per cent in those years. This represents a major loss of the Church's primary recruitment mechanism, and one that undoubtedly contributed to the fall in church communicants.

Success in recruitment of baptised persons into full membership of the Church of England and the Church of Scotland (which took place usually between 12 and 18 years of age) was remarkably resilient until the mid-1950s, and then after 1956 plunged in the Church of Scotland, and fell significantly in the Church of England, whilst both churches experienced a sustained (and as yet unended) recruitment catastrophe from 1966 with, by the mid-1990s, only 17–20 per cent of baptised persons entering full communion. More clearly than any other statistics, these show that the two world wars did not have a permanent impact on internal recruitment – it was the period after 1956 that did. Recent studies of youth attitudes to religion have explored more fully than ever before the mechanism of youth alienation from religion – including how 'religion' and 'the church' are perceived as 'uncool', whilst 'spirituality' and the new moral agenda of environmentalism and respect between human beings can be deeply attractive, yet unfulfilled by conventional religion.[6]

One of the key characteristics of Britain between 1900 and 1960 was that, though church attendance fell, passive association was strongly sustained. Both the Church of England and the Church of Scotland suffered comparatively little loss of adherence during the first half of the twentieth century, with peak of communicants as a proportion of population coming in 1911 and 1934 respectively, whilst their low points in 1947 and 1948 respectively were only marginally lower. The real fall in their constituency came after 1956. Aggregation of data across Christian denominations is nigh impossible for purposes of per capita analysis of church membership in England and Wales, but it is more possible in Scotland. Here, it is possible to construct year-on-year data on church adherence or membership between 1840 and 1994 (including Presbyterian Sunday school enrolment), expressed as a percentage of total population at annual intervals.[7] This shows that nearly all the permanent loss of church adherence per capita in Scotland since church statistics began occurred after 1956, and it was between 1963 and c. 1975 that the gradient of decline reached unprecedented proportions. All Protestant churches suffered, and only a small number (like the Baptist Church) experienced a stabilisation of membership loss in the later

twentieth century. Though the decline in the Scottish Catholic Church (as measured by a variety of indicators) only started in the mid-1970s, it has since the
mid-1980s experienced an accelerating decline that has reached a gradient un-
matched by any other Scottish church before. In short, Catholic Church decline
started late, but it is proving to be incredibly sharp.

A final major area of statistical analysis is that of opinion poll data on religious
attitudes and claimed religious activities. These data largely apply to the period
since the 1960s, and most of them have been extensively analysed by Clive
Field.[8] He showed that there has been a marked decline in most self-claimed
indicators of religious activity since the 1970s, a decline which is steepest at the
end of the period. He also noted how the evidence suggests that by the 1990s
the influence of religion is about the same in England and Scotland, is higher
than in France and Scandinavia, is much lower in Britain than in most Catholic
countries of Europe, and is very much lower than in North and South America.
Overall, he agrees with the proposition that in zones previously thought to be
'highly religious' (such as Scotland) there has been a haemorrhage of faith
underway in the later decades of the twentieth century.

To summarise, all of the indicators bar two (church-going and opinion poll
data) show that the period between 1956 and 1973 witnessed unprecedented
rapidity in the fall of religiosity in British society. In most cases, at least half of
the overall decline in each indicator recorded during the century was concentrated into those years or a smaller period within them. That in itself makes the
'long sixties' highly significant in the history of British secularisation. What
heightens the significance is the fact that so many indices of religiosity fell
simultaneously. Across the board, the British people started to reduce the role
of religion in their lives: for their marriages, as a place to baptise their children,
as an institution to send their children to Sunday school and church recruitment,
and as a place for affiliation. The next generation, which came to adulthood in
the 1970s, exhibited even more marked disaffiliation from church connection
of any sort, and *their* children were largely raised in a domestic routine free
from the intrusions of organised religion. Meanwhile, the long-term decline of
church-going has continued, and together with the evidence from opinion poll
data, there seems every reason to conclude that the data indicate little short of
a 'mass' dissolution of popular faith in Britain in the last three decades of the
twentieth century.

Deconstructing the data, redefining the study

If the data emphasise the suddenness of religious change in Britain in the late
twentieth century, they also suggest much greater continuity in the measurable
social significance of religion between the mid-nineteenth and mid-twentieth
centuries than has long been assumed. This fits quite comfortably with trends

in recent 'revisionist' scholarship that have downplayed the extent of damage to organised religion rendered by industrialisation and urbanisation in the eighteenth and nineteenth centuries. However, the data also suggest that the focus of traditional social history of religion on the 1880–1930 period as a turning-point in Britain has only partial validity. Only church-going decline seems significant then, and it is counterbalanced by much evidence of the vibrancy of religious culture in both plebeian and bourgeois life in the late Victorian, Edwardian and inter-war periods. The modern puritan revolution was very far from exhausted by the 1930s, and was to revitalise in the vigour of church growth and the 'crusade evangelism' of Billy Graham in the mid-1950s.

By contrast, despite the difficulty of church-going data, the 'long 1960s' from 1956 to 1973 appear as a cataclysm for the place of religion in British society. The sheer scale of religious change in that decade puts in the shade the more equivocal change of the 1790s and 1840s and the 1880–1910 period so beloved of historical debate. The years 1963–65 appear striking as the turning-point at which virtually all indices of religious adherence, youth education and rites of passage passed below the known scale. It is from 1963 that historians have to recalibrate their barometer of religiosity.

Two important sets of interpretational points arise from these observations. First, the obvious – the 1960s can be empirically identified as the commencement of the first period of steep, multi-factorial, long-term and (statistically) secular (as distinct from cyclical) dechristianisation of Britain. Though the characteristics of a multi-faith society first become significant from the 1960s, the rise of non-Christian religions and quasi-religions (including New Religions and New Age movements) did not, have not and will not fill the void of religiosity left by the decline of Christianity. Thus, it also seems irrefutable that what Britain has experienced since 1963 is 'genuine' secularisation. Though this argument deserves much greater focus on theoretical, conceptual and empirical issues, it strikes me as as clear commonsense. This will be deeply unsatisfying to some observers, but they will mostly have flags of faith to fly.

The second interpretational point arises from the first. It is that it is only the 1960s – and our experience of it – that actually provides a sensory, empirical and conceptual understanding of what 'secularisation' is, and of what kind of society it produces. If you think of those efforts of historians to argue that secularisation started in the Enlightenment or the Industrial Revolution, then the nature of the process they are able to describe as taking place is *at most* merely one of 'forgetting to observe' Christianity, and the society produced out of it is a strongly self-reflectively neglectful religious society. There was nothing 'secular' whatever in nineteenth-century British society. It was a society which knew well, from top to bottom, what it knew it *ought* to believe and *ought* to do religiously, and what it was that some were alleging was being 'lost' in the midst of urban–industrial change. When members of society did not do the expected and observable 'religious' things, they were loudly harangued by moral and religious gatekeepers from pulpit, corner gossip shop and Sunday lunch table. This was the discursivity of faith-power. It was the power of late modern puritanism which enveloped British (as well as European) society until the 1950s. That power was only challenged effectively by a cultural revolt (not a revolt of neglect or secularism or politics), and it did not happen until the 1960s. The sixties produced not the end but the beginning of the revolt against the discursivity of Christian culture in Europe.

Therefore, there was no conception of what secular society was until after the 1960s had been fully absorbed into our consciousness. For this reason, each book on the subject written before or without that understanding (including most famously Bryan Wilson's *Religion in Secular Society* of 1966) is not a book which did or could conceptualise what secular society looked like or felt like. Our ability to conceptualise that society is dawning bit by bit as we progress in Britain through to third- and fourth-generation secularists.

The third interpretational point is potentially more far-reaching for the social history of religion. I will give a bald statement of it first and elaborate on it after. The bald statement is this: secularisation fillets the religious spine out of the body of human culture. When that happens, as in Britain since the 1960s, it is not possible to continue to study the subject by looking at the churches, church membership, religious observance or opinion polls. The basis of the academic subject has fundamentally changed. The churches are now less relevant; indeed, to be frank, they become increasingly irrelevant with every year. They are so marginal to the place of religion in society that the academic game has to change fundamentally.

Church history could once claim to encompass the social history of religion. It can't any more. Religious studies – the academic discipline, with all its research and theorising about the diversity, overlap, decentredness and fluidity of spiritual and religious experience – have done enough to convince that the study of the spiritual and religious past needs to change with it, and adopt the same conceptual challenges and diversity of empirical investigation. At the same time, religious studies must change because of major weaknesses in empiricism, conceptualisation of historical change and obsession with theorising (faults drawn, I suspect, from sociology). But that is another matter. Let me be plain. Religious studies represents the future of the past. The secularisation decade in Britain has destroyed the conceptual validity of religious history as we have known it, just as it has destroyed what we once understood to be 'religion'.

Of secularisation and other concepts

'Secularisation' represents a number of different things to scholars. First, it is a *theory* which, broadly speaking, defines the decline in the social significance of religion as a long-term and inevitable historical process, with short-term accelerants (such as the Reformation, the Enlightenment, industrialisation and urbanisation) and also short-term retardants (generally referred to as 'revivals'). In general terms, this *theory* of secularisation is regarded by some scholars as now being in tatters. Intellectually and – above all – empirically, the notion that the decline of religion has been an inevitable and inexorable accompaniment of 'modernisation' is now enjoying diminishing support amongst British social historians of religion.[9] Sociologists of religion, who were the most ardent promoters of the theory in the 1950s, 1960s and 1970s,[10] have become since the 1980s and 1990s largely silent on the issue.[11] Even in the United States, a 'revisionist' group of sociologists have turned full square against the notion that cities secularise and, instead, have argued that cities are centres of increased religious activity.[12] The language of academic debate has now started to change from religious 'decline' to religious 'change', marking the growing acknowledgement of not merely the ability of religion to survive modern social and economic change but its ability to change and grow in parallel to it and, perhaps, because of it.[13]

Second, secularisation is, as Jeff Cox has called it, a 'master narrative'. As a history, it is a narrative predominantly written of the period since the eighteenth century, and centred in the historiography between 1780 and 1914. This history encompasses most of western Europe, Great Britain and the United States, and though it varies its causative forces according to national (and sometimes regional) context, fundamentally the course, timing and scale of change is similar across this territory. Secularisation is thus an international historical development, drawn by scholars both in incredible detail at local level and in broad brush on an international canvas.[14] This history or master narrative has been fairly constantly revised, updated, qualified and empirically enriched by scholars since the 1960s. Indeed, so qualified has the secularisation story researched for the 1780–1914 period become, that many scholars seek now to replace the master narrative. 'Secularisation' has become a *bête noir* for revisionists who maintain that not only did religion not decline during the eighteenth and nineteenth centuries, it could just as well have grown.[15]

Many scholars have thus increasingly devalued the concept of 'secularisation' as an historical development. As a result, the demise of secularisation as a theory ('it is a social-scientific illogicality') has been accompanied during the 1980s and 1990s by the decline of secularisation as an acknowledged historical process of the eighteenth and nineteenth centuries ('it didn't happen that way'). Amongst sociologists of religion, there has been a secularisation side-show concerning debate about 'secular society', with one tradition arguing that Britain is not a secular society – or not as secular as is often thought[16] – whilst the other tradition argues that it is patently obvious that Britain of the mid-1990s was radically secular in comparison to the Britain of, say, the mid-1890s.[17] This is a debate which is poorly invested with an historical perspective; even if it is charitably classified as contributing a 'narrative', it fails critically to be interested in identifying when the transitions to secularity occurred. It resonates too much with a similarly forlorn debate in the 1960s, and neither of these really does anything to enhance understanding of historical change.

The failure in theory and in narrative gives rise to a third status to secularisation: as a postmodernist (and poststructuralist) *problematic*. A methodological revolution is underway in how scholars study religiosity. Much of the work of unpicking the stranglehold of secularisation theory now involves discourse analysis upon those sources (authors, institutions, media) in which were intellectualised, refined and circulated the key discourses on what it was to be 'religious' and what it was to be 'irreligious' in industrial society. These discourses (or representations) were framed within complex class, gender and ethnic structures, and they had a resilience which rendered them still relevant well into the third quarter of the twentieth century. (Thus, incidentally, they became the active discourses of analysis in most of the scholarship on the social history of religion during the 1950s, 1960s and early 1970s.[18]) The effect of these discourses in the English-speaking world was to make religiosity be perceived as something intrinsically good rather than bad, Christian rather than non-Christian, rural and pre-industrial rather than urban and industrial, middle-class rather than working-class, feminine rather than masculine, and white Anglo-Saxon Protestant rather than, for example, black (or African American), Irish or Roman Catholic. This is to simplify enormously complex discourses which varied over time, country and region, but they were surprisingly common features within world Protestantism.

Secularisation, like religiosity itself, thus becomes a problematic requiring changes in scholarship.[19] The remainder of this section explores the impact of postmodernism on this work.

1. First, the poststructuralist agenda involves decoupling concepts of religiosity from social structures, and liberating the working classes from 'blame' in the decline of religion by a conscious effort of devaluing the class dialectics which have in the past dominated how historians understood the declining social significance of religion. The prominence previously given to working-class alienation from the churches as the long-run cause of secularisation in Britain from the late eighteenth century to the present has been under assault since the late 1970s from studies showing the relative strength of working-class involvement in church membership and worship,[20] and from the mid-1980s by a growing awareness from experiential sources concerning the continuities in, and strength of, proletarian religiosity.[21] This must continue.

2. Second, the simultaneous postmodernist agenda stresses the importance of understanding religious experience through individuals' subjectification of discourse in negotiation with their own economic and social experience. This

demands two main things: first, discourse analysis of the 'self' (in this case the religious self, as part of a wider construction of the individual), through study of circulating discourses in the dominant media (books, newspapers, popular song, sermons, and so on); and second, study of personal testimony (such as autobiography, oral history, and personal testimony reconstructed from third-party sources (such as judicial and ecclesiastical records)). An important and key criterion of analysis in recent years using these methods has been gender and religion – principally femininity and Christian piety.[22] Studies of England and North America in the eighteenth century have suggested that there was a complex feminisation of religion in which Protestantism especially came to play different roles in women's and men's identities in modern society.[23] Within evangelicalism, the increasing tendency to emotionalism alienated men, leading to them perceiving in the evangelical conversion a much less intimate relationship with God than was felt by women.[24] Evangelicalism focused religious discourse with increasing intensity upon the home and family, and upon the inculcation of religious and moral values in the next generation through the piety of mothers.[25] The way in which religion (specifically Protestantism) operated within personal identities, and the way in which men and women associated with the churches, diverged, and continued to diverge until well into the twentieth century.[26] Clearly, gender cannot be the only criterion for analysis in the study of the social history of religion in the way social class was for decades. To state the obvious, there are also the vital categories of race, ethnicity, geography and so on. But, I would argue that gender is emerging as possibly the single most important definer of the timing and content of long-term change to the Christian religion of Europe.

3. Third, secularisation as a concept (the decline of religion) has to be problematised as linked to the meta-narrative 'theory of secularisation' which emerged from the Enlightenment and modernity. This linkage has created particular ways of viewing religion (and irreligion and the decline of religion) which rely on social science method (principally either/or notions of religiosity, and the counting of heads). Now, the implication of poststructuralist and postmodernist theories and methods is that the historian of modern religion must contemplate the implications of 'the end of the social' in the social history of religion, and 'the rise of the self' or 'the personal'. A new twin-pronged agenda should be unfolding: a postmodernist discourse analysis of the conceptions of piety in Britain, and a poststructuralist approach to the role of religion in multifarious non-class identities. Secularisation as the decline of the *social* significance of religion thus becomes itself in need of deconstruction. It is a term which imputes change and which, in academic terms, urges scholars to the pursuit of revelation of that change; it does not tend to admit of the possibility of 'sameness' in religiosity over the long term. It even urges those (like the revisionists) who refute the timing of secularisation to the nineteenth century

to think again about using terms like religious 'growth' or 'adaptability' or 'survival' or 'revival'. The language spawned of the secularisation debate is loaded, and in need of linguistic turn.

The postmodernist challenge to the social historian of religion is to turn on our terms (the linguistic turn), to examine discourses of religion (the social construction of religiosity as ideals and anti-ideals – their content, the manner of their circulation, and who benefited from them) and explore experiences of religion (through the rescue, commissioning, reconstruction and study of personal testimony), and thereby to reassess our accepted chronologies and understanding of the nature of change to religion, the churches, spirituality, piety and culture. This will leave secularisation under a three-pronged assault: as a 'false' theory (based on modelling by outmoded methods of sociology which do not match the empirical evidence), as a 'false' narrative (principally of the eighteenth, nineteenth and early twentieth centuries which erroneously chronicled religious decline), and as a 'false' discourse (of the upward progress of the rational western mind evidenced in the false narrative).

4. The revelation that 'religious decline' and 'secularisation' are narratives to be discussed in the way I have attempted above, and in the way previously addressed by scholars like Jeff Cox, is a product of the postmodern condition. It is, in my view, more directly a product of the 1960s and the grievous wound inflicted by that decade upon western Europe's Christianity and culture. It may have taken time (a few decades) for scholarship to catch up with the spiritual turn of the people of that continent, but we are here now discussing the concept of religious change because 'decline' and 'secularisation' are now revealed as uncentred realities. The concept caused few problems to Christian clerics or atheist sociologists in the 1950s and 1960s (beyond some bizarre accusations that it was anti-Christian). We can see now that secularisation is a concept of Christian modernity, wholly produced to bolster the power of the salvation industry in the new rational intellectual economy thrown up by the Enlightenment, and attracting the subscription of those (like Marx and Engels) who wished the process well. The concept and theory of secularisation was intrinsic to the concept and theory of modernisation. It was intrinsic to social science itself – indeed, the latter was constructed upon the former. How can you conceive of social science without a notion of the death of revelatory premodern Christianity? How can you conceive of the concept of modernisation without a faith (yea, a faith) in the decline of a putative religiously inspired ignorance of the cosmos?

And so secularisation emerges to us now, after forty years of postmodern turning away from centred realities in white, Anglo-Saxon, Protestant, Eurocentric, gendered supremacies, as yet another centred reality that 'is being dispersed in clouds of narrative language elements'.[27]

5. This leaves unfinished business. The refashioning of the agenda in the 'post-secularisation-theory' age does not remove the issue of the *cause* of the

new age. For all that the theory, history and discourse of 'secularisation' may be fundamentally flawed on all three counts, secularisation may still plausibly and logically exist. The *theory* of secularisation may be a myth, but *secularisation* is not. Though the theory of secularisation may be wrong, and though the secularisation discourse neglects 'the personal' in piety, the falseness of the narrative history of secularisation should lead not to its *abandonment* but to its *correction*.

There is still an empirical task to be performed. The postmodernist agenda may rightly imply greater continuity in personal piety over the centuries than the structuralist social historian has thus far allowed. But by the same token it is entirely possible that personal piety itself can undergo and has undergone enormous change. It is vital that scholars are willing and able to recognise secularisation when we see it; and if it is to be seen anywhere in British history, it is to be seen most strikingly as starting in the 1960s and continuing in the last forty years of the twentieth century.

Statisticising secularisation

So, we are 'turned back' upon empiricism. There is no conceptual difficulty with this. The decline of religion since 1960 has disturbed the stability of meaning in 'secularisation'. The decline needs to be studied. But how it is done has to change as a result of the lessons of the 1960s.

The medium is the message,[28] and statistics of religion are a striking example of this aphorism. The collection and circulation of statistics of religion have virtually always been linked to a discourse of approval of 'the religious persons' and disapproval of 'the irreligious persons' counted, have implied that religiosity is reducable to an either/or choice, and signal the message that what is being measured is the moral as well as the religious state of the nation. It seems to be self-evident and inescapable that statistics of religion are moral messages. I want to approach that issue through a brief discussion of the problems of religious statistics.

In the first instance, there is the measurement problem: statistics of religion measure formal actions, some of them requiring commitment, some of them requiring very little commitment but merely conformity. Statistics of church membership may not necessarily show what people are doing for their faith (such as going to church), whilst statistics of church-going may not show what people are believing religiously in what they are doing by attending worship. So, the first problem is that such statistics are not necessarily measuring what it is we actually might want to measure. And what we actually want to measure is defined by the social constructions of religiosity employed by the historian. (For the latter, see the third instance below.)

In the second instance, there are the statistical compilation problems: of reliability, comparability and continuity. Religious statistics are those compiled by diverse sources – the churches themselves, government agencies, newspapers, evangelical organisations, and (in some cases) academics. These have diverse origins, and the means of measurement vary, and in very many cases time-series data involve important elements of discontinuity (in definitions of church membership, for instance) which require careful consideration during the compilation of datasets. Such problems are not insuperable in most cases, but they require careful preparation of data.

In the third instance, religious statistics deserve problematisation in a postmodernist sense. The way in which statistics operate is by demanding the imposition of structures upon the field of inquiry, dividing people into the categories needed for counting: church-goers and non-church-goers, church-members and non-members, weddings into church- and civil-solemnised occasions, and so on. In this field of inquiry, one can safely say that such structures induce considerable statistical inaccuracy because (i) those counted as church-goers on one occasion will be non-church-goers on others, and vice versa, and thus impose a false structure; because (ii) changes in the numerical balance between 'opposite' categories in a structure conceal other (sometimes unmeasurable) continuities; because (iii) many of the ways in which religiosity can be measured have rarely been counted; and because (iv) it is clear that we now understand religiosity (from modern cultural theory, if from nowhere else) as something that is composed of characteristics and categories which are not countable.

Domestic and personal religious rituals have rarely been measured in any depth over time, and even social surveys (asking about belief in God, for instance) require a binary structure (in this case, yes/no) which conceals rather than reveals the graduated, complex and often confused nature of faith. More fundamentally, postmodernist analysis of the sort undertaken by Sarah Williams reveals that religious statistics are measuring that which the churches (or clergymen) take to be the gauge of religiosity; they miss the highly gendered and class-based forms of religiosity – sometimes characterised as 'superstition' – which have been prevalent in industrial society, but yet little investigated by scholars of any discipline.[29]

Such examples show that statistics of religion are not 'neutral' measures. Statistics of religion (as of other, perhaps most, fields of inquiry, certainly in the social sciences) are discursively active. They are, in short, judgements which accrue power – faith-power – to those who collect and wield them. Those in use by historians, sociologists and churches since the eighteenth century are an element of a discourse, or series of discourses, on religiosity and secularisation. The churches – male-dominated institutions of a competitive capitalist society – developed categories to be counted because they could show denominational success against other denominations, organisational growth and prosperity, and success in evangelising 'the ungodly' (principally the working classes).

When national religious statistics were collected (by the state in its church-going census of 1851 for instance), it was to show the strength or weakness of Britain as a Christian nation in the midst of its imperial mission. Similar exercises by both individual churches and ecumenical groups in the twentieth century were concerned almost uniformly to display the *failure* of Christian Britain. Diverse discourses lie in these statistical series: a focus on change (in minute shifts in church membership from year to year); a preoccupation with denominational competition which seeks 'growth' in specific forms of measurement; an elite obsession with the scale of 'the lapsed masses' in the Victorian and Edwardian periods; and gendered and class-based approaches which fail to measure those forms of pious expression which were scorned or ignored by the self-appointed judges – the clergymen. Religious statistics, as one Edwardian compiler opined, are 'unimpeachable witnesses to vigour, progress and interest'.[30]

In short, religious statistics are invariably circulating discourses on ecclesias-tical machismo, national righteousness, class commentary or moral judgement (sometimes all at once), and require to be treated as such. The social construc-tion of religious statistics is thus an issue for the historian, as is the historian's employment of them. *The tendency and the danger implicit in that action lie in the perpetuation of that social construction – the discourses of religiosity – into scholarly understanding of the social history of religion.* This leaves the social scientist with the task of justifying the conceptual validity of statistical measurement. The range of measures of religiosity needs to display a number of things. First, there needs to be an awareness of structures (of gender, class and ethnicity, for instance). The on/off binary approach of religious statistics needs to be most carefully reassessed to expose the structures imposed so cav-alierly upon the past and the present. Second, there needs to be awareness of the many different ways in which piety or religiosity may be expressed (now and in the past, in Britain and other places, in different branches of Christianity and other faiths, and, very importantly, in forms independent from conventional church traditions). Third, there must be an appreciation that valid expressions of personal faith may be beyond practical forms of measurement in society (whether now or in the past). And fourth, there needs to be an understand-ing that the implication of 'measurement' is an imposition of discontinuities (however graduated) upon the past; in other words, statistics may not only be impersonal, but take the personal out of the past, and treat it as 'another world' *which it may not be.*

Advocates of secularisation theory in the 1950s, 1960s and 1970s can be accused of failure in most if not all of the above points when they assessed the impact of industrialisation and city growth upon religion in the late eighteenth and early nineteenth centuries. But by the same token, there is a real danger that the postmodernist awareness of the social construction of religious statistics may lead to an overlooking of real historical change when it *did* occur. That remains the task.

Conclusion

The ways religion is studied in the periods of the 1960s, since the 1960s and before the 1960s need to coalesce. There needs to be a sharing of concept and method in the study of religion and society between historians of medieval, early modern and late modern periods, and between the historian, the anthropologist, the cultural- and religious-studies scholar. The postcolonial, the gender and the post-class perspectives of our age need to be brought to bear on all those familiar themes of nineteenth- and twentieth-century British religious history. This means active deployment of reflexivity in our work, involving amongst other things a very keen re-examination of the vocabulary of our field. This in turn needs to feed into how social-science method and postmodernist method fuse together. In such ways, the 1960s not only marked an epoch change in the social history of the religious history of the nation (and of Europe). The sixties also changed the way in which we understand religion and secularisation across human history.

NOTES

1. H. McLeod, *Piety and Poverty: Working-Class Religion in Berlin, London and New York 1870–1914* (New York, 1996); C. G. Brown, 'A revisionist approach to religious change', in S. Bruce (ed.), *Religion and Modernization: Sociologists and Historians Debate the Secularization Thesis* (Oxford, 1992), 37–58 and his 'The mechanism of religious growth in urban societies', in H. McLeod (ed.), *European Religion in the Age of Great Cities 1830–1930* (London, 1995), 239–62.
2. C. G. Brown, *The Death of Christian Britain: Understanding Secularisation 1800–2000* (London, 2001).
3. These estimates come from a variety of sources; see C. G. Brown, 'Religion', in R. Pope (ed.), *Atlas of British Social and Economic History* (London, 1989), 213.
4. Discussion of Sunday school data is to be found in C. G. Brown, 'The Sunday-school movement in Scotland, 1780–1914', *Records of the Scottish Church History Society* 21 (1981), 3–26.
5. A fuller discussion of the crisis in youth recruitment methods to the churches is contained in C. G. Brown, *Religion and Society in Scotland since 1707* (Edinburgh, 1997), chapter 7.
6. S. Wiltshire, 'Spirit of our age: dimensions of religiosity amongst Scottish youth', unpublished PhD thesis, University of Edinburgh, 2001.
7. A full denominationally divided version of this graph appears in Brown, *Religion and Society*, 62–3.
8. C. D. Field, '"The Haemorrhage of Faith?": opinion polls as sources for religious practices, beliefs and attitudes in Scotland since the 1970s', *Journal of Contemporary Religion*, 16 (2001), 157–75.

9. See, for instance, S. J. D. Green, *Religion in the Age of Decline: Organisation and Experience in Industrial Yorkshire 1870–1920* (Cambridge, 1996); M. Smith, *Religion in Industrial Society: Oldham and Saddleworth 1740–1865* (Oxford, 1994); J. Morris, *Religion and Urban Change: Croydon 1840–1914* (Woodbridge, 1992).

10. B. Wilson, *Religion in Secular Society* (Harmondsworth, 1966); D. Martin, *A General Theory of Secularisation* (Oxford, 1978).

11. A notable exception is Steve Bruce. See for instance Bruce (ed.), *Religion and Modernization*.

12. R. Finke and R. Stark, 'Religious economies and sacred canopies: religious mobilisation in American cities, 1906', *American Sociological Review*, 53 (1988), 41–9.

13. Brown, 'A revisionist approach'.

14. An impressive broad-brush account is Hugh McLeod, *Religion and the People of Western Europe 1789–1970* (Oxford, 1981).

15. J. Cox, *The English Churches in a Secular Society: Lambeth 1870–1930* (Oxford, 1981); C. G. Brown, 'Did urbanisation secularise Britain?', *Urban History Yearbook* 1987, 1–15.

16. The most recent advocate of the first is Grace Davie, *Religion in Britain since 1945* (Oxford, 1994), and G. Davie, 'Religion in post-war Britain: a sociological viewpoint', in J. Obelkevich and P. Catterall (eds.), *Understanding Post-War British Society* (London and New York, 1994), 165–78.

17. Steve Bruce, 'Religion in Britain at the close of the twentieth century: a challenge to the silver lining perspective', *Journal of Contemporary Religion*, 11 (1996), 261–75.

18. They are most powerfully to be found in E. R. Wickham, *Church and People in an Industrial City* (London, 1957); K. S. Inglis, *Churches and the Working Classes in Victorian England* (London, 1963); and A. D. Gilbert, *Religion and Society in Industrial England: Church, Chapel and Social Change 1740–1914* (London, 1976).

19. Sarah Williams, 'Urban popular religion and the rites of passage', in McLeod (ed.), *European Religion*, 216–36; S. Williams, 'The problem of belief: the place of oral history in the study of popular religion', *Oral History*, 24 (1996), 27–34; S. Williams, 'The language of belief: an alternative agenda for the study of Victorian working-class religion', *Journal of Victorian Culture*, 1 (1996), 303–16; S. C. Williams, *Religious Belief and Popular Culture in Southwark c. 1880–1939* (Oxford, 1999).

20. C. D. Field, 'The social structure of English Methodism, eighteenth–twentieth centuries', *British Journal of Sociology*, 28 (1977), 199–225; P. Hillis, 'Presbyterianism and social class in mid-nineteenth-century Glasgow: a study of nine churches', *Journal of Ecclesiastical History*, 32 (1981), 47–64.

21. As well as the work of S. Williams, see H. McLeod, 'New perspectives on Victorian working-class religion: the oral evidence', *Oral History*, 14 (1986), 31–49, and C. G. Brown and J. D. Stephenson, ' "Sprouting wings"? Women and religion in Scotland c.1890–c.1950', in E. Gordon and E. Breitenbach (eds.), *Out of Bounds: Women and Religion in Scotland in the Nineteenth and Twentieth Centuries* (Edinburgh, 1992), 95–120.

22. For the medieval period, see for instance P. Ranft, *Women and the Religious Life in Premodern Europe* (Basingstoke, 1996). For the early modern period, see P. Crawford, *Women and Religion in England 1500–1720* (London, 1993). For the late modern period, see Brown, *Death of Christian Britain*.

23. Crawford, *Women and Religion*, 204–8; A. Fletcher, *Gender, Sex and Subordination in England 1500–1800* (New Haven and London, 1995), 347–63; S. Gill, *Women and the Church of England from the Eighteenth Century to the Present* (London, 1994), 83–98; H. McLeod, *Religion and Society in England 1850–1914* (Basingstoke, 1996), 156–68.

24. B. L. Epstein, *The Politics of Domesticity: Women, Evangelism and Temperance in Nineteenth-Century America* (Middletown, CT, 1981), 45–66.

25. J. Rendall, *The Origins of Modern Feminism: Women in Britain, France and the United States 1780–1860* (London, 1985), 73–107.

26. Brown, *Death of Christian Britain*; Brown, *Religion and Society*, chapter 8.

27. J.-F. Lyotard, *The Postmodern Condition: A Report on Knowledge* (Manchester, 1979; 2nd edition 1984), p. xxiv.

28. M. McLuhan, *Understanding Media: The Extensions of Man* (Cambridge, MA, 1964; 2nd edition 1994), p. 15.

29. Williams, 'Urban popular religion and the rites of passage'.

30. R. Mudie-Smith (ed.), *The Religious Life of London* (London, 1904), 6–7.

3   Christendom in decline: the Swedish case

Eva M. Hamberg

Available data indicate that the share of the population who adhere to Christian beliefs or who devote themselves to such traditional religious activities as prayer and church attendance declined in Sweden during the twentieth century. The decline in church attendance can easily be documented. Information on religious beliefs is available only for comparatively recent times; hence, we may run the risk of overestimating the former prevalence of such beliefs.[1] The same is true of information on prayer habits.

It should also be borne in mind that certain forms of religious practice that in the contemporary Swedish situation may be regarded as expressions of religious commitment, e.g. church attendance, formerly were part of a social and cultural pattern to which individuals were expected to conform. While nowadays the share of the population who attend public worship is considerably lower than the share who believe in God, the reverse may have been true in times when church attendance was the prevailing social norm.[2]

Available data indicate a decline not only in the prevalence of religious beliefs, but also in the saliency of these beliefs. A smaller share of the population adhere to the Christian faith, and among those who still do hold on to this faith (or to certain parts of it) many seem to do so with a low degree of personal commitment.[3]

According to the European Values Studies which were carried out in 1981 and 1990, Sweden is one of the most secularised countries in western Europe, in the sense that very low percentages of the population adhere to the Christian faith or attend public worship. In 1990, only 15 per cent of the adult Swedish population (aged 16–74 years) said that they believed in the existence of a personal God, 27 per cent believed in heaven, and 19 per cent in the resurrection of the dead. Only 4 per cent attended church weekly, while another 6 per cent did so monthly. A similar pattern can be found for prayer and Bible reading. In 1990 only 10 per cent of adult Swedes said that they often prayed, while 49 per cent never prayed and 10 per cent hardly ever did so. Bible reading is even less common: according to a Swedish survey undertaken in the mid-1980s, only 8 per cent of the adult population read the Bible at least once a month. Moreover, a comparison of the results of the second European Values Study, undertaken in

1990, with those of the first study, undertaken in 1981, shows that both church attendance and belief in God had decreased in Sweden during the 1980s.[4]

Religious beliefs

Not only can Sweden be described as a very secularised country, in the above-mentioned sense. In addition, available evidence indicates that a large share of those who still believe in God do so with a low degree of personal commitment: using a concept introduced by Thomas Luckmann, one might say that this belief increasingly tends to be accepted as a 'rhetorical system' only.[5] Thus, the European Values Studies show that only a minority of Swedes accord God an important role in their lives. These surveys contained a question on the importance of God in the respondents' lives. Answers were to be given on a ten-point scale, where 1 stood for 'not at all important' and 10 for 'very important'. In 1981, 10 per cent of the adult Swedish population chose the highest point on the scale, and 29 per cent the lowest. A point on the upper half of the scale was chosen by 29 per cent. In 1990, only 8 per cent chose the highest point on the scale, while 35 per cent chose the lowest. A point on the upper half of the scale, i.e. from 6 to 10, was selected by 25 per cent.[6]

Thus, for many of those Swedes who still believe in God, this belief is more or less unimportant. Moreover, conceptions of divinity seem to be changing, the traditional Christian faith in a personal God being superseded by a more unspecified belief in a transcendent power. According to the European Values Study of 1981, 20 per cent of Swedes believed in a personal God and 37 per cent affirmed belief in 'some kind of spirit or life force'.[7] In 1990, the corresponding shares were 15 and 44 per cent, respectively. Evidence of this may also be found in a study of world-views and value-systems in Sweden undertaken in 1986. In this survey some of the questions were 'open', i.e. respondents were asked to answer in their own words. The respondents often expressed a vague belief that there may exist a God, a transcendent power or 'Something'.[8] The following quotations may serve as examples:[9]

That there is something. Perhaps a God or some superior power, don't know. (Man, born in 1968)

Believe that there's something. Not exactly a God, but something else. Cannot say what. (Woman, born in 1968)

I believe in something, I don't quite know what. (Woman, born in 1922)

Believe that there's something divine or spiritual, but don't know what. (Woman, born in 1917)

It is noteworthy that very few respondents mentioned Jesus, even as an historical person. A connection between a decline in belief in Christ and the emergence of a vague belief in 'Something' seems probable. Moreover, a connection between changing concepts of divinity and a decline in the importance accorded to God may be assumed: belief in a vaguely conceived transcendent power would probably tend to be less salient to those who hold it than would belief in a personal God.[10]

While adherence to traditional Christian beliefs has reached very low levels, these seem to have been partly replaced by less orthodox ones.[11] Belief not only in the existence of a transcendent power, not understood as a personal God, but also in reincarnation, has gained ground: in 1990, 17 per cent of adult Swedes stated belief in reincarnation.[12] In particular, this position was held by young people: in the age group 16–24 years, belief in reincarnation was twice as common as in the age group 65–74 years (20 and 10 per cent, respectively).

Other types of non-traditional beliefs may be gaining ground as well. Recent survey data indicate that particularly among young persons interest in various occult phenomena, such as astrology, ghosts and extra-terrestrial beings visiting the earth, is fairly common.[13] Thus, both a decline in traditional Christian beliefs and an increase in other types of religious faith characterise Swedish society today. This process may also be described as an increasing individualisation of life-philosophies or world-views.[14]

Not only is adherence to the basic tenets of the Christian faith low; the decline of traditional religion is even more evident in the very low prevalence of church attendance, prayer and Bible reading. This might be expected if, as suggested above, many of those who still hold a Christian faith do so with a low degree of personal commitment. To the extent that belief in God becomes less important to individuals and/or is replaced by a vague belief in a transcendent power, people would be less likely to engage in religious activities. In addition, these developments may be mutually reinforcing: while declining religious commitment results in declining religious practice, a decline in religious practice may contribute to a development where traditional religious beliefs are replaced by less orthodox ones. This may in turn further contribute to the decline in religious practice, etc.[15]

Religious affiliation

While the level of church attendance is very low in Sweden, the overwhelming majority of the population, 80 per cent , are members of the Church of Sweden. This is true in spite of the fact that Sweden has received a large number of immigrants in recent decades.[16] Among these a considerable proportion belong to the Catholic and Orthodox churches and there are also many Muslims. Approximately 5 per cent of the population belong to one of the so-called 'free churches', including the Congregational, Baptist, Methodist and Pentecostal denominations.

Considering the low numbers of the population who adhere to traditional Christian beliefs and practices, it may seem paradoxical that eight Swedes out of ten belong to the Church of Sweden, which is Evangelical-Lutheran, and was until 2000 the state church, partly governed by the political system. In the Swedish context, however, membership of the state church need not be associated with religious beliefs or religious practice. Even a large majority of those who do not regard themselves as Christian and/or who do not believe in the existence of God are members of the church. For instance, the study of worldviews and value-systems mentioned above found that more than 80 per cent of those who did *not* regard themselves as Christians or who did *not* believe in the existence of God or a transcendent power were members of the Church of Sweden.[17] Moreover, although eight Swedes out of ten are members of this church, they express little confidence in the church. According to the 1990 European Values Study, only 6 per cent of the adult population had great confidence in the church, and 29 per cent had rather great confidence. The majority had little or no confidence in the church!

Probably several factors must be taken into account in an attempt to explain why an overwhelming majority of Swedes continue to be members of the Church of Sweden, regardless of their religious beliefs or lack of such beliefs and regardless of their lack of confidence in the church.

One reason for the continued high membership may be that the church is regarded as a symbol and warrantor of moral decency. This attitude may be exemplified by the statement of a respondent who, although he declared that he did not believe in God, said: 'I still belong to the Church of Sweden. It may be good from a moral point of view' (Man, born in 1917).

It has also been suggested that the high level of affiliation in the Scandinavian national churches may express a form of 'civil religion': membership in these churches may be seen as a way of expressing solidarity with society and its basic values.[18]

Another factor which probably contributes to the low level of non-affiliation is that, until 1996, Swedes automatically became members of the Church of Sweden by birth, unless both parents were non-members. In many cases, membership in the church seems to be taken for granted. In a survey undertaken in 1991, 77 per cent of the respondents said that they had never considered leaving the church. A similar result was obtained in a survey in 1978.[19] Indeed, until 1951, Swedes were prohibited by law from leaving the Church of Sweden, unless they became members of another church or denomination.

Thus, several factors may contribute to explain why formal non-affiliation is comparatively rare in Sweden. While in an American context, the phenomenon of people who are 'believers but not belongers' has been discussed,[20] many Swedes might be described as 'belongers but not believers', with the important qualification that in the Swedish context 'belonging' may be of a formal nature only: most of the 'belongers' rarely engage in religious activities.[21] Obviously, the fact that an overwhelming majority of Swedes are members of the Church of Sweden cannot be seen as evidence of religious commitment.

As mentioned above, one reason why most Swedes, regardless of their religious beliefs or lack of such beliefs, still belong to the Church of Sweden may be that the church is seen as representing certain moral values. This assumption is supported by many of the interviews from the previously mentioned 1986 nationwide study of world-views and value-systems.[22]

In this study, almost two thirds of the respondents chose to describe themselves as 'Christians in their own personal way'.[23] When asked to give their reasons for choosing this self-description 33 per cent of the respondents answered that they adhered to certain ethical principles or lived in a certain way. For many of the respondents, being a Christian (albeit in 'one's own personal way') apparently meant doing one's best, and being honest, considerate and ready to help others. The following quotations may serve as examples:

You should be as decent as possible in your daily life. (Man, born in 1919)

To live as I consider right, to be an honest person. (Man, born in 1920)

I do my best, don't hurt anyone, try to help. I leave people alone. Cannot stand slander. (Woman, born in 1917)

The answers implied in some cases that the respondents adhered to certain ethical principles, in other cases that they lived in a certain way. The answers convey the impression that both types of answers tend to express the same thing: the respondents think that they ought to live according to certain moral standards, and they also think that they do so. Sometimes this is stated explicitly; often it seems to be implied. In many cases the ethical standards seem to be such that they should not be too difficult to live up to. The responses do not give the impression that the high ethical standards of the Sermon on the Mount were considered binding. Rather, the respondents seemed to think that one should do one's best within reasonable limits.[24]

Thus, the study indicates that for many Swedes Christianity is associated primarily with certain moral standards: one should be a kind, honest and law-abiding person, and lead a decent life. Probably this is an important reason why an overwhelming majority of Swedes still belong to the Church of Sweden regardless of their religious beliefs or lack of them.

Are the Swedes 'privately religious'?

While the decline in traditional, church-oriented religion has been very pronounced in Sweden, it has sometimes been alleged that other forms of religion, often called 'private religion', have emerged. These forms have been assumed to contain such elements as belief in a transcendent power and/or belief in some form of life after death.[25] In addition, the 'privately religious' often are assumed to practise certain forms of religious behaviour, such as private prayer or meditation, and to be very interested in questions relating to religion.

Contributing to the assumptions of an emerging 'private religiosity' have been the results from several surveys, where a majority of the population, when asked to choose between alternatives for a religious self-description, have chosen to describe themselves as 'Christians in their own personal way'. Hence, a study of this group may shed light on the question of the prevalence of beliefs and practices which may be seen as expressions of private religiosity.

In the 1986 survey, 41 per cent of those respondents who described themselves as 'Christians in their own personal way' affirmed belief in God or a transcendent power, while 59 per cent either repudiated this belief or were uncertain. The beliefs held often seemed to be vague: rather than belief in a personal God, the respondents expressed a diffuse belief in a transcendent power of some kind. In addition, the answers convey the impression that belief in a divine power, where it existed, often played a minor role in the respondents' lives.[26]

Beliefs concerning the possibility of a life after death also varied among the 'Christians in their own way'. While 23 per cent affirmed belief in a life after death, 19 per cent replied in the negative; the majority, or 59 per cent, were uncertain. As might be expected, belief in God and belief in life after death were related: of those who expressed belief in God or a transcendent power, 50 per cent believed in a life after death, and of those who did *not* believe in God or a transcendent power almost 70 per cent stated that they did not believe in a life after death.[27]

An overwhelming majority (95 per cent) of the 'Christians in their own way' seldom or never participated in public worship. Neither did they devote themselves to private religious activities, such as prayer or meditation. The answers indicate that no kind of religious activity – either public or private – was common among those who chose this self-description.[28]

Thus, the group who described themselves as 'Christian in their own personal way' was far from homogeneous with respect to religiosity. This self-description was chosen for a variety of reasons, not necessarily connected with religious faith or religious commitment. Widely differing religious beliefs – or the absence of such beliefs – were represented among this group. Hence, the fact that a majority of Swedes choose this self-description cannot be interpreted as evidence of a widespread existence of forms of religion which may reasonably be termed 'private' or 'implicit' – at least not if the term 'religion' is substantively defined.

Changing values: a result of secularisation?

Animals and human beings regarded as having equal value

Concomitant with the decline in traditional religious beliefs, other changes in values appear to have taken place. For instance, a world-view where human beings are no longer regarded as being intrinsically different from animals now seems to be fairly widespread in Sweden. In recent years, several surveys have shown that only a minority of Swedes think that human beings have greater value than animals. In the previously mentioned nationwide survey undertaken in 1986, 38 per cent of the respondents agreed that human beings ought to be treated with more respect than animals, while 43 per cent disagreed with this view and 19 per cent were uncertain. According to the European Values Study of 1990, 55 per cent held the opinion that human beings and animals are equally valuable, while 40 per cent accorded a higher value to human beings and the rest were uncertain.[29]

In the 1986 survey, the respondents also were asked to explain the reasons for their answers. Those who held the opinion that human beings should *not* be treated differently usually considered human beings and animals to be in principle of equal value and therefore entitled to the same respect. The reasons for holding the opinion that human beings *should* be treated in a special way were somewhat more varied. The reason most commonly given (by approximately one fifth of the respondents) was that biological factors entitle human beings to special respect. In particular, the fact that human beings are more intelligent than animals was frequently mentioned. Other respondents referred to established custom or gave pragmatic reasons for their opinion (e.g. that we depend on animals for food), while still others were unable to give a reason for their opinion. Very few, however, only a few per cent of the respondents, justified their opinion by referring to the special status accorded to human beings in Christian doctrine.[30]

Thus, only a minority of Swedes think that human beings have greater value and should be treated with more respect than animals. Of course, the fact that many Swedes regard animals and human beings as having equal value does not imply that they actually treat animals and human beings in the same way. Only a minority are vegetarians, for instance, and one may assume that almost everyone, if having to choose between saving a human being or an animal, would opt for saving a human life. Moreover, there is a tendency to distinguish between different types of animals.[31] In particular, a very high value is accorded to dogs, while insects sometimes are mentioned as exceptions to the rule, as illustrated by the following answer: 'One ought to show respect for all living beings, except mosquitoes, spiders, and flies' (Woman, born in 1950). Thus, while in fact human beings are treated differently from animals, this special treatment now tends to be based on biological or pragmatic grounds rather than on theological or ideological principles. Although we cannot be certain that the tendency to regard animals as being in principle on a par with human beings is a new phenomenon, it would seem plausible that this may be one aspect of the secularisation process. In the absence of theological reasons for ascribing a special status to human beings, people may find it difficult to base such a status on grounds of principle.

It is also conceivable that the view that animals should be treated with the same respect as human beings may be connected to belief in reincarnation, as suggested by this response in an interview: 'I don't kill an insect – you never know. The bumble-bee may be Mrs Johansson' (Man, born in 1925). If animals are regarded as possibly being deceased relatives or friends, a tendency to see animals and human beings as meriting the same degree of respect would perhaps not be surprising! Thus, changes in views concerning animals may conceivably reflect several aspects of the secularisation process.

Health as the most important value in life

Another aspect of the secularisation process may be a change in the importance attached to health. Survey data indicate that many Swedes see good health as the most important value in life. In the 1986 survey, the respondents were asked what they regarded as most important in their lives. The value most often given (mentioned by 45 per cent) was health. About a third mentioned families or friends and about a quarter of the respondents gave answers related to their economic situation.[32]

While we have no means of knowing the importance attached to this value some fifty or hundred years ago, it seems probable that the concern for health has increased in recent decades. One of the reasons for this assumption is the fact that the market for health-food, magazines and other products catering to the interest in preserving or improving one's health has expanded rapidly, as has the number of health centres and institutes for physical training.

Several factors may conceivably contribute to the interest taken in health. One may be a trend towards individualisation, including such themes as self-expression, self-realisation and personal autonomy, which tend to bestow a sacred status upon the individual.[33] Illness and death being the ultimate threat to the individual's existence, the increasing importance accorded to self-realisation and personal autonomy may well lead to a growing concern for preserving or improving one's health.

Another factor, related to individualisation, may be the declining adherence to traditional religious beliefs. As belief in a personal God becomes less widespread, fewer people hold the belief that life and health ultimately depend on a divine power. As a result, people may to an increasing extent see themselves as responsible for their health and well-being. Moreover, changing beliefs about life after death may well have an impact on the importance attached to health: the declining prevalence of belief in a life hereafter may lead to an increased interest in prolonging the present life. Hence, it seems possible that the importance attached to health may be yet another result of the secularisation process.

Factors behind the secularisation process

While Sweden is one of the most secularised countries in western Europe, in the sense that low numbers of the population adhere to the Christian faith or attend public worship, survey data indicate that Swedes, living in the modern welfare state, are on average more happy and satisfied with their lives than are Europeans in general. The possibility of a connection between these facts has been suggested: it has been assumed that the demand for religion may have declined as a result of the rise in material welfare.[34]

It should be pointed out, however, that even if a correlation can be established between low levels of traditional religiosity and high levels of subjectively experienced satisfaction with life, this need not be interpreted as evidence of a direct causal relationship; for instance, such a correlation, if it does exist, may be due to underlying factors influencing both religiosity and life satisfaction. To the extent that satisfaction with life is related to material welfare, it seems more likely that *both* the increase in material welfare and life satisfaction *and* a decline in demand for traditional religion may be different aspects of the process of modern economic growth, which since the beginning of the Industrial Revolution, to varying degrees, has been transforming western societies. Several aspects of this process, notably migration and urbanisation, may conceivably have contributed to the decline in traditional religiosity.[35]

Such explanations assume that the present low levels of religiosity in countries like Sweden are caused by a low *demand* for religion, possibly related to the high levels of social welfare and subjective life satisfaction. This assumption, however, is not uncontested. While scholarly attempts to explain the low levels of traditional religiosity in many European countries often have been focused on the demand for religion, a trend in recent research has been to shift the attention to factors associated with the *supply* of religion.

The lack of religious pluralism as a factor contributing to the secularisation process

Although the secularisation process has gone further in Sweden than in most other European countries, the European countries in general can, with few exceptions, be described as secularised. Hence Sweden stands out less as an exception from the rest of Europe, than as a country where the European trend towards secularisation is particularly evident. Typically, European countries are characterised by low levels of religious participation.[36] This is in sharp contrast to the United States, where over the last two centuries religious participation has been increasing and where today approximately 65 per cent of the population belong to a church congregation.[37]

The reasons for the difference in levels of participation in most European countries and in America have been much discussed among scholars. While previously many scholars have taken for granted that religious pluralism weakens religious adherence, a growing number of studies have suggested that high levels of religious pluralism are in fact associated with high levels of religious participation.[38]

As a matter of fact, the connection between religious pluralism and religious participation was observed long ago. In the nineteenth century, American visitors to Europe were surprised by the low levels of religious activity they found there. Conversely, European visitors to the United States remarked on the high level of religious participation. Moreover, Europeans discussing the American religious situation often gave the same explanation for the difference between Europe and America: whereas Europe was characterised by religious monopolies, in America a number of churches vigorously competed in a free religious market.[39]

Hence, the difference between the strong position of religion in the United States and the low levels of religious participation in many European countries can be understood as an effect of religious pluralism versus monopoly. As stated in one of the major studies in this field: 'There is ample evidence that in societies with putative monopoly faiths, religious indifference, not piety, is rife.'[40]

The religious market structure in Sweden

According to Laurence R. Iannaccone, religious pluralism forces religious organisations to be responsive to their members and to make efficient use of their resources, and ensures a rich religious supply.[41] Iannaccone has also presented empirical evidence in support of this hypothesis, e.g. in a cross-cultural study of seventeen western nations, where he found the levels of church attendance and religious belief to be significantly higher in countries with high levels of religious pluralism.[42]

It should be noted, however, that the absence of religious pluralism need not *necessarily* lead to low religious participation.[43] An obvious case occurs when regulations enable a state-supported monopoly church to enforce participation. Historically this has not been unusual in the European context. Thus, in Sweden attendance was high during the period when the Church of Sweden still enjoyed a full religious monopoly, a situation which lasted until the mid-nineteenth century.[44] The high level of attendance can be attributed not only to conformity with the prevailing social norms, but also to state regulations, which enforced a certain level of attendance. For instance, receiving Holy Communion at least once a year was mandatory until 1862, and those who abstained did not enjoy full citizenship.[45] Thus, under certain circumstances religious participation may be high even when one church has a religious monopoly.[46]

While the Church of Sweden no longer enjoys a full monopoly on 'the religious market', it did so until the mid-nineteenth century. As people's religious choices tend to display considerable inertia, the effects of religious regulation and monopoly may, however, be long-lived: 'Even after a state church is disestablished and the religious market is legally opened, it may take generations for the situation to approach that of a perfectly competitive market.'[47] This inertia is attributed not only to the effects of indoctrination and habit formation, but also to the special character of religion: in order to appreciate a particular kind of religion, a person needs specific knowledge, a knowledge which may be regarded as a form of 'human capital'. As switching to another form of religion would make much of this human capital obsolete, people will be reluctant to change their affiliation.[48]

Moreover, although the separation between the church and the state in Sweden accelerated during the twentieth century, full separation took place only in the year 2000.[49]

Thus, the Swedish religious market, while no longer monopolistic, is in fact still of a nearly monopolistic character. It would seem to correspond rather well to Iannaccone's description of 'a heavily subsidized dominant firm, run or regulated by the state. A large number of smaller, independent, and competing firms may exist at the dominant firm's periphery.'[50] Iannaccone expects the public provision of religion in this type of market to be characterised by inefficiency, and the overall level of religious consumption to be lower than it would be if the market were competitive. Thus, 'we might predict that in countries or regions where the government's role in the provision of religion is unusually high, actual levels of religious practice and belief will be unusually low'.[51] As should be evident from the above, Iannaccone's statement would serve well as a description of the Swedish situation.

From a supply-side perspective, the religious situation in contemporary Sweden can be seen as the result of a long period of religious monopoly or near-monopoly, when almost the whole population has belonged to the Church of Sweden. With the exception of certain rites such as baptisms, weddings and funerals, the religion supplied by the dominant church appears to be in low demand.

Moreover, recent studies support the assumption that religious pluralism – or the lack of pluralism – may have important effects on religious participation. Although the overall degree of religious pluralism in Sweden still is very low, empirical studies indicate that regional differences in religious pluralism, although small, do have an impact on participation.

In two studies based on Swedish church statistics, the hypothesis of a positive relationship between the degree of religious pluralism and the level of religious participation was tested.[52] The results were consistent with the assumption that pluralism has an impact on participation: in those municipalities where the degree of religious pluralism was higher than average, religious participation also was higher. These studies indicate that the different degrees of pluralism in Swedish local religious economies may partially explain the regional differences in participation. However, the results do not indicate that the degree of pluralism can be regarded as the *only* factor influencing the level of religious participation. Rather, the degree of pluralism seems to be one among several factors that influence participation.

The effects of religious supply on religious participation have also been empirically studied from another perspective. In a recent study, changes in the supply of worship services and in church attendance within the Church of Sweden were studied. This study showed that attendance had developed better in parishes which had considerably increased the diversity and/or availability of worship services than in parishes which had not. Both increased availability of services and increased diversity between types of services were positively related to attendance. Thus, a rich supply of worship services seems to lead to increased attendance. *Possibly, the very low levels of church attendance which generally prevail in Sweden may be due less to a general lack of demand for worship services than to a lack in demand for the types of services which usually are provided.*[53]

Supply and demand factors in the secularisation process

Obviously, attempts to understand the secularisation process need to take both demand and supply factors into account. For an equilibrium situation to exist, the supply of religious 'goods' provided by religious organisations should equal the demand for religion in a given 'market'. In a pluralistic religious market this can be expected to occur, at least in the long run.

In a nearly monopolistic or oligopolistic religious market, however, a latent demand for religion may exist which is not met by the existing churches or denominations. In such a market, although demand for the existing religious 'goods' may be low, there may exist a latent demand for other types of religion not supplied by the existing organisations. However, the market structure may not provide enough incentives for other religious organisations to emerge.[54]

Thus, in a country like Sweden there may conceivably exist a latent demand for religious consumption, which is not met by the religious organisations presently existing. What appears to be a low level of demand for religion may be a low level of demand for *the available forms of religion*. Although the level of latent demand may be impossible to estimate, an attempt to understand processes of religious change needs to take both demand and supply factors into account.

Although probably several factors contribute to explain the religious situation in contemporary Sweden, empirical data indicate that this situation may *at least partly* be understood as the result of a long period of religious monopoly: for centuries the religious market has been dominated by the Church of Sweden. The empirical data presented in this chapter certainly seem to support the assertion that 'in societies with putative monopoly faiths, religious indifference, not piety, is rife'.[55]

NOTES

1. See e.g. Karel Dobbelaere, 'Secularization: a multi-dimensional concept', *Current Sociology*, 29(2) (1981), 31–5; Rodney Stark and Laurence R. Iannaccone, 'A supply-side reinterpretation of the "Secularization" of Europe', *Journal for the Scientific Study of Religion*, 33(3) (1994), 241–4, 249.
2. Eva M. Hamberg, *Studies in the Prevalence of Religious Beliefs and Religious Practice in Contemporary Sweden* (Uppsala, 1990), 55.
3. *Ibid.*
4. Eva M. Hamberg, 'Secularization and value change in Sweden', in Thorleif Pettersson and Ole Riis (eds.), *Scandinavian Values: Religion and Morality in the Nordic Countries* (Uppsala, 1994), 179–83.
5. Cf. Thomas Luckmann, *The Invisible Religion: The Problem of Religion in Modern Society* (New York, 1967), 88–90.
6. Hamberg, 'Secularization and value change', 188.
7. *Ibid.*, 179.
8. Hamberg, *Studies in the Prevalence of Religious Beliefs*, 44.
9. The quotations cited here and elsewhere in the text have been translated from the Swedish language as literally as possible.
10. Hamberg, 'Secularization and value change', 183.
11. Similar developments can be traced in other, less secularised, European countries as well. See, e.g., Peter Ester, Loek Halman and Ruud de Moor, 'Value shift in western societies', in Peter Ester, Loek Halman and Ruud de Moor (eds.), *The Individualizing Society: Value Change in Europe and North America* (Tilburg, 1993), 9, and Stephen Harding and David Phillips with Michael Fogarty, *Contrasting Values in Western Europe: Unity, Diversity and Change* (London, 1986), 46–9.
12. Hamberg, 'Secularization and value change', 186.
13. Ulf Sjödin, *En skola – flera världar: värderingar hos elever och lärare i religionskunskap i Gymnasieskolan* (Helsingborg, 1995), 80–101.
14. For a definition of the terms 'life-philosophy' and 'world-view', see Eva M. Hamberg, 'Migration and religious change: changes of life-philosophies in connection with migration', in Sven Gustavsson and Harald Runblom (eds.), *Language, Minority, Migration: Yearbook 1994/95 from the Centre for Multiethnic Research* (Uppsala, 1995), 153–4.

15. Eva M. Hamberg, 'Stability and change in religious beliefs, practice and attitudes: a Swedish panel study', *Journal for the Scientific Study of Religion*, 30(1) (1991), 63–80; Hamberg, 'Secularization and value change', 183.

16. Eva M. Hamberg, 'World-views and value systems among immigrants: long-term stability or change? A study of Hungarian immigrants in Sweden', *Sociale Wetenschappen*, 38(4) (1995), 86–7.

17. Hamberg, *Studies in the Prevalence of Religious Beliefs*, 39.

18. Göran Gustafsson, *Tro, samfund och samhälle: sociologiska perspektiv*, 2nd edition (Örebro, 1997), 184–5.

19. Jonas Alwall, Göran Gustafsson and Thorleif Pettersson, *Svenska kyrkans medlemmar och kyrka-statfrågan* (Stockholm, 1991), 36.

20. Wade Clark Roof and William McKinney, *American Mainline Religion: Its Changing Shape and Future* (New Brunswick, NJ, 1987), 52.

21. Hamberg, *Studies in the Prevalence of Religious Beliefs*, 39. Cf. Grace Davie, 'Believing without belonging: is this the future of religion in Britain?', *Social Compass*, 37(4) (1990), 455–69, for a discussion of 'believing without belonging' in Britain.

22. The results of this study are reported in Hamberg, *Studies in the Prevalence of Religious Beliefs*.

23. The respondents were asked to choose between the following alternatives (the percentage choosing each alternative is given in parentheses): 'I'm a practising Christian' (9 per cent); 'I'm a Christian in my own personal way' (63 per cent); 'I'm not a Christian' (26 per cent).

24. Hamberg, *Studies in the Prevalence of Religious Beliefs*, 46–7.

25. When the term 'private religion' is used in this way, it denotes a phenomenon rather similar to what has been termed 'implicit religion'. See Davie, 'Believing without belonging', 455–7 *et passim*.

    As the term 'private religion' is used here it presupposes a substantive definition of religion. However, other definitions would be possible. With a functional definition of religion, 'private religion' might be used to denote what has been called 'invisible religion'. See Thomas Luckmann, *The Invisible Religion: The Problem of Religion in Modern Society* (New York, 1967) and Thomas Luckmann, 'Shrinking transcendence, expanding religion?', *Sociological Analysis*, 50(2) (1990), 137. For substantive versus functional definitions of religion, see e.g. Peter Berger, *The Sacred Canopy: Elements of a Sociological Theory of Religion* (Garden City, NY, 1967), Appendix I.

26. Hamberg, *Studies in the Prevalence of Religious Beliefs*, 44, 53–4.

27. Hamberg, 'Secularization and value change', 186.

28. *Ibid.*, 186–7.

29. *Ibid.*, 189.

30. *Ibid.*, 189–90.

31. *Ibid.*, 190.

32. *Ibid.*, 191.

33. See Luckmann, 'Shrinking transcendence', 138.

34. Thorleif Pettersson, *Bakom dubbla lås: en studie av små och långsamma värderingsförändringar* (Stockholm, 1988), 108–13; Thorleif Pettersson, 'Welfare policies, religious commitment and happiness', in Laurence Brown (ed.), *Religion, Personality and Mental Health* (New York, 1994), 174–92.

35. Hamberg, 'Secularization and value change', 193.
36. See, e.g., Loek Halman and Ruud de Moor, 'Religion, churches and moral values', in Peter Ester, Loek Halman and Ruud de Moor (eds.), *The Individualizing Society: Value Change in Europe and North America* (Tilburg, 1993), 42–7 and Harding *et al.*, *Contrasting Values in Western Europe*, 35–45.
37. Roger Finke and Rodney Stark, *The Churching of America, 1776–1990: Winners and Losers in our Religious Economy* (New Brunswick, NJ, 1992), 15; Stark and Iannaccone, 'A supply-side reinterpretation', 249.
38. See, e.g., Roger Finke and Rodney Stark, 'Religious economies and sacred canopies: religious mobilization in American cities, 1906', *American Sociological Review*, 53(1) (1988), 41–9; Roger Finke and Rodney Stark, 'How the upstart sects won America: 1776–1850', *Journal for the Scientific Study of Religion* 28(1) (1989), 27–44; Finke and Stark, *The Churching of America*; Roger Finke and Laurence R. Iannaccone, 'Supply-side explanations for religious change', *The Annals of the American Academy of Political and Social Science*, 527 (1993), 27–39; Laurence R. Iannaccone, 'The consequences of religious market structure: Adam Smith and the economics of religion', *Rationality and Society*, 3(2) (1991), 156–77; Laurence R. Iannaccone, 'Religious markets and the economics of religion', *Social Compass*, 39(1) (1992), 123–31; Rodney Stark, 'German and German-American religiousness: approximating a crucial experiment', *Journal for the Scientific Study of Religion*, 36(2) (1997), 182–93; Rodney Stark, Roger Finke and Laurence R. Iannaccone, 'Pluralism and piety: England and Wales, 1851', *Journal for the Scientific Study of Religion*, 34(4) (1995), 431–44; Stark and Iannaccone, 'A supply-side reinterpretation'; Rodney Stark and James C. McCann, 'Market forces and Catholic commitment: exploring the new paradigm', *Journal for the Scientific Study of Religion*, 32(2) (1993), 111–24; Eva M. Hamberg and Thorleif Pettersson, 'The religious market: denominational competition and religious participation in contemporary Sweden', *Journal for the Scientific Study of Religion*, 33(3) (1994), 205–16; Hamberg and Pettersson, 'Short-term changes in religious supply and church attendance in contemporary Sweden', *Research in the Social Scientific Study of Religion*, 8 (1997).
39. Stark, 'German and German-American religiousness', 183.
40. Finke and Stark, *The Churching of America*, 19.
41. Iannaccone, 'Religious markets', 123–31.
42. Iannaccone, 'The consequences of religious market structure', 169–72.
43. See Hamberg and Pettersson, 'The religious market', 208.
44. In Sweden, church records containing both general population information and information on various aspects of religious life have been kept since the seventeenth century, making it possible to study religious participation in a long historical perspective. See Thorleif Pettersson, 'Swedish church statistics: unique data for sociological research', *Social Compass*, 35 (1988), 15–31.
45. Pettersson, 'Swedish church statistics', 19.
46. In contemporary Ireland and Poland religious participation has remained high despite the lack of religious pluralism. In these societies, however, the church has played an important role in the political resistance to external domination; hence, religious participation there also has served the function of expressing commitment to nationalism (Finke and Stark, 'Religious economies', 42).
47. Iannaccone, 'The consequences of religious market structure', 163.

48. *Ibid.*
49. Hamberg and Pettersson, 'The religious market', 206–7.
50. Iannaccone, 'The consequences of religious market structure', 160.
51. *Ibid.*, 162.
52. Hamberg and Pettersson, 'The religious market'; Thorleif Pettersson and Eva M. Hamberg, 'Denominational pluralism and church membership in contemporary Sweden: a longitudinal study of the period 1974–1995', *Journal of Empirical Theology*, 10 (1997), 61–78.
53. Hamberg and Pettersson, 'Short-term changes', 35–51.
54. For a fuller discussion of this, see Hamberg and Pettersson, 'The religious market', 214–15.
55. Finke and Stark, *The Churching of America*, 19.

4   New Christianity, indifference and diffused spirituality

Yves Lambert

When theories of secularisation came to the forefront in the 1960s and 1970s,[1] western religious evolution appeared to be *The Decline of the Sacred in Industrial Society*,[2] especially in Europe. It is well known that the last thirty years have further complicated this pattern. We have witnessed the rise of the NRMs (New Religious Movements), the expansion of Pentecostal, Evangelical and Charismatic tendencies (throughout Christianity), the worldwide success of Pope John Paul II, the diffusion of parallel beliefs (astrology, telepathy, near death experiences, and so on), the development of religious fundamentalism, although essentially in the non-western world (especially the Islamic countries), and the collapse of communism in eastern Europe. Now we speak of desecularisation[3] and the recomposition of religion.[4] Meanwhile, in western Europe, the erosion of religious belonging paradoxically continues and the secularisation thesis remains the only master narrative, as Jeffrey Cox observes. But how can we explain both of these tendencies?

From the beginning of modernity until now, we can in fact observe five principal trends at work in current western religious evolutions: the development of secular systems, religious decline, transformations/revivals of Christianity, traditionalist-fundamentalist reactions, and innovations, especially new religious forms (NRMs, para-scientific beliefs, self-spirituality). Lester Kurtz[5] refers to: (1) the substitution of religious traditions by rationalism, scientism and individualism; (2) secularisation; (3) the revitalisation of traditional forms; (4) the construction of quasi-religious forms, such as civil religion or ideologies (the latter I personally consider as secular forms); (5) the creation of new forms of religious beliefs and practices. I propose an analytical model that can explain all of these aspects. We can construct such a model if we identify the distinguishing features of modernity and their typical religious effects. Then, we can consider the transformation of Christendom into Christianity and other ongoing changes.

Modernity as a new 'axial age': a comparative approach to religious changes

In order to identify the features and changes previously mentioned, it is useful to treat modernity as a new 'axial age', as compared to the former one. The concept of 'axial age' was first used to refer to one historical period: the emergence of universalism, philosophy, the great religions and early science.[6] This was especially true of the fifth and sixth centuries BCE, which were a key stage in this process (Deutero-Isaiah, the era of Pericles, the Upanishads, Jain, Buddha, Confucius, Lao-Tze), of which Christianity and Islam are the offspring. This age is considered as 'axial' because we continue to be its heirs, particularly through the principal religions. Jaspers regarded the turn taken by modernity in the nineteenth century as the harbinger of a probable 'second axial period' because radically new features were reshaping whole societies.[7] His only hesitation was that globalisation was not yet a widespread phenomenon when he first wrote his thesis in 1949; undoubtedly, we can assume that this is the case today. Jaspers identified modernity through four fundamental distinguishing features: modern science and technology; a longing for freedom; the emergence of the masses on the historical stage (nationalism, democracy, socialism, social movements); and globalisation. We should add to this list the primacy of reason (a point that Jaspers implicitly includes in the four features), and the development of capitalism and functional differentiation (the rise of the modern state, and Parsons' and Luhmann's concept of differentiation of the spheres of activity in society).[8] We could select a set of criteria more or less different, but the main thing is not to miss something of importance.

In a very schematic fashion, we can periodise modernity, that is, trace it historically through four periods. It starts essentially with the fifteenth and sixteenth centuries, which are the beginning not only of the 'modern age' according to historians, but also of modern science, capitalism and the bourgeoisie. But modernity only becomes a major phenomenon at the end of this period, with the Enlightenment, the English, American and French revolutions, and the birth of the experimental method and industry (the second analytic phase). The third phase includes the development and triumph of industrial society and of capitalism (nineteenth to mid-twentieth centuries), the development of class conflicts, socialism and communism, the spread of nationalism and colonialism up to its breaking point with the eruption of the two world wars. And finally decolonisation, as well as the triumph of democracy, the affluent society and the welfare state in the west. The 1960s and 1970s are often considered as a turning-point towards post-industrial society and the so-called knowledge-based society (information, communication, new technologies), marked by the predominance of the tertiary sector, the decline of the working class, and finally the collapse of communism, and also the development of a consumer society, the moral and anti-authoritarian revolution, new social movements (fourth phase) and full globalisation.

Are we still in the age of modernity or in a postmodernity? I share the opinion of Anthony Giddens,[9] who writes that 'rather than entering a period of post-modernism, we are moving into one in which the consequences of modernity are becoming more radicalized and universalized than before'. We can then refer to the present phase as 'ultra-modernity', following the term proposed by Jean-Paul Willaime.[10] However, if we consider modernity as a new axial period, we cannot know at what exact point we are in this process, in as much as modernity involves permanent change, even change at an accelerated pace, which could produce a kind of permanent turning-point, instead of following a prolonged phase of stabilisation.

Before returning to modernity, let us first remind ourselves of the characteristics of the religions of salvation (especially Buddhism, Christianity and Islam), when they emerged in the preceding axial age, in comparison with those of ancient polytheistic religions. One can briefly mention the following characteristics: an extension to everyone and everywhere (universalism); a major advance in the 'demythologisation' of nature (with regard to the divinisation of natural forces); consequently, the abandonment of animal sacrifice, as the once central rite of agrarian and polytheistic religions; the rejection of the notion of divine affiliation of sovereigns or of aristocracy; the unification and rationalisation of religious concepts in reference to a single God (monotheism) or to a sole principle (atman-brahman); an emphasis on ethical and spiritual aspects, especially the instilling of perfect justice for all, either under the judgement of God or under the logic of karma; post-mortem destiny (salvation) being rendered dependent on one's behaviour in this world; a pre-eminence bestowed on 'other-worldly' accomplishment in replacement of 'this-worldly' success (paradise/hell, rebirth/nirvana), thus, the human condition being perceived as an imperfect and provisional state from which one needs to be saved (hence, the expression 'religions of salvation'); a greater importance placed upon the inner faith as opposed to the scrupulous execution of religious rites; a formal equality of every individual before ethical and religious law and before salvation, to which even the sovereign is subservient; the development of theological and philosophical speculation with the emergence of clerics; proselytism as a consequence of universalism and the call to salvation.

These characteristics are to be considered in relation to general changes with which they are intertwined: a greater mastery of nature on a large scale; urbanisation; the emergence of new social spheres, in particular a middle class and clerics who claimed an ethico-spiritual wisdom;[11] the formation of vast empires, which were themselves sources of universalism owing to the encountering of different religions and the imposition of rules and destinies upon indigenous populations; the widening of the distance between extreme social conditions, which became a cause for the demands for perfect justice and compensation in the future; finally, a greater independence of individuals in relation to primary groups, which brought about a more personal religiosity. Indeed, an internal Christian interpretation would consider all these changes as the conditions leading to the time of the final revelation, but in this case we are trying to provide an explanation in the field of social sciences.

This turning-point was a radical rupture with regard to former religions. Almost all the polytheistic religions were eliminated. After their triumph, Christianity, Buddhism and Islam acquired characteristics that, in some respects, brought them closer to the preceding religions: remythologisation of nature, multiplication of mediators, ritualism, hierarchisation and institutionalisation, patriarchalism, and religious legitimisation of power. Christianity, Buddhism and Islam became agents of the symbolic unification of empires; Christianity, starting with the emperor Theodosius, also eliminated 'pagan' religions and philosophies. It placed its stamp on all aspects of civilisation, which led to Christendom.

We may assume that modernity, if it is in a new axial age, also stands as a major challenge to established religions, especially in its phase of radicalisation and generalisation. In theory, the disappearance of earlier religions is even possible. 'I am reasonably sure', said Bellah,[12] that 'even though we must speak from the midst of it, the modern situation represents a stage of religious development in many ways profoundly different from that of historic religion.' In addition, as Gordon Melton[13] remarks,

during the twentieth century, the West has experienced a phenomenon it has not encountered since the reign of Constantine: the growth of and significant visible presence of a variety of non-Christian and non-orthodox Christian bodies competing for the religious allegiance of the public. This growth of so many religious alternatives is forcing the West into a new situation in which the still dominant Christian religion must share its centuries-old hegemony in a new pluralistic religious environment.

Religious declines, transformations, traditionalist reactions and innovations

Sociologists of religion generally use only three or four criteria to define modernity (rationalisation, individualisation, functional differentiation, globalisation) and do not carry out an historical analysis of their effects (and reciprocal effects) on religion; furthermore, sociologists of secularisation overestimate the aspects of decline and privatisation. Therefore, let us consider the diverse and contradictory effects of each of the seven features of modernity on religion, as well as the combination of such effects: the primacy of reason, science and technology, the longing for freedom, the emergence of the masses, economic development, modern functional differentiation and globalisation. The way these factors have historically worked could explain the religious situation in each country. Conversely, we could analyse the influence of religion on the modernisation process but, owing to space constraints, I shall not proceed to this type of analysis here. Instead, I shall summarise the main conclusions of an analysis which was originally published in 1999;[14] with some exceptions, I shall refrain from any reference to empirical data for the study of the current situation.

1. As we know, on the one hand, the exercise of reason led to the contesting of the primacy of revelation and religious authority, criticism of religion (to the point of making religion a human invention), autonomy of thought, secular ethics and philosophies, and even a purely rational vision of the world (rationalism). On the other hand, reason has been seen as emanating from God and as a powerful factor for adapting to modernity by means of rationalisation, as Ernst Troeltsch and Max Weber emphasised. Partially, in reaction against the excesses of rationalisation, ultra-modernity opens towards a relativisation of reason, a marginalisation of rationalism and a revalorisation of intuition and emotion. This change is undoubtedly by its very nature capable of creating a context that is more favourable to a religious or spiritual attitude. Knowing that other changes are moving in the same direction, as we shall see, undoubtedly contributes to explaining the expansion of a religiosity of emotional community (Pentecostalism, Evangelicalism, Charismatism), the diffusion of NRMs and the progression of self-spirituality, all typical phenomena of ultra-modernity.

2. The development of science and technology revolutionised ways of seeing and living. It could lead to religious decline (atheism, agnosticism, scientism, materialism), as well as to reinterpretations (demythologisation, critical exegesis, 'this-worldliness'), fundamentalist reactions (creationism), or religious innovations (deism, para-scientific beliefs and New Religious Movements: modern astrology, telepathy, notions of positive and negative waves, and notions of cosmic energy). Here again, ultra-modernity is synonymous with relativisation: indeed, faith in science and technology remains high but, henceforth, it runs the risk of being dangerous to mankind; in other respects, there is no longer a belief in indefinite progress and Marxism suffered the after-effects of the failure of communism. Finally, what emerges today is a renewed landscape. It is acknowledged that one cannot prove or invalidate the existence of God by science. New conflicts have emerged (genetic manipulation, euthanasia, etc.), but they do not seem to question religion itself, and they are divisive among all camps. We can obtain an indirect idea of the impact of reason and science, for example, through research data on belief in God and on the perception of the Bible, even if these are indicative of a more general effect.

3. Likewise, individual freedom may give rise to a rejection of religion, indifference, as well as to a more personal faith or to the adoption of new religious insights and practices, as the above mentioned comparatists have already highlighted. Indeed, Protestantism was the first widespread religious expression of

the desire for liberty and freedom. The triumph of freedom at first had its effects on religious freedom and on freedom of thought, and then expanded towards other areas. This triumph of freedom also had effects which were rather irreligious when churches opposed it, and rather religious when they supported it: the Catholic Church did not fully recognise freedom of conscience until the Second Vatican Council (1962–65). Ultra-modernity is characterised by an individualisation that is even more advanced in conquering the areas of sexuality and family life; the longing for freedom has further inflamed the conflict between permissiveness and Christian ethics, especially sexual freedom, divorce, living out of wedlock, homosexuality, abortion. However, recent data demonstrate a decline of permissiveness and a convergence in the morals of the more and the less religious.

4. The emergence of the masses on the historical stage (nationalism, democracy, socialism, communism, fascism, social movements) has also had contradictory effects on religion, depending on the historical role of the church or religious groups (i.e., support, neutrality or opposition) and the attitude of the masses *vis-à-vis* religion, as David Martin[15] has already pointed out. For instance, opposition in the cases of the unification of Italy (the problem of the Papal States), the beginnings of the French Republic, socialism and communism; support in the cases of Polish and Irish nationalism, English working-class Methodism, and democracy in other countries. Previous authors have underestimated these questions, but have noticed all the aspects concerning the lay tendency, the approach to the masses, the revalorisation of man ('poor sinner' in the past). Ultra-modernity turns the page of all these conflicts (with the exception of Northern Ireland) for the benefit of defending democracy and human rights, while communism has collapsed. Thus, even here, we observe a renewed landscape. The research data indicate that religious differences between the working class and the upper class have diminished and that, if the religious profiles of the left and right electorates remain contrasting, they are less so than before.

5. The effects of economic development are more difficult to identify because they are more indirect, except if we consider the social consequences of the development of capitalism (proletarisation, and so on, see above). Economic development has been a factor in the rise of materialism, secular 'this-wordliness', cynicism, and the emergence of vocational ethics (as was illustrated by the famous Weber thesis), and 'this-worldly' religious reinterpretation and commitment. The correlation between the per capita GDP and religiosity is not very conclusive; the same applies to the level of income. According to Dobbelaere and Jagodzinski,[16] among the ten countries included in the survey, the least developed have the highest levels of religiosity (Ireland, followed by Spain and Italy), while the most developed have a moderate or low level of religiosity (Germany, followed by France and Sweden). But that would no longer be

confirmed if the analysis took into account Luxembourg, Switzerland, Austria, Canada and, above all, the United States, which are among the most developed nations but have the highest levels of religiosity.

6. By functional differentiation we mean modern state building, differentiation between the public sphere and the private sphere, and the autonomisation, as described by Luhmann, of the spheres of activity (subsystems): politics, economics, science, education, law, art, health, family, religion. Functional differentiation contributed to depriving churches of their monopoly in education, culture and the legitimisation of the socio-political order. However, functional differentiation favoured a redefinition of the role of the churches in education, culture, health, social aid and welfare, human rights and peace, while keeping up with the pluralistic context that is characteristic of ultra-modernity. According to Luhmann,[17] religion has become an optional subsystem, which is a very significant aspect in the process of secularisation.

7. Globalisation could further a radical relativisation of religion (in so far as the truths of various religions are incompatible), a reinterpretation with a more pluralist view (all religions are acceptable, or give interesting clues), and expand not only the worldwide diffusion of religion (missions, NRMs, papal visits, etc.), but also ecumenism, inter-religious dialogue, fundamentalist reactions, and innovations (borrowings, 'do-it-yourself', syncretism, NRMs). Each of these effects is growing increasingly acute in the current phase of accelerated globalisation.[18] According to the 1981 European Values Study, 25 per cent (17 per cent of 18–29-year-olds) of those surveyed thought that there was only one true religion; 53 per cent (56 per cent of 18–29-year-olds) said that there were interesting insights in all the great religions; and 14 per cent (19 per cent of 18–29-year-olds) said that no religion has any truth to offer. In France, those who believed that there is only one true religion decreased from 50 per cent in 1952 to 14 per cent in 1981 (11 per cent of 18–29-year-olds).

Europe at a religious turning-point

Each of these factors, and modernity in its entirety, has multiple effects, two of the most important ones being undoubtedly the production of secular systems and the transformation of Christendom into Christianity. How can we assess the religious situation in western Europe and its current evolution from the major surveys, namely the European Values Study (EVS: 1981, 1990 and 1999) and the International Social Survey Programme (ISSP: 1991, 1998)?[19] Essentially, the surveys concern Christianity, constituting 70 per cent of the population of the nine countries where figures for both 1981 and 1999 are available (85 per cent in 1981). In these countries we find that church attendance at least once a month has decreased from 36 per cent in 1981 to 30 per cent in 1999; 68 per cent in the nine countries believe in God, compared to 74 per cent in 1981. Only 7 per cent say they are 'a convinced atheist', the maximum being in France (14 per cent), the home of positivism; this rate has increased, though very slightly (from 5 per cent in 1981). The other respondents are agnostic or hesitating. When asked what kind of God they believed in, the responses were: 'a personal God' (38 per cent), 'a spirit or life force' (30 per cent), 'I don't really think there is any sort of spirit, God or life force' (15 per cent), 'I don't know' (13 per cent), and 'no answer' (4 per cent). The proportion saying they believed in 'a personal God' has increased a little since 1981, when it was 30 per cent. In order to capture these new perceptions, we should also identify God as the origin of the Big Bang, as the energy or the divine within each creature, or as cosmic consciousness. (See Table 4.1 for a country-by-country breakdown of the figures for the European Union in 1999.)

Regarding the Bible, the 1991 ISSP produced the following responses: 'the Bible is the actual word of God and it is to be taken literally, word for word', 'the inspired word of God but not everything should be taken literally, word for word', 'an ancient book of fables, legends, history, and moral precepts recorded by man', 'this does not apply to me', and 'can't choose'. The rates for 'actual word' and 'inspired word' were 13 per cent and 40 per cent respectively in the western European sample group, that is to say, in total only a small majority (this sample includes six countries: Germany, Great Britain, Ireland, Italy, Denmark, the Netherlands); in the United States, the rates for 'actual word' and 'inspired word' were 32 per cent and 47 per cent respectively in 1991. The response 'the actual word' was more frequent among older people, farmers, the working classes and the lower middle classes, which suggests that this type of answer might decline in the future; this type of response is also indicative of the importance of creationism.

The research data thus show that biblical fundamentalism is very limited and, presumably, in decline in the countries surveyed. This conclusion applies also to what we could call 'social fundamentalism', defined as the desire to structure life in society according to religious principles. The 1991 ISSP allows us to identify 'social fundamentalism' through a survey of opinions on six issues: there should be daily prayers in schools; right and wrong should be based on divine law; we should ban books and films attacking religions; religious leaders should not try to influence government decisions; those who do not believe in God are unfit for public office; church and religious organisations have far too little power/far too much power. If we calculate the average percentages of extreme responses to these six issues for the six European countries, the secular focal area proves to be twice as large as the fundamentalist focal area, with an average of 24 per cent as opposed to 12 per cent respectively, and even 32 per cent as opposed to 7 per cent, among young adults; thus, social fundamentalism is characterised by the same features as biblical fundamentalism, which is an area that can be considered as a remnant of the ancient spirit of Christendom.

Table 4.1. *The religious state of the western European countries in 1999 (European Values Study) (read for instance: in Ireland, 71 per cent define themselves as a religious person).*

	Ireland*	Portugal	Italy*	Austria	Spain*	Luxembourg	Belgium*	France*	West Germany*	United Kingdom*	Netherlands*	Denmark*	Sweden	Finland	Greece	Europe 81*	Europe 99*	Europe 18–29; 81*	Europe 18–29; 99*
General religiosity																			
Define self as a religious person	71	85	83	75	56	58	62	44	58	37	63	71	37	62	81	62	56	47	45
Convinced athest	*2*	*3*	*3*	*2*	*6*	*7*	*8*	*14*	*4*	*4*	*6*	*5*	*6*	*3*	*2*	*5*	*7*	*8*	*9*
Comfort and strength from religion	80	77	68	58	49	45	47	32	49	33	44	30	29	51	79	48	45	32	33
Religion: important 1990/1999	61	75	71	53	42	45	47	36	29	37	40	27	35	45	79	46	43	34	32
Children's religious faith: important	38	24	31	20	20	17	16	8	15	18	10	8	5	16	54	17	17	9	12
Religious belonging																			
Belong to a religious denomination	90	88	82	86	82	72	63	57	86	82	46	88	76	88	97	85	75	78	68
Belong to Catholicism	87	85	81	79	81	68	55	53	38	13	24	1	2	0	0	55	49	52	46
Belong to Protestantism	2	0	0	6	0	1	3	2	41	51	17	87	70	84	0	30	21	23	18
Do not belong to a religion	10	12	18	14	18	28	37	43	14	18	54	11	24	12	3	18	25	19	30
Practices																			
Church attendance: ≥once a month	67	51	53	42	36	31	28	12	34	19	26	12	9	14	43	36	30	25	19
Prayer to God: ≥once a week	68	62	61	43	39	31	35	19	38	27	34	20	NA	39	67	NA	36	NA	NA
Religious volunteer work	7	3	7	7	4	6	6	3	6	6	12	3	NA	8	9	6	6	4	4
Want religious service/birth	89	89	86	79	75	68	66	60	71	55	41	64	58	83	66	65	66	57	60
Religious service/marriage	91	87	82	74	72	64	67	64	74	64	46	62	61	81	89	68	68	61	64
Religious service/death	95	91	86	83	77	75	70	70	78	74	56	79	76	88	91	74	74	68	72
Church image																			
Confidence in church	52	79	66	38	41	46	42	44	40	33	29	55	44	57	63	51	43	35	34
Church gives adequate answers:																			
– to people's spiritual need	57	65	66	53	48	38	46	51	49	47	37	40	44	59	66	44	52	34	48
– to moral problems and needs	27	52	55	33	33	28	32	33	39	26	29	16	20	36	48	35	38	22	31
– to the problems of family life	25	42	43	26	29	21	29	26	56	23	24	12	14	34	40	34	31	21	24
– to social problems	24	32	38	26	23	20	24	20	32	21	29	9	14	26	38	28	26	22	19
Beliefs																			
God	93	93	88	83	81	68	66	56	70	61	61	62	47	74	90	74	68	61	60
A personal God	*63*	*77*	*70*	*31*	*46*	*31*	*29*	*21*	*37*	*28*	*23*	*24*	*16*	*49*	*70*	*30*	*38*	*24*	*31*
A sort of spirit or vital force	*25*	*15*	*19*	*51*	*27*	*32*	*34*	*29*	*34*	*37*	*49*	*36*	*52*	*31*	*17*	*35*	*30*	*35*	*33*
God important (6 to 10/1 to 10 scale)	76	83	76	65	56	47	48	33	53	40	46	25	28	56	83	51	49	38	35
Sin	79	65	67	57	44	42	41	37	43	57	39	18	23	58	79	57	47	44	42
A life after death	68	37	61	50	40	46	40	39	39	43	46	32	39	45	50	43	43	38	44
Hell	46	31	42	16	27	19	18	18	20	28	13	8	9	25	45	22	25	16	23
Heaven	77	51	50	38	42	29	30	28	32	45	35	16	28	50	53	39	38	30	35
Reincarnation	19	24	15	19	16	21	17	25	19	NA	20	15	19	15	19	12	18	20	22

- The asterisk designates the nine countries of the EEC that were surveyed in 1981, 1990 and 1999 (the mean is weighted according to the population of each country).
- NA indicates no data available.

Regarding the after-life, 43 per cent say they believe in 'a life after death' (which may include reincarnation), the percentage being the same as that found in 1981; 38 per cent say they believe in heaven (39 per cent in 1981); 25 per cent in hell (22 per cent in 1981). It seems that the better side of the hereafter is preserved more willingly. Eighteen per cent believe in reincarnation (12 per cent in 1981) (1999 EVS). Belief in sin drops from 57 per cent in 1981 to 47 per cent in 1999; as Walter also indicates,[20] we can see that belief in heaven or in hell is not necessarily linked to belief in sin. The research data illustrate the fact that the importance formerly given to an other-worldly salvation has collapsed. The notion of salvation has become even more problematic: for example, the research group 'Religious and Moral Pluralism in Europe' had to abandon a question on the idea of salvation because, according to the preliminary tests, it was understood by only a third of those questioned.

Of course, we note great differences between countries (see Table 4.1) and across age groups. Mostly, we observe a notable change in the religious landscape in western Europe: next to the tendency towards religious decline, which was a dominant trend, particularly among young people, we note a movement of Christian revival and the development of an autonomous spirituality, with these last two phenomena being manifested even more so among young people. Circumstances now vary according to the countries, even though in the past they were rather homogeneous. Thus, the tendency towards decline dominates in the most secularised countries, such as France, Belgium, Great Britain, the Netherlands and Sweden, and also in Spain, but this tendency has slowed down among young people. All criteria of Christian religiosity, except for church membership, are rising in Portugal, Italy and Denmark, and among the young people in the former West Germany (Catholics and Protestants), with an increase in the belief in a personal God. Finally, among those with no religion, we note the development of a vague autonomous religiosity, which is detached from Christianity and is also characterised by an increased belief in the after-life: in 1999, 33 per cent of those with no religion 'take some moments of prayer, meditation or contemplation or something like that' (27 per cent in 1981), 31 per cent believed in God (22 per cent in 1981), and 24 per cent believed in an after-life (12 per cent in 1981). It is undoubtedly the most original phenomenon and it is among young people that it is developing the most, particularly in the least Christian countries, as if some kind of substitution were going on.

This change in the religious landscape will certainly make Europe a less 'exceptional case', to refer to the debate initiated by Grace Davie.[21] The change can be explained in two ways: there is a pendulum effect with regard to the religious fracture of the 1960s and 1970s; we can equally observe a pendulum effect with respect to permissiveness, which, as a characteristic of current ultra-modernity, as we have already seen, seems to be more favourable to the religious. Concerning the return of beliefs connected to the after-life, they are part of a general reversal with regard to death, after a phase of denial, which might be explained by the general sentiment of a greater precariousness in different areas; the rebound of the overvalorisation of self-actualisation, which renders death more unacceptable; the influence of videos and games among adolescents, in which the players reach paradise or are driven to hell.

The typical transformations of Christianity in ultra-modernity

Modernity produces secularisation, as well as intense religious transformations. Besides the non-Christian innovations (New Religious Movements, parallel beliefs, diffused spiritualities), let us draw out the main new religious features that can be singled out in the case of Christianity. First, we will review what we can learn from the comparatists who analysed religious modernity by reference to what preceded it; then, we will focus on ultra-modern Christianity.

Modern Christianity according to the comparatists

Jaspers[22] confined himself to some brief but insightful remarks: 'if a transcendent aid does manifest', he predicted about completed modernity, 'it can only be to free a man and by virtue of his autonomy', for 'he that feels free lets his beliefs fluctuate, regardless of any clearly defined credo . . . in accordance to an unfettered faith, which escapes any specific definition, which remains unattached while retaining the sense of the absolute and seriousness, along with their strong vitality'. This faith, he adds (in 1949), 'still has not found any resonance with the masses' and is 'despised by the representatives of the official, dogmatic and doctrinaire creeds', but it has become typical of ultra-modern individualised religiosity.

Joseph M. Kitagawa[23] distinguished four related characteristics in the modern mentality: a single cosmos, this-worldly orientation, man as the centre and the search for freedom (he speaks of the scientific single cosmos as contrasted to the former dualistic cosmos: the sky, home of God/the earth, home of man). As a global consequence, 'this phenomenal world is the only real order of existence, and life here and now is the center of the world of meaning'. But 'all classical religions tended to take negative attitudes towards phenomenal existence and recognised another realm of reality', which was the most important, and 'in this life, man was thought to be a sojourner or prisoner' yearning for heaven or nirvana which would release him from suffering, sin, imperfection, finitude. So religions are compelled 'to find the meaning of human destiny in this world – in culture, society and human personality' in order to fulfil the human vocation, meaning soteriologies which are recentred on this world.

'The historic religions discovered the self', Bellah reminds us, but only early modern religion (Protestantism) concentrated 'on the direct relation between the individual and the transcendent reality', on salvation by faith alone, which 'is not to be found in any kind of withdrawal from the world but in the midst of worldly activities', hence 'especially in its Calvinist wing, a whole series of developments from economics to science, from education to law' (cf. Weber, Merton).[24] With modern religion, 'the central feature of the change is the collapse of the dualism that was so crucial to all the historic religions' (cf. Kitagawa), the dehierarchisation, which reduces the distance between the terrestrial and the celestial, the human and the divine, and hence between the laity and the clergy, thus favouring individual freedom.

The idea that all creedal statements must receive a personal interpretation is widely accepted . . . I expect traditional religions to be maintained and developed in new directions, but with growing awareness that it is *symbolism* and that man in the last analysis is responsible for the choice of his symbolism . . . each individual must work out his own ultimate solutions, and the most the church can do is provide him a favourable environment for doing so, without imposing on him a prefabricated set of answers.[25]

He speaks of 'a much more open and flexible pattern of membership', and even, 'one might almost be tempted to see in Thomas Paine's "My mind is my church" or in Thomas Jefferson's "I am a sect myself" the typical expression of religious organisation in the near future'. Like Kitagawa, he thinks that 'the search for adequate standards of action, which is at the same time a search for personal maturity and social relevance, is in itself the heart of the modern quest for salvation', concluding that the analysis of modern man as non-religious is fundamentally misguided.

Nakamura[26] refers to similar points, adding pluralism and insisting that religions must emphasise their positive and humanistic aspects (service to people, development, human rights), including the value of the body rather than asceticism or fear of damnation.

Ultra-modern Christianity according to the latest studies

These latest studies either confirm or allow us to complete the following insights:

1. *Centring on 'this-worldly' salvation.* In the study of a Breton parish, I observed that Catholicism had been *de facto* reinterpreted as a transcendental humanism, aimed towards earthly fulfilment, while being open to an after-life devoid of eternal damnation;[27] the evocation of hell disappeared slightly after Vatican II (1962–65). The thematic of Pope John Paul II is centred not on salvation in the hereafter, but on the construction of 'civilisation of love'. The revalorisation of pilgrimages and the expansion of Evangelical and Charismatic currents proceed from this adaptation to the extent that demands for 'grace', oriented towards present life, play an important role (health, family, success);

moreover, belief in miracles remains very high (ISSP 1998). On the extreme side, televangelists put forth an analogous argument by showing that the expiation of sin and fidelity to God are infallible ways of assuring heavenly grace and benediction, especially in matters of health, family and employment. The title of a book written by the televangelist Roberts, who was heard on the Euronews channel in 1998, is significant: *God's Formula for Success and Prosperity*. New millenarisms, proposing an earthly fulfilment (Jehovah's Witnesses, Mormons, Adventists), are expanding in popularity.

2. An important consequence of 'this-worldliness' is the *dissociation between sin and one's fate after death*, the desoteriologisation of guilt (hence, the collapse of the practice of confession in Catholicism?) or a more worldly interpretation: sin distances one from God and prevents one from benefiting from His grace, from being fully happy, from communicating with others.

3. *The bringing together of the divine and the human*, more typical of Protestantism (direct relation with God), is gradually happening within Catholicism too. Vatican II abolished the constraints required for taking communion (fasting, etc.) and emphasised the fact that God is love and father, to the detriment, we could say, of the Lord God Almighty who judges and punishes. Surveys verify this shift among Catholics and Protestants: between a God of Judgement and God of Love, and a God as King and God as Friend, the second term clearly prevails (ISSP 1998). Christianity is recentred on Christ, the incarnate God, the God who is close to us. This characteristic undoubtedly helps to explain the success of Pentecostalist and Charismatic movements, the followers of which experience the divine within themselves through the outpouring of the Holy Spirit. Televangelists invite people to walk 'hand in hand with the Lord'.

4. *Religious individualisation* has been sufficiently described. We must simply emphasise that in ultra-modernity religious individualisation can go as far as self-spirituality, whether it is about a strong autonomy within a church that is treated as a free resource, a borrowing of many sources, a rather loose link with a spiritual domain, or, up to a point, a total independence. According to a survey conducted in the United States in 1988–89 among the baby-boom generation, 31 per cent agree with the following statement: 'People have God within them, so Churches aren't really necessary.'[28] What is partially developing here is a reaction against excessive individualisation, as well as a *religiosity of emotional communities.*[29]

5. We note a much larger *religious mobility*, in connection, of course, with individualisation, pluralisation and relativisation, but weaker in Europe in comparison with the case of the United States. Danièle Hervieu-Léger has revealed the typical faces of the pilgrim and the convert.[30]

6. Following Wade Clark Roof, we can refer to a *culture of a spiritual quest* (*seeker spirituality*). Thus, facing the alternatives, 'Is it good to explore many differing religious teachings and learn from them, or should one stick to a

particular faith?', 60 per cent of American baby-boomers preferred to explore. In France, the latest Values Survey puts an alternative: 'stick to a particular faith' or 'explore the teachings of different religious traditions', with the last view clearly progressing from older (18 per cent) to younger people (34 per cent), half of whom were Catholics.

7. *Religious pragmatism* appears as a consequence of relativism, of the focusing on the 'here below' and of individualisation. In sum, the important thing is not for a religion to be 'true', but that it can bring something in terms of fulfilment. Religious practice is itself reconsidered in light of this criterion.

8. We will not return to *relativism*, except to specify that it is tempered by pragmatism and by the sentiment of the universality of Christianity, present in every continent. We must also mention 'probabilism': when questions on beliefs allow a gradation of responses of the type 'certainly yes/probably yes/probably not/certainly not', as in the ISSP survey, probable responses are in the majority, almost always among young people. The *probabilist* belief also originates in the culture of uncertainty, typical of ultra-modernity. Thinking that the existence of God is not certain does not prevent one from adhering, because, as we just saw, what counts the most is what this adherence can convey.

9. The phenomenon specified under the term *religion à la carte* is typical of ultra-modernity, to the extent that it is connected to individual freedom, pragmatism and religious pluralism. It is illuminating to examine in what proportion individuals satisfy the following four conditions at the same time: practice at least once a year (outside ceremonies), belief in God, belief in sin, and belief in an after-life, which seem to constitute a least demanding and inevitable Christian minimum. However, this minimal core does not gather more than 31 per cent of Christians, that is 60 per cent of regular church-goers and 21 per cent of irregular church-goers.

Conclusion

If we compare these challenges to the religious characteristics of the preceding axial age, we can put forth the following conclusions. Although reason, science and technology have helped to bring about a radical rationalisation and de-mythologisation, Christianity had none the less originally made great progress in this direction (ethico-spiritual rationalisation, demagification), which has effectively allowed it the opportunity to adapt to modernity, even to be purged, since Christianity had brought about a relative remythologisation. Similarly, in relation to religion, we know that modernity signifies the large autonomisation of social and political life, yet we can also acknowledge that Christianity had, in the beginning, carried out this autonomy, before becoming the instrument of symbolic legitimisation of the socio-political order, so that it might be able to adapt to this transformation. Likewise, Christianity might adapt to a large extent to individualisation, which it promoted *at the beginning*. Probably 'this-worldliness', globalisation and relativisation are major challenges. But the most important global effect of modernity on religion was the loss of the monopoly of religions in the 'symbolic field' (conceptions of life and the world), which is now structured both by religions and by secular systems (science, philosophies, ideologies, values).

We can then come to the conclusion that there has been an astonishing adaptation of Christianity to modernity and ultra-modernity. But the price to pay is, as we have seen, the abandonment of what rendered religion absolutely indispensable: the reaching of eternal salvation. Can we still speak of Christianity when the Christian basic core is not shared any more? Jacques Sutter[31] sees it as a decomposition of Christianity. Is this the only possible interpretation? Could this also be a radically symbolist reinterpretation? To go even further in the analysis, we are particularly missing qualitative surveys like those undertaken by John Fulton.[32] Jim Beckford complains that we can learn little about the contemporary religious landscape from sociologists of postmodernity. But if we take account of the decisive transformations mentioned above, the main features of this landscape start to become clear.[33]

NOTES

Many thanks to Lina Molokotos Liederman, who was responsible for most of the translation. This is a revised and updated version of 'Religion in modernity as a new axial age: secularization or new religious forms?', published in *Sociology of Religion*, 60(3) (1999), 303–33 (© Association for the Sociology of Religion, Inc. All rights reserved.)

1. P. Berger, *The Sacred Canopy* (New York, 1967); K. Dobbelaere, 'Secularization: a multi-dimensional concept', *Current Sociology*, 29(2), (1981), 3–213.
2. S. S. Acquaviva, *The Decline of the Sacred in Industrial Society* (Oxford, 1969).
3. P. Berger, *The Desecularization of the World: Resurgent Religion and World Politics* (Washington, DC, 1999).
4. D. Hervieu-Léger, *Le Pèlerin et le converti* (Paris, 1999).
5. L. Kurtz, *Gods in the Global Village: The World's Religions in a Sociological Perspective* (London, 1995).
6. K. Jaspers, *Origine et sens de l'histoire*, French translation (Paris, 1954); R. N. Bellah, *Beyond Belief: Essays on Religion in a Post-traditional World* (New York, 1976); S. Eisenstadt, *The Origins and Diversity of Axial Age Civilizations* (Albany, NY, 1986).
7. Jaspers, *Origine*, 38.
8. N. Luhmann, *Funktion der Religion* (Frankfurt am Main, 1976); N. Luhmann, *The Differentiation of Society* (New York, 1982).
9. A. Giddens, *The Consequences of Modernity* (Cambridge, 1991).
10. J.-P. Willaime, *Sociologie des religions* (Paris, 1995).
11. Eisenstadt, *Origins*.
12. Bellah, *Beyond Belief*, 39.

13. J. G. Melton, 'Modern alternative religions in the west', in J. R. Hinnells (ed.), *A Handbook on Living Religions* (Harmondworth, 1985).

14. Y. Lambert, 'Religion in modernity as a new axial age: secularization or new religious forms?', *Sociology of Religion*, 60 (1999), 303–33.

15. D. A. Martin, *A General Theory of Secularization* (Oxford, 1978).

16. K. Dobbelaere and W. Jagodzinski, 'Secularisation and church religiosity' (chapter 4), in J. W. V. Deth and E. Scarbrough (eds.), *The Impact of Values* (Oxford, 1995); J. Casanova, *Public Religion in the Modern World* (Chicago, 1994).

17. Luhmann, *Funktion*; Luhmann, *Differentiation*.

18. P. Beyer, *Religion and Globalization* (London, 1994).

19. Y. Lambert, 'The scope and limits of religious functions according to the European Value and ISSP surveys', in J. Billiet and R. Laermans (eds.), *Secularization and Social Integration: Papers in Honor of Karel Dobbelaere* (Leuven, 1998), 211–12; Y. Lambert, 'Religion: l'Europe à un tournant. Les valeurs des Européens', *Futuribles*, 277 (2002), 129–59.

20. Tony Walter, *The Eclipse of Eternity: A Sociology of the Afterlife*, London, 1996.

21. Grace Davie, *The Exceptional Case: Parameters of Faith in the Modern World* (London, 2002).

22. Jaspers, *Origine*, 278–80.

23. J. M. Kitagawa, 'Primitive, classical, and modern religions', in J. M. Kitagawa (ed.), *The History of Religion: Essays on Problems of Understanding* (Chicago, 1967), 39–65.

24. Bellah, *Beyond Belief*, 36–9.

25. *Ibid.*, 39–44.

26. H. Nakamura, *A Comparative History of Ideas* (London, 1986).

27. Y. Lambert, *Dieu change en Bretagne* (Paris, 1985).

28. W. C. Roof, 'The spiritual seeking in the United States', *Archives de Sciences Sociales des Religions*, 109 (2000), 56.

29. F. Champion and D. Hervieu-Léger (eds.), *De l'Emotion en religion* (Paris, 1993).

30. Hervieu-Léger, *Pèlerin*.

31. J. Sutter, *Les Français sont-ils encore catholiques?* (Paris, 1991).

32. J. Fulton *et al.*, *Young Catholics at the New Millennium* (Dublin, 2000).

33. J. A. Beckford, 'Postmodernity, high modernity and new modernity: three concepts in search of religion', in K. Flanagan and P. C. Jupp (eds.), *Postmodernity, Sociology and Religion* (London, 1996), 30–47.

Part II

5 Established churches and the growth of religious pluralism: a case study of christianisation and secularisation in England since 1700

David Hempton

Secularisation theories have largely been abandoned by most of their erstwhile inventors as being inapplicable to most parts of the world except western Europe. Indeed all kinds of theories of historical inevitability have taken a fearful pounding in the half-century since the publication of Sir Isaiah Berlin's famous lecture on the subject at the London School of Economics in 1953.[1] History without contingencies is like life without choice, but contingencies require explanatory frameworks. The purpose of this chapter is to advance an argument about the process of religious change in England from around 1700 which takes account of contingencies, but which seeks to establish analytical structures of more general application. The argument is that in England the rise of a more pluralistic religious society in the nineteenth century led to an increase in the social significance of religion (however that is to be measured) in the short run, but that the distinctive way in which it happened posed more serious problems for churches in the twentieth century. Ironically, the rise of a more voluntaristic and competitive religious environment in England helped erode some of the conditions that had nurtured its own development. What follows, therefore, is a tentative explanation of that story in England which is markedly different from the religious trajectories of other countries in the same period, including, for the sake of comparison, Ireland and the United States.

In the eighteenth century, established churches, largely untroubled by notions of social utility and still preoccupied by the theological battles of the Reformation period, 'were not so much expected to do things as to be things'.[2] Within Anglicanism the allegedly consensual Thirty Nine Articles were often bitterly fought over by those in search of the true Reformation principles of the Church of England, but the ancient administrative *structures* of the Church were relatively uncontentious. The Reformation had not disturbed the old medieval parish structure but it did bring the laity, as governors and property owners, firmly into the centre of ecclesiastical management.[3] What had to be managed was a system of territorial parishes of uneven size and importance serviced by the largest single profession in the eighteenth-century state. The system had never been designed with pastoral efficiency in mind and bore no more relation to demographic realities than the eighteenth-century electoral structure, which was an equally ramshackle inheritance from the past.[4] In a society in which patronage, property rights and social hierarchy were the really vital ingredients it is well to be reminded that religion was part of a wider social system and not a separate spiritual sphere entire unto itself.[5] Established churches have therefore to be judged not against the criteria employed by later generations for whom religion had become mostly a matter of voluntary commitment, but within frameworks of meaning appropriate to eighteenth-century culture and conditions. In essence that means less concentration on the performance of the Church and more on its social significance. This is no easy task, however, for not only were the clergy of established churches themselves a far from homogeneous social group, but they had to serve an even more socially variegated laity.[6] Moreover, as early modern historians have shown, understanding the social function of religion poses obvious difficulties in societies where 'a wide range of people share the same symbols, texts and rituals, yet may understand them in a multitude of different ways'.[7] Many churches bear the same labels now as they did in early modern Britain, but their social significance has changed dramatically. Familiarity has all too often restricted historical imagination.

The Church of England in the eighteenth century was both a formidably strong and deceptively weak institution. Episcopalianism had spread to most corners of the British Isles, but it did not command the loyalties of the majority of the Scots or the Irish. Roman Catholicism had not been eradicated, Protestant Dissent had become a permanent feature of British society and the Toleration Act of 1689 had seriously undermined the legal basis for the enforcement of religious uniformity and moral discipline. Although the general tendency of recent scholarship has been to show that church courts in the eighteenth century did not wither away as quickly as was once assumed, there is no denying their general decline from mid-century onwards. The decline of Puritanism, the expansion of the economy, the growth of the population and the erosion of the coercive powers of the deanery courts all contributed to a freer atmosphere. Assiduous bishops, like Samuel Peploe of Chester, could still crank the machinery against fornication, bastardy, adultery and cohabitation in the 1730s and 1740s, but the growth of non-appearance before the courts, especially in the more populous and industrial areas, was a sure sign that the old order was simply fading away.[8] By the late eighteenth century churchmen were forced to conclude that persuasion offered better returns than coercion and that the future lay more in clerical example, religious education and internal reform of the church than in the legal enforcement of its moral prescriptions.

The diminution of coercive power was not necessarily disastrous for the Church of England, which had always valued acquiescence in the Church's rites more highly than enthusiastic devotion to its ministry, but it did point up a more general shift in the relations between Church and people over the course of the eighteenth century. Attendance at church services, participation in catechising and the practice of communion all became more dependent on the inclination of parishioners than on the insistence of the clergy. This subtle shift in the balance of power between producer and consumer was an inevitable consequence of the Toleration Act and made the established churches more vulnerable to the possible attraction of religious alternatives. This was disguised for much of the century, because the alternatives were thought not to be, and indeed were not, very threatening. One of the most consistent features of clerical responses to visitation enquiries before 1780 is their relatively dismissive attitude to the activities of Dissenters, Roman Catholics and Methodists.[9] The first two were thought not to be on the march and the Methodists were divided up between those of 'Mr John Wesley's persuasion' who 'attend the church constantly and communicate regularly' and those who were regarded as propertyless and brainless enthusiasts.[10] Some clergymen grudgingly welcomed the former while the latter were regarded as beyond the communion of the Church and peripheral to the functioning of civil society. There were of course sporadic attempts to stop them, but outside periods of national emergency most Anglicans ignored them because they thought that Methodists of low social degree simply did not count for anything in the political commonwealth. The Church of England's much maligned complacency in the eighteenth century, in so far as it existed, was therefore part of an ecclesiastical mentality which assumed that the worst excesses of the seventeenth century had been survived, and that the great bulk of men of property and influence at the centre and in the localities were friends of the Church.[11] Both assumptions were in fact correct.

The extent to which the Church of England had become dominated by a propertied frame of mind is only now receiving proper treatment.[12] Commercial dealing in advowsons, tithe farming and litigation, pew rents and disputes based on social status, concern for church fabric and the upkeep of parsonages, and an almost obsessional interest in the value of livings all contributed to a propertied mentality which came to dominate the church. God and Mammon apparently could be served together and this was reflected also in an important shift in attitudes to poor relief and charity. A decline in benefactions for charitable purposes was accompanied by an ideological shift away from charity as a form of relief from suffering to a concept based more on a strategy for securing self-improvement. Furthermore, Gilbert's Act of 1786 was an indication that concern about the funding of poor relief was moving beyond the confines of the parish to the doors of Parliament. Here, as in so many other areas, there were straws in the wind which scarcely threatened the Church's position in the eighteenth century, but which boded ill for the more trying conditions of the nineteenth century. The invasion by the laity of the Church's privileged position in the construction and delivery of social policy, therefore, has roots deep within the eighteenth century and beyond.[13]

The argument being developed is that the Church of England was an institution reasonably well attuned to the social conditions of the eighteenth century. It had legal powers and privileges, but was not unduly inquisitorial or persecuting. It was supported by property owners and in turn both upheld property and was itself a form of property. Its clergy in the main were neither pious enthusiasts nor scandalously negligent. Its parish churches were focal points of a genuinely popular Anglicanism which valued tradition, community, ritual, obedience and harmony.[14] The great explosion of literature in the past decade either defending the Church's record or attacking its shortcomings has considerably enriched our understanding of how the Church functioned, but seems to have arrived at a predictable stalemate.[15] The eighteenth-century Church was not as mediocre as its subsequent evangelical, tractarian and utilitarian critics thought it was, but neither was it a paragon of pastoral devotion and evangelical zeal. It was a working establishment with all the structural and administrative problems associated with a large institution with weak central authority, little proper control over clerical recruitment and training, and no clear statement of what it wanted to achieve beyond the steady performance of Christian ordinances and the maintenance of social cohesion. As Professor Ward has observed (after a quarter of a century's study of the eighteenth-century Church), the historian neither has a god's eye view of its operation nor ought to spend very much time enquiring how successful the Church was in fulfilling purposes which it never set itself. The point of this discussion is not to induce despair in the historian, but to suggest that the traditional way of explaining the rise of religious pluralism in England as a direct consequence of the mediocrity of the Church of England is not a very fruitful line of enquiry. The Church was not self-evidently more mediocre in 1780 than it was in 1680, yet its fortunes in the half-century following each date could hardly be more different. Whereas in the former period the Church shrugged off political attacks from without and internecine conflicts within to emerge as the almost unchallenged church of the English,[16] in the latter period it was on the brink of becoming a minority religious establishment, and some of its most ardent defenders expected it to be disestablished within a decade.[17]

A more profitable, though admittedly more complex and risky, way of investigating the rise of religious pluralism is to suggest that established churches, through relatively generous religious toleration and the extensive dissemination of basic Christian knowledge throughout the population, helped create the minimum conditions within which others could mount a challenge to their hegemony. Early Methodists, for example, by claiming devotion to the creeds, liturgies and sacraments of the Church, and by refusing to shelter under the legal protection afforded by the Act of Toleration, were in reality acting as Trojan horses within the establishment.[18] The principles of voluntarism and associationalism, which were clearly antithetical to the ideals of a truly national church, became deeply rooted long before formal separation in the late 1790s flushed the issues out into the open. Methodism not only organised pious Anglicans into independent religious societies, but also forged new links with Dissenters. Perhaps even more importantly, the intense piety of its adherents set up tensions within parishes between the religious and the irreligious, the saved and the lost, and the rough and the respectable. Such divisions helped disturb the parochial consensus upon which a truly popular Anglicanism was based.[19] By the end of the eighteenth century the Church of England could rely neither on the church courts nor on old-style Church and King sentiment to maintain parochial discipline against 'impudent, new fangled, rambling teachers, called Methodists'. By the time the Church's diocesan leaders hit on the idea of prohibiting itinerant preaching as a means of reimposing Anglican control, neither Parliament nor the country was prepared to co-operate.[20] Voluntarism, albeit still circumscribed by social pressures to conform, had arrived and was not going to go away.

If the eighteenth-century Church of England had unconsciously offered legal and sacramental shelter for one of its most vigorous nineteenth-century competitors, all of the established churches in the British Isles contributed to the later success of evangelical dissenters by successfully laying the foundations of religious knowledge upon which evangelical zeal depended. By concentrating their efforts on controversial conflicts within Anglicanism or in assessing the role of the Church in periods of national crisis, historians have been guilty of underestimating the efforts made by the Church to disseminate basic Christian knowledge. Catechisms in particular were used extensively in churches, schools and homes to inculcate knowledge of the four basic staples of Creed, Decalogue, Lord's Prayer and Sacraments.[21] Several hundred catechisms designed for different levels of personal and religious maturity were composed, printed and distributed to all parts of the country between the Reformation and the middle of the eighteenth century. Clearly too much should not be claimed for the effects of the rote memorising of basic statements of Christian belief, but with millions of cheap versions in circulation it is clear there is at least some connection between catechising and popular literacy. Moreover catechising was reinforced by prayers, collects, canticles, religious verse and metrical psalms which resulted in a growing attachment of parishioners to the Book of Common Prayer.[22] Ian Green has shown that even in the post-Reformation Church the words of the catechisms were visually reinforced in parish churches by commandment boards, painted scripture texts, sacred utensils, religious monuments and gravestones.[23] But perhaps most intriguing of all is his suggestion that, in the interests of simplifying complex doctrines and of offering reassurance to the anxious, catechetical instruction may have reinforced the popular Pelagianism of ordinary parishioners.[24] It was this very characteristic that evangelical enthusiasts most deplored, and perhaps most exploited, among the people instructed by the Established Church. A vigorous appeal to justification by faith and the new birth had particular resonance for those schooled in basic Christian concepts and persuaded of the need to live a godly life, but apparently denied the compelling attraction of the immediate efficacy of divine forgiveness. In such circumstances John Wesley's 'evangelical catholicism', which was 'a theological fusion of faith and good works, scripture and tradition, revelation and reason, God's sovereignty and human freedom, universal redemption and conditional election, Christian liberty and an ordered polity, the assurance of pardon and the risks of falling from grace, original sin and Christian perfection', was particularly well suited to the religious training of the population he sought to influence.[25]

Catechisms, though probably the most historically neglected form of popular print and instruction employed by the Church of England, were only part of a much more extensive flow of religious literature in the eighteenth century. Collections of sermons, biblical commentaries, classic devotional works, religious tracts and chapbooks, provincial newspapers, godly broadsheets and pamphlets appealed in different ways to different social classes.[26] Some of this material was crudely sensationalist, most of it never reached the lowest social groups, and much of it failed to connect with, or eradicate, the unorthodox supernaturalism of popular belief and practice, but cumulatively it had an impact. Michael Snape, whose study of religion in the northern parish of Whalley in the eighteenth century serves as a valuable antidote to too much Anglican hagiography, nevertheless quotes with approval the following extract from Samuel Bamford's memoirs showing the 'primacy – if not exclusiveness' of Christian concepts within a popular view of the world that was 'hybrid, heterodox and eclectic'.

Owler Bridge . . . was to be much dreaded. Woe to the wight or the wean, who had to pass that way on starless windy night! My father, when a boy, went to take lessons from a wise-man at Hilton-fold, and consequently had to traverse the haunted field, and to pass the perilous bridge; but he seldom forgot to hum a psalm or hymn tune whilst on his way.[27]

Eighteenth-century revival movements in all parts of Britain relied on the Christianising functions of inclusive established churches to lay the foundations of basic religious knowledge upon which they could make their more emotive appeals. Systematic studies of the Cambuslang conversion narratives of 1742, for example, have shown that although the converts were of humble social status, all of them could read.[28] Although the sample of 110 narratives (seventy women and forty men) is too small to allow any general conclusions, it supports the conventional wisdom that in the Scottish lowlands in the mid-eighteenth century most women and around half of the men could not write.[29] If the ability to write, therefore, is taken to be the appropriate measurement of literacy then the great majority of the Cambuslang converts were illiterate; but in reality they were not. They acquired their ability to read primarily from catechetical instruction and Bible reading at home, in parish schools and in the kirk. Peer pressure, accompanied by the availability of other forms of religious literature including psalm books, chapbooks and popular works of devotion, resulted in a further development of reading skills in teenage years. The Cambuslang converts were chiefly women of relatively low social status, but they were neither unfamiliar with the ordinances of the kirk nor unaware of the foundational concepts of the Christian faith when they felt themselves 'awakened' by the evangelical preaching of the New Birth.

A similar pattern has been identified in eighteenth-century Wales, where the growth of Methodism coincided directly with the setting up of Griffith Jones' remarkable network of circulating schools.[30] The schools were successful because they were cheap to run, were mostly conducted in the vernacular language and concentrated on the teaching of reading by means of catechisms, psalms and popular religious literature. As a country parson embarking upon a major parochial experiment, Jones could ill afford to lose the support of the clergy and patrons of the Established Church and he was consequently forced to distance himself from the religious enthusiasts he had once embraced. By his death in 1761 it has been estimated that he was responsible for founding over 3000 parochial schools in which some quarter of a million pupils, about half the Welsh population, were taught to read religious literature.[31] Although the chief beneficiary of Jones' remarkable achievement in the short term was the Established Church, which reported increases in attendance at parish services, in the longer term, improvements in 'religious literacy' benefited both Methodism and the more radical forms of Dissent which coalesced to deal such a heavy blow to the fortunes of the Established Church in the nineteenth century.[32]

The tidy proposition advanced so far that the established churches of the eighteenth century, through their relatively high levels of religious toleration and their often unrecognised efforts to christianise the masses, helped lay the foundation for the remarkable rise of evangelical Dissent in the nineteenth century is in need of further refinement in the light of the most recent and most extensive study of the subject in England and Wales from the 1790s to the 1850s.[33] The main argument of Michael Watts' book is that evangelical Nonconformity benefited from the religious seed sown by the Established Church in the eighteenth century, but was unable to harvest it in the more trying conditions of the nineteenth century. In the subsequent harvesting of the crop by Dissenters, the author draws a sharp contrast between the predominantly middle-class Quakers and Unitarians and the predominantly working-class evangelical Nonconformists. Paradoxically perhaps, the former were this-worldly and largely becalmed while the latter were other-worldly and expansionist. Watts vigorously combats the alleged economic and political reductionism of Marxist scholars of religion by suggesting that the majority of evangelical Nonconformists were poor, female, superstitious, illiterate (the measurement employed is writing not reading) and unsophisticated. Most were converted before the age of 26; most were from religious backgrounds of some sort; most were psychologically prepared for conversion by incomplete youthful rebellion, sexual guilt, and fear of disease, death and eternal punishment; most were uninterested in radical politics except in periods of acute economic depression; and most were resident either in the countryside or in towns of less than 5000 people. Indeed, it is hard to resist the conclusion that in his efforts to ward off Marxist and Weberian arguments of social control and the Protestant ethic, the author portrays evangelical Nonconformists as the off-scouring of all things. It is difficult, at first sight, to square this argument with his emphasis on the achievements of the Established Church in the eighteenth century in preparing the religious ground for the evangelistic efforts of the Dissenters, but Watts does attempt a resolution of the problem. In a vigorous rebuttal of Keith Thomas' thesis that the Reformation led inexorably to the diminution of popular belief in magic and superstition, Watts suggests that established churches played an important part in reinforcing a supernaturalist view of the world in a predominantly superstitious popular culture.

> There is consequently no contradiction between the conclusion drawn above from the study of the geographic distribution of Dissent, that Nonconformity often flourished in areas where the ground had been prepared by the Church of England, and the conclusion of this section, that Methodism and Dissent found their largest body of supporters in the worst educated and most superstitious parts of England and Wales. Both the teachings of the established church and beliefs inherited from pre-Christian paganism reinforced a frame of mind which accepted the supernatural as normal and which predisposed their holders to accept Evangelical beliefs in sin, judgement, instantaneous conversion, and heaven and hell . . . it was this mixture of Anglicanism and superstition that was to prove the most fertile ground for the growth of Methodism.[34]

Ironically Watts' argument mirrors the view articulated over a quarter of a century ago by E. P. Thompson, an historian to whom Watts is implacably opposed (on ideological grounds) in all other respects. In one of his less well-known essays, 'Anthropology and the discipline of historical context', Thompson portrayed Methodism as a 'psychologically compelling' attempt to bridge the cultural gap between the erastianism and materialism of the Established Church and the superstitions of the poor. He suggested that Wesleyanism was explicitly a movement of counter-enlightenment in which Wesley reaffirmed scores of superstitions which Thomas described as being in decline: 'Among these were bibliomancy, old wives' medical remedies, the casting of lots, the belief in diabolical possession and in exorcism by prayer, in the hand of providence, in the punishment (by lightning-stroke or epilepsy or cholera) of ill-livers and reprobates.'[35] Thompson's suggestion that Methodism traded on the unorthodox supernaturalism of the poor is undoubtedly correct, but his emphasis on the erastianism, rationalism and materialism of the Church of England seriously underestimated the extent to which it too benefited from and collaborated with the 'superstitions' of the rural poor. Anglicanism in the eighteenth century was a broad church, not only in the conventional sense of embracing different traditions of churchmanship, but also in the more popular sense of making connections with the diverse supernatural beliefs of its humble parishioners. Once that point is grasped the rise of Methodism can be seen from a different perspective, namely that 'widespread popular belief in the supernatural actually fostered the growth of early Methodism and Primitive Methodism rather than the other way round'.[36]

What is ultimately at stake in Watts' wide-ranging study of the rise of religious pluralism in England and Wales is a self-conscious attempt to shift the debate away from explanations based on economic and political processes alone to take account of other important issues, including the existence of long-term patterns of religious geography in Britain,[37] the importance of psychological processes of guilt and fear among adolescents and young adults, and the attraction of dissenting communities as extended families of the faithful inculcating religious and social discipline.[38] But such explanations do not of themselves explain why evangelical Dissent made its most striking gains in rural areas and in towns of between 500 and 5000 inhabitants, while its progress was less spectacular in small villages and large cities. Small-scale industrialisation, short-distance population migrations and the growth of regional markets all helped erode the parochial stability and deferential relationships upon which established churches thrived. The mechanisms by which this took place are still shrouded in some mystery, largely because it has been assumed for too long that urban and rural religion were self-contained and separate, when in reality migratory patterns in early industrial societies were as much circulatory as linear.[39] The problem for historians is that many of the available source materials supply only cross-sectional data which obscure as much as they reveal. 'As soon as people are considered longitudinally', state Langton and Hoppe, 'that is, as living continuously through whole life-times rather than momentarily whilst a census count is made, some awkward questions about the urbanisation process arise immediately.'[40] What they are suggesting is that there was a much greater reactive exchange between urban and rural cultures in eighteenth- and nineteenth-century Europe than is allowed for in crude statistical categories of urbanisation, and this clearly has implications for the study of religious belief and practice.[41] It is now becoming clear from a number of studies that short-distance population migration facilitated the transmission of evangelical Dissent in early industrial Britain and helped shape the religious geography of larger towns and cities.[42]

Established churches, as much through their pastoral efficiency as their pastoral neglect, their *de facto* legal tolerance as much as their propertied privileges, and their supernaturalist message as much as their Pelagian imperatives, helped nurture the conditions within which religious alternatives could flourish. Evangelical religion supplied the fervour, economic transformation opened up the opportunities, and the erosion of social and political deference set the tone for a more competitive religious environment. Competition both expanded the market and divided the suppliers. In precisely the same period of time it took Wesleyan Methodism to separate formally from the Church of England (from the 1730s to the 1790s), it suffered manifold secessions from its own ranks as conflicts over religious styles and ecclesiastical government produced several new species and scores of regional mutations (from the 1790s to the 1850s).[43] Competition affected everything. Denominational self-consciousness triumphed over interdenominational co-operation, first in the Sunday schools,[44] then in the establishment of foreign missions[45] and finally in the contests for supremacy over elementary education.[46] But the market brought religious discipline as well as ecclesiastical fragmentation. Pan-evangelical co-operation in the interests of reclaiming the ungodly operated both at the metropolitan centre and in the provincial peripheries of the British state.[47]

The argument advanced so far requires careful elucidation. My emphasis on the role of established churches in creating some of the conditions for the rise of evangelical Nonconformity and hence of greater religious pluralism is intended to be neither a defence of Anglican deficiencies in the eighteenth century nor a repudiation of the view that evangelical Dissenters were as much reacting against the inadequacies of Anglican paternalism (in all its social, political and ecclesiastical manifestations) as they were benefiting from its limited pastoral success.[48] The point is simply that in explaining the remarkable surge of evangelical Nonconformity in the period 1780–1850, in all its regional complexity, not all the explanations line up conveniently in the same direction. Religious endeavour, as with all other aspects of human action, can give rise to quite unintentional results. In that respect, time will probably show that established churches in the British Isles in the eighteenth century were both educationally more successful and ecclesiastically more vulnerable than appeared to most contemporaries in the 1780s and 1790s and to most historians in the 1980s and 1990s.

The energy unleashed by religious zeal and religious competition at the turn of the century undoubtedly led to an increase in the religiosity of the British people in the nineteenth century, but the longer-term implications are not quite so clear. The chief victims of the rise of religious pluralism were the established churches, with their older notions of an inclusive, territorial and truly national church. The established churches in Ireland and Wales were first undermined, then reformed and finally disestablished. The Church of Scotland was split asunder in 1843 and never again threatened to deliver Thomas Chalmers' intellectually coherent, but hopelessly unrealistic, ideal of the Godly Commonwealth.[49] In England, the Church was first supported by money from the state, was then reformed in a utilitarian direction, and was finally left to its own devices.[50] Despite the unrivalled popularity of its rites of passage and its ability to ward off disestablishment sentiment, the Church of England's role as a truly national church was undermined from three different directions. First, the very social and political forces which made it impossible for the state to restrict religious toleration at the turn of the century soon made it impracticable for it to fund the expansion of established churches in the early Victorian period. The contrast between Lord Liverpool's willingness to grant one million pounds to build new churches in 1818 and Peel's flat refusal under pressure to do something similar in 1842 could hardly be more striking.[51] Peel's political instincts had told him that taxpayers would no longer willingly contribute to a national church and that any attempt to coerce them would simply rebound on the established churches themselves. Not only would the state not fund expansion, but also Parliament, under pressure from Irish Catholics and British Dissenters, acquiesced in the erosion of the Church's ancient privileges in the sphere of what came to be known as social policy. Second, both evangelicals and tractarians, with the best of intentions, established more rigorous criteria for acceptable Anglican devotion which almost certainly alienated as many as they were able to attract.[52] The same could be said for the extension of the practices of double duty and monthly communion, which may only have served to scare away the half-committed. Finally, the Church of England was increasingly forced to accept that it was only one (albeit the most important one) denomination among many in English society. Parish churches came to be used solely for services of worship; clergymen, revealingly, began to speak of parishioners and non-parishioners; and attempts to create a committed laity all too often produced a social elite as much as a pious elite. By 1870 the Church of England could no longer claim to be *the* church of the English nation, and by the end of the century the old inclusive parish church had become more of a resort for the decent than a resource for the community.[53]

The truth of the matter is that by the end of the nineteenth century the establishmentarian foundations of the Church of England had been substantially eroded. The result was an Established Church forced increasingly to act as a religious denomination, but without the voluntaristic assumptions and resources that would have enabled it to perform that role more effectively.[54] Ironically, the Church of England's unconvincing lurch to voluntarism was matched by a reverse lurch to establishmentarian practices among many erstwhile populist Dissenters. Moreover, some have argued that a combination of free-market Nonconformity and the residual establishmentarian attitudes of the Church of England produced an over-supply of churches in late Victorian

English cities, which, if anything, only hastened the speed of secularisation in the twentieth century.[55] For good or for ill, the territorial, inclusive and national ideals of the eighteenth-century Church of England have all but gone. But gone also, or at least steadily going, is the broad base of Christian knowledge and religious literacy which evangelical Dissenters were able to exploit so successfully in the late eighteenth and early nineteenth centuries. In England at least, religious pluralism may have delivered impressive short-term gains at the expense of a centuries-old pattern of religious provision which was unspectacular but remarkably durable. It seems likely that, notwithstanding the additional emotional pizzazz of Pentecostal and charismatic renewal movements, there is no longer a sufficient bedrock of basic Christian concepts or of supernaturalist beliefs in modern English society for there to be a new surge of religious pluralism on anything like the same scale as was the case in the nineteenth century.

The contrast between what happened in England and the patterns that emerged in Ireland and the United States in the same period could hardly be more striking. In Ireland the official Protestant Established Church was more or less replaced in the twentieth century by a Roman Catholic quasi-established church in which territorial parishes survived, the church retained a major say in the construction of the state's social policy (especially over ethics and education) and the church was able to express the cultural and political objectives of the great mass of the population. In such circumstances, religion retained its influence over a broad social constituency and, crucially, was able to offer different levels of religiosity to suit different degrees of commitment.[56] In the United States the relatively early collapse of established churches and the ability of other churches to adapt to the conditions of the marketplace have produced a remarkably pluralistic and flexible religious culture.[57] New pockets of religious enthusiasm, in harmony with the democratic egalitarian values of the new republic, expanded without risk of falling foul of established churches or of being absorbed by them.[58] There were, for example, more African American Methodists in the United States at the end of the nineteenth century than there were Methodists in England.[59] In order to understand a fact like that, historians and sociologists interested in secularisation need also to be aware of different patterns of Christianisation. Understanding how a religious movement formed in England achieved dramatically better results in the United States explains a good deal about the reasons for the different patterns of religious growth and decline in the two countries. In England the Established Church, despite its traditions and its apparently unassailable position in the middle of the eighteenth century, was able neither to survive as an establishment on anything like the same terms as the Irish Roman Catholic Church, nor to adapt successfully to the religion of the marketplace. What it did achieve was to lay the foundations, both positively and negatively, for a remarkable explosion of religious pluralism which transformed the old denominational order and contributed to the expansion of English forms of Christianity to many parts of the world. Anglicanism, as a result both of its own energy and of the dissenting competition it provoked, helped Christianise populations far from its own English heartlands, but could not stem the tide of religious voluntarism, nor ultimately of secularisation, in England itself.

My aim has been to approach the theme of the decline of Christendom in western Europe by investigating the themes of the social significance of established religion, the rise of religious pluralism, and the growth of secularisation in England from the early eighteenth to the early twentieth century. It has been suggested that the rise of religious pluralism was not so much a reaction against the Established Church's shortcomings (though clearly it was partly that) so much as a product of conditions created by the Church itself, including the mass dissemination of basic Christian knowledge, the maintenance of a *de facto* religious toleration and the proclamation of a supernaturalist view of the world, albeit overlain with semi-Pelagian theological ideas. Evangelical Dissenters benefited from all three conditions and were consequently well placed to take advantage of changing demographic, economic and political patterns at the end of the eighteenth century without which its spectacular growth would simply not have taken place. The rise of religious pluralism, propelled mostly by evangelical enthusiasm, amounted to an English religious revolution and undoubtedly led to an increase in public and private religiosity, however they are to be measured. Short-term gains were more difficult to secure in the longer term, however, as the combination of a weakened establishment and the gathered church inclinations of its competitors undermined the inclusivist principles of a truly national Christian culture. Throughout the nineteenth century the ubiquitous Sunday schools and the astonishing influence of hymns performed the same kind of function as catechising had in an earlier period, but they also failed to arrest the increasing associationalism and diminishing communalism of all the Christian denominations.[60] By the mid-twentieth century the hard slog of disseminating basic Christian knowledge to the whole population, parish-by-parish (however inadequate this had been in the past) and school-by-school, had been considerably eroded. The Established Church had neither the resources nor the inclination to go on doing it, the state emerged as only a lukewarm supporter of such an enterprise, and most religious Nonconformists were more concerned with recruitment to gathered congregations than with spreading Christian knowledge to all and sundry. Given the distinctive patterns of religious belief and practice that existed in early modern England, it may well be that no other pattern would have delivered better results for the English churches than the one described in this chapter, but the different patterns that emerged in Ireland and the United States at least offer scope for intriguing comparisons.

NOTES

1. Isaiah Berlin, *Historical Inevitability* (London, 1954). For more refined treatments of this theme see Pieter Geyl, *Debates with Historians* (The Hague, 1955); E. H. Carr, *What Is History?* (London, 1961); and G. R. Elton, *Return to Essentials: Some Reflections on the Current State of Historical Study* (Cambridge, 1991).
2. W. R. Ward (ed.), *Parson and Parish in Eighteenth-Century Hampshire: Replies to Bishops' Visitations* (Winchester, 1995), xvii.
3. Peter Virgin, *The Church in an Age of Negligence: Ecclesiastical Structure and Problems of Church Reform 1700–1840* (Cambridge, 1989), 191–6.
4. For a useful summary of recent scholarship on the eighteenth-century Church of England see John Walsh, Colin Haydon and Stephen Taylor (eds.), *The Church of England c. 1689–c. 1833: From Toleration to Tractarianism* (Cambridge, 1993). For a more traditional account see E. G. Rupp, *Religion in England 1688–1791* (Oxford, 1986).
5. S. J. C. Taylor, 'Church and state in England in the mid-eighteenth century: the Newcastle years 1742–1762', PhD dissertation, Cambridge University, 1988.
6. Anthony Russell, *The Clerical Profession* (London, 1980).
7. Martin Ingram, 'From Reformation to toleration: popular religious cultures in England, 1540–1690', in Tim Harris (ed.), *Popular Culture in England, c. 1500–1850* (London, 1995), 95–123.
8. M. F. Snape, '"Our Happy Reformation": Anglicanism and society in a northern parish, 1689–1789', PhD dissertation, University of Birmingham, 1994.
9. W. R. Ward, *Parson and Parish in Eighteenth-Century Surrey: Replies to Bishops' Visitations* (Guildford, 1994).
10. Ward, *Parson and Parish* (Hampshire), 334.
11. J. C. D. Clark, *English Society, 1688–1832* (Cambridge, 1986); Linda Colley, *In Defiance of Oligarchy: The Tory Party 1714–60* (Cambridge, 1982).
12. Paul Langford, *Public Life and the Propertied Englishman 1689–1798* (Oxford, 1991), 14–24.
13. See T. J. F. Kendrick, 'Sir Robert Walpole, the Old Whigs and the bishops 1733–36', *Historical Journal*, 11 (1968), 421–45; W. M. Jacob, *Lay People and Religion in the Early Eighteenth Century* (Cambridge, 1996), 46–51; and Snape, '"Our Happy Reformation"', chapter 9.
14. The same could perhaps be said of any period from the mid-sixteenth to the late eighteenth century. See, for example, Christopher Marsh, '*Holding Their Peace': Popular Religion in Sixteenth Century England* (London, 1997); Bob Bushaway, *By Rite: Custom, Ceremony and Community in England 1700–1800* (London, 1982); Ian Green, 'Anglicanism in Stuart and Hanoverian England', in Sheridan Gilley and W. J. Sheils (eds.), *A History of Religion in Britain* (Oxford, 1994), 168–87; and David Hempton, *Religion and Political Culture in Britain and Ireland: From the Glorious Revolution to the Decline of Empire* (Cambridge, 1996), 15–18.
15. On the whole, the debate has led to a more optimistic assessment of the Church's performance. See John Walsh, Colin Haydon and Stephen Taylor (eds.), *The Church of England c. 1689–1833: From Toleration to Tractarianism* (Cambridge, 1993) and Mark Smith, *Religion in Industrial Society: Oldham and Saddleworth 1740–1865* (Oxford, 1994). The most important modern critics of the Church are Peter Virgin, W. R. Ward and M. F. Snape.

16. See G. V. Bennett, *The Tory Crisis in Church and State 1688–1730* (Oxford, 1975).

17. Owen Chadwick, *The Victorian Church*, vol. I (London, 1966), 7–100.

18. For the complex legal issues raised by JPs see Lambeth Palace Library MSS, Secker Papers, 8 (Methodists), folios 4–5. Much of this correspondence has been reproduced in a more accessible form by O. A. Beckerlegg, 'The Lavington correspondence', in *Proceedings of the Wesley Historical Society*, 42 (1980), 101–11, 139–49 and 167–80.

19. David Hempton, *The Religion of the People: Methodism and Popular Religion c. 1750–1900* (London, 1996), 145–61.

20. D. W. Lovegrove, *Established Church, Sectarian People: Itinerancy and the Transformation of English Dissent, 1780–1830* (Cambridge, 1988) and W. R. Ward, *Religion and Society in England 1790–1850* (London, 1972).

21. Ian Green, *The Christian's ABC: Catechisms and Catechizing in England c. 1530–1740* (Oxford, 1996), 558.

22. J. Maltby, ' "By this Book": parishioners, the Prayer Book and the Established Church', in K. Fincham (ed.), *The Early Stuart Church, 1603–42* (London, 1993), 115–37.

23. Green, *The Christian's ABC*, 563.

24. *Ibid.*, 569.

25. A. C. Outler (ed.), *John Wesley* (New York, 1974), viii. See also Frederick Dreyer, 'Faith and experience in the thought of John Wesley', *American Historical Review*, 88(1) (1983), 12–30.

26. For a useful summary of this material see W. M. Jacob, *Lay People and Religion in the Early Eighteenth Century* (Cambridge, 1996), 101–23. See also, T. Watt, *Cheap Print and Popular Piety 1550–1640* (Cambridge, 1991); D. M. Valenze, 'Prophecy and popular literature in eighteenth-century England', *Journal of Ecclesiastical History*, 29 (1987), 75–92; and S. Pedersen, 'Hannah More meets Simple Simon: tracts, chapbooks, and popular culture in late eighteenth-century England', *Journal of British Studies*, 25 (1986), 84–113.

27. Snape, ' "Our Happy Reformation" ', chapter 2, ' "The doctrines of exploded superstition": Anglicanism and popular heterodoxy'.

28. T. C. Smout, 'Born again at Cambuslang: new evidence on popular religion and literacy in eighteenth-century Scotland', *Past and Present*, 97 (1982), 114–27. See also, Arthur Fawcett, *The Cambuslang Revival: The Scottish Evangelical Revival of the Eighteenth Century* (London, 1971) and Ned Landsman, 'The Evangelists and their hearers: popular interpretations of revivalist preaching in eighteenth-century Scotland', *Journal of British Studies*, 28 (1989), 120–49.

29. Rab Houston, 'The literacy myth? Illiteracy in Scotland, 1630–1760', *Past and Present*, 96 (1982), 81–102.

30. G. H. Jenkins, *The Foundations of Modern Wales: Wales 1642–1780* (Oxford, 1987), 370–81, and *Literature, Religion and Society in Wales 1660–1730* (Cardiff, 1978).

31. Jenkins, *The Foundations of Modern Wales*, 377.

32. T. Herbert and G. E. Jones (eds.), *People and Protest: Wales 1815–1880* (Cardiff, 1988); I. G. Jones, *Communities: Essays in the Social History of Victorian Wales* (Llandysul, Dyfed, 1987); E. T. Davies, *A New History of Wales: Religion and Society in the Nineteenth Century* (Llandybie, Dyfed, 1981); and Hempton, *Religion and Political Culture*, 49–63.

33. M. R. Watts, *The Dissenters*, Vol. II: *The Expansion of Evangelical Nonconformity 1791–1859* (Oxford, 1995).

34. *Ibid.*, 109–10.

35. E. P. Thompson, 'Anthropology and the discipline of historical context', *Midland History*, 1(3) (1972), 41–55, and 'Patrician society, plebeian culture', *Journal of Social History*, 7(4) (1974), 382–405. See also, John Rule, 'Methodism, popular beliefs and village culture in Cornwall, 1800–50', in R. D. Storch (ed.), *Popular Culture and Custom in Nineteenth-Century England* (London, 1972), 48–70; James Obelkevich, *Religion and Rural Society: South Lindsey 1825–1875* (Oxford, 1976); and David Luker, 'Revivalism in theory and practice: the case of Cornish Methodism', *Journal of Ecclesiastical History*, 37(4) (1986), 603–19.

36. Owen Davies, 'Methodism, the clergy, and the popular belief in witchcraft and magic', *History*, 82(266) (1997), 252–65.

37. See, for example, John Langton, 'The Industrial Revolution and the regional geography of England', *Transactions of the Institute of British Geographers*, new series 9 (1984), 145–67.

38. Watts is impatient both with those historians who relate Methodist expansion too closely to the emergence of social class and with those who see it as an expression of class protest. These include E. P. Thompson, *The Making of the English Working Class* (London, 1968) and W. R. Ward, *Religion and Society in England 1790–1850* (London, 1972). He is also critical of the economic and social assumptions about the appeal of evangelical dissent to a self-improving artisanry in A. D. Gilbert, *Religion and Society in Industrial England, 1740–1914* (London, 1976) and Robert Currie, Alan Gilbert and Lee Horsley, *Churches and Churchgoers: Patterns of Church Growth in the British Isles since 1700* (Oxford, 1977).

39. See, for example, John Langton and Goran Hoppe, 'Urbanization, social structure and population circulation in pre-industrial times: flows of people through Vadstena (Sweden) in the mid-nineteenth century', in P. J. Corfield and D. Keene (eds.), *Work in Towns 850–1850* (Leicester, 1990), 138–63; Michael Anderson, *Family Structure in Nineteenth-Century Lancashire* (London, 1971). See also, H. McLeod, 'Class, community and religion: the religious geography of nineteenth-century England', in M. Hill (ed.), *A Sociological Yearbook of Religion in Britain* 6 (London, 1973), 29–72, and D. M. Thompson, 'The churches and society in nineteenth-century England: a rural perspective', *Studies in Church History*, 8 (1972), 267–76.

40. Langton and Hoppe, 'Urbanization', 141.

41. See, for example, the creative suggestions of Albion Urdank, *Religion and Society in a Cotswold Vale: Nailsworth, Gloucestershire 1760–1865* (Berkeley, CA, 1990).

42. See C. G. Brown, 'The mechanism of religious growth in urban societies: British cities since the eighteenth century', in Hugh McLeod (ed.), *Religion in the Age of Great Cities 1830–1930* (London, 1995), 239–62.

43. See J. S. Werner, *The Primitive Methodist Connexion: Its Background and Early History* (Madison, WI, 1984); D. A. Gowland, *Methodist Secessions: The Origins of Free Methodism in Three Lancashire Towns* (Manchester, 1979); J. H. S. Kent, *The Age of Disunity* (London, 1966); and Robert Currie, *Methodism Divided* (London, 1968).

44. T. W. Laqueur, *Religion and Respectability: Sunday Schools and Working-Class Culture, 1780–1850* (London and New Haven, 1976).

45. Bernard Semmel, *The Methodist Revolution* (London, 1974), 152–66. See also Stuart Piggin, 'Halevy revisited: the origins of the Wesleyan Methodist Missionary Society: an examination of Semmel's thesis', *The Journal of Imperial and Commonwealth History*, 9(1) (1980), 19–20; R. H. Martin, 'Missionary competition between Evangelical Dissenters and Wesleyan Methodists in the early nineteenth century: a footnote to the founding of the Methodist Missionary Society', *Proceedings of the Wesley Historical Society*, 42 (1979), 81–6; and R. H. Martin, *Evangelicals United: Ecumenical Stirrings in Pre-Victorian Britain, 1795–1830* (London, 1983).

46. G. F. A. Best, 'The religious difficulties of national education in England, 1800–70', *Cambridge Historical Journal*, 12 (1956), 105–27; D. G. Paz, *The Politics of Working-Class Education in Britain 1830–50* (Manchester, 1980); and David Hempton, *Methodism and Politics in British Society 1750–1850* (London, 1984), 149–78.

47. Smith, *Religion in Industrial Society*.

48. For more extensive treatment of this subject see Hempton, *Religion and Political Culture*, 1–48 and *The Religion of the People*, 162–78.

49. S. J. Brown, *Thomas Chalmers and the Godly Commonwealth* (Oxford, 1982).

50. O. J. Brose, *Church and Parliament: The Reshaping of the Church of England 1828–1860* (Stanford, 1959).

51. N. Gash, 'The crisis of the Anglican establishment in the early nineteenth century', in his *Pillars of Government and Other Essays on State and Society c. 1770–c. 1880* (London, 1986), 16–25. See also Gash, *Reaction and Reconstruction in English Politics 1832–1852* (Oxford, 1965).

52. Obelkevich, *Religion and Rural Society*. The idea that evangelical zeal could stimulate short-term religious excitement at the expense of the durability of long-term religious cultures is vigorously pursued in relation to Presbyterianism in Northern Ireland by Peter Brooke, *Ulster Presbyterianism: The Historical Perspective* (Dublin, 1987).

53. Frances Knight, *The Nineteenth-Century Church and English Society* (Cambridge, 1995), 201–2.

54. See, for example, Jeffrey Cox, *The English Churches in a Secular Society: Lambeth, 1870–1930* (Oxford, 1982).

55. Robin Gill, 'Secularization and the Census data', in Steve Bruce (ed.), *Religion and Modernization: Sociologists and Historians Debate the Secularization Thesis* (Oxford, 1992), 90–117, and Gill, *The Myth of the Empty Church* (London, 1993).

56. J. H. Whyte, *Church and State in Modern Ireland 1923–1970* (Dublin, 1971).

57. R. L. Moore, *Selling God: American Religion in the Marketplace of Culture* (New York, 1994); N. O. Hatch, *The Democratization of American Christianity* (New Haven, 1989); M. A. Noll, *A History of Christianity in the United States and Canada* (Grand Rapids, 1992); and M. A. Noll (ed.), *God and Mammon: Protestants, Money and the Market, 1790–1860* (New York, 2001).

58. Finke and Stark, *The Churching of America*.

59. W. B. Townsend, H. B. Workman and George Eayrs, *A New History of Methodism*, 2 vols. (London, 1909), vol. II, 532. For an interpretation of those statistics see David Hempton, 'Methodist growth in Transatlantic perspective, ca 1770–1850', in Nathan Hatch and John Wigger (eds.), *Methodism and the Shaping of American*

Culture (Nashville, 2001), 41–85, and Sylvia Frey and Betty Wood, *Come Shouting to Zion* (Chapel Hill, NJ, 1998).

60. See Laqueur, *Religion and Respectability*; P. B. Cliff, *The Rise and Development of the Sunday School Movement in England 1780–1980* (Redhill, Surrey, 1986); and Jim Obelkevich, 'Music and religion in the nineteenth century', in J. Obelkevich, L. Roper and R. Samuel (eds.), *Disciplines of Faith* (London, 1987), 550–65.

6   Catholicism in Ireland

Sheridan Gilley

Modern Ireland has appeared distinctive in two ways: first, in the complete identification of Irish nationalism with Irish Catholicism; and second, in the high levels of religious practice in Catholic Ireland until very recently, with over 90 per cent of the population attending mass every Sunday. Ireland has been unusual if not unique since the sixteenth century as a country in which the Counter-Reformation largely prevailed in the very teeth of persecution by a Protestant state, so that its Catholic faith was forged in the fire of suffering. Thus it has always been granted that in Ireland, at least from the time of Daniel O'Connell (1775–1847), Catholicism and Irish nationalism have reinforced each other. This relationship was sometimes troubled, and O'Connell himself drew the line against papal interventions in Irish politics by declaring 'Our religion from Rome: our politics from home', while the Irish Catholic nationalist movement was liberal in its sympathies in honouring its Protestant leaders, like the main protagonist of Home Rule for Ireland, Charles Stewart Parnell.[1] Yet by drawing the priesthood into politics in the 1820s as the instruments of the first mass democratic movement in the modern world, the Catholic Association, O'Connell gave the clergy a perilous responsibility as the guardians of his pacific constitutionalist and democratic nationalism with its overt hostility to violence. Thus most churchmen suspected Irish nationalism in its revolutionary form, and they publicly denounced the main revolutions against British Protestant rule in Ireland in 1798, 1848 and 1867.

For all that hostility, and the occasional unpopular papal intervention in Irish politics on the conservative side, Irish Catholic anticlericalism was the dog that did not bark. Why this was so requires a complicated explanation. A minority of the clergy sanctioned revolution, and even the official Church was usually prepared to give a retrospective blessing or baptism to dead revolutionaries. This occurred most famously after the Easter Rising of 1916, which was at first largely opposed by both the people and their priests, but was, for the most part, the work of devout Catholics and was heavily overlain with Catholic symbolism. Even the Socialist James Connolly attempted to create a reconciliation between Catholicism and revolutionary nationalism, and died with the rites of the Church. By dying like Christian martyrs at the hands of the British army, the revolutionaries of 1916 won in death the legitimacy that they had lacked in life, and dictated the character of the newly independent Ireland, leaving an ambiguous legacy of the creation of a state by violence which is still invoked by the Provisional IRA in Ulster.

So between 1800 and 1916, the adjectives Irish and Catholic thereby became so interchangeable that Irish Catholic devotion could be simply taken for granted, as an unchanging part of the national character, and it was only in the 1970s that Irish historians questioned whether the high levels of modern Irish religious practice have always obtained. The seminal essay by David Miller in 1975 argued that before 1840, in rural parishes in which Irish-speakers were most numerous, especially in the west of Ireland, only 20 to 40 per cent of the population went to mass every Sunday. In rural parishes with fewer Irish-speakers, in the east, the rates of churchgoing were 30 to 60 per cent of the population; it was only in the towns (and in a rural area of County Wexford) that mass attendance rose to over 70 per cent.[2] Miller's figures have been questioned and revised upward by Professor Patrick Corish,[3] the doyen of Irish church historians, to take account of the sick, the aged and mothers with children under 7 and these children, who were not obliged to attend Sunday mass and who, he calculates, comprised a fifth of the population.[4] Even so, Miller powerfully suggested that the universal mass attendance rates in the modern period in Ireland came after the Famine; that it was the better-off and better educated, in Ireland before 1850, as in Protestant England, who went to church every Sunday,[5] and that it was only after 1850 that regular church-going became characteristic of the great masses of the Irish Catholic poor.

Miller's figures were used even before their formal publication by the most prolific of Irish church historians, Emmet Larkin. Larkin has an unrivalled knowledge of nineteenth-century ecclesiastical archives, and his books have tended to project a view of religious history as a form of epistolary intercourse between bishops.[6] Arguably his best interpretations have appeared in articles, as in his essay on what he called the 'Devotional Revolution' in Ireland for the *American Historical Review* in 1972.[7] Larkin argued that the Famine was the watershed in Irish religious history, for it bore most severely upon the poorest sections of the population, of landless labourers and cottiers, especially in the west, where church-going was weakest, while sparing the well-to-do farming classes among whom church-going was strong. The Famine also corrected the decline in the ratio of the Catholic clergy to the total population. In the first half of the century, the number of priests went up 35 per cent, but fell in relative terms as the population doubled. At a stroke the Famine improved the ratio of priests to people, and the number of priests and nuns continued to rise through the second half of the nineteenth century while the population continued to fall through continuing emigration. In a manner unusual in nineteenth-century Europe, Ireland after 1850 experienced a more numerous clergy evangelising a declining population.

Both Miller and Larkin cut across the tendency to derive the strength of Catholicism from the native Gaelic tradition, by arguing that formal Tridentine religious practice was strongest among the most urban and Anglicised section of the population. Indeed it could be argued that in their new degree of Sunday observance the Irish became more like the Victorian British, not less so; it is the decline of religious observance in the twentieth century in Britain which made the Irish look distinctive. By the same token, the increasing sexual puritanism of nineteenth-century Ireland, in part the result of a trend to late marriages to preserve farms for a single heir after the Famine, also looks like an approach to the British norm. Larkin argued that the Famine dealt a final blow to the already weakened Gaelic-speaking culture, so that a population traumatised by the Famine was acutely susceptible to the redefinition of their old traditions. The people who died were mostly poor and Gaelic-speaking. The people who survived were comparatively well-to-do and spoke English.

Larkin saw the central figure in this 'revolution' as Paul Cullen, who became archbishop of Armagh in 1849 and was translated in 1852 to Dublin. A cold and reserved figure, 'Paul the Prudent' was Ireland's first cardinal, and his knowledge of Rome and his special office as Apostolic Delegate gave him enormous influence in the Irish Church as well as in the church of the Irish diaspora in North America and Australasia.[8] Cullen had been Rector of the Irish College in Rome, and from his experience of the Roman revolution of 1848, he tended to see Ireland through Italian spectacles. Thus he interpreted the Young Ireland movement responsible for the Irish revolt in 1848 as an anti-Catholic imitation of Mazzini's Young Italy, and he has always borne a bad reputation among Irish nationalists for his crusade against the Fenians who rose against Protestant rule in 1867, and for disciplining priests who were caught up in radical or revolutionary politics. Yet here, in Larkin's theory, he was being recast as a kind of revolutionary himself.[9]

In Larkin's argument, Cullen transformed Irish Catholicism by imposing a stricter Roman discipline upon the clergy, and by attacking pastorally neglectful priests and those guilty of drunkenness, avarice and sexual immorality. Cullen also promoted missions and retreats and enriched popular piety by introducing and promoting a new wealth of Roman devotions: 'the rosary, forty hours, perpetual adoration, novenas, blessed altars, *Via Crucis*, benediction, vespers, devotion to the Sacred Heart and to the Immaculate Conception, jubilees, triduums, pilgrimages, shrines, processions, and retreats', the whole reinforced 'by the use of devotional tools and aids: beads, scapulars, medals, missals, prayer books, catechisms, holy pictures, and *Agnus Dei*',[10] and by a body of new vernacular hymns which were mostly written by English converts to Rome from Anglicanism.

Larkin called this a 'Devotional Revolution' and related it to the huge expenditure after 1850 on highly decorated churches, with marble altars, paintings, stained glass and a Roman liturgy rich in image and symbol, exploring the senses through candles and flowers, coloured and embroidered vestments and the entrancing odours of beeswax and incense. The 'Devotional Revolution' meant that religion was increasingly under direct clerical control, and it had its theological counterpart in the Romanisation or Ultramontanisation of the Irish Church through a new emphasis on papal authority, which destroyed a lingering Gallican tradition imparted to Irish Catholicism by its earlier links with France. Irish Gallicanism is like Irish Jansenism, which has sometimes been held responsible for Irish sexual puritanism, a bit of a will o' the wisp, without much proper historical substance, and a matter of preservation more of local than of national tradition as in France. Yet Cullen did get the Maynooth Professor of Theology George Crolly sent to Rome to be reinstructed in Roman ways,[11] while two of the bishops, MacHale of Tuam and Moriarty of Kerry, voted on the inopportunist side against papal infallibility at the First Vatican Council. This was, however, arguably a storm in a theological teacup, or to change the metaphor, at an intellectual level remote from the ordinary Irish Catholic. Much more dramatic and immediate to him was the stronger Roman feel to the actual church building, which was now the holy place, with its rituals, especially attendance at mass, the new heart of religion. In the second half of the nineteenth century, these new churches multiplied and the poor rates of mass attendance were reversed, and the Irish became what they have been until quite recently, the most practising Catholics in the world.

This picture of the consequences of the Famine also makes sense of the rather late and forlorn attempt by a minority of Protestant Evangelical clergy within the Church of Ireland to evangelise the hungry Catholic multitudes, to make them both literate and Protestant allegedly by offering them free soup, which won them the nickname of 'Soupers' among the hostile Catholic population. This 'Second Reformation'[12] had been endorsed by a Protestant archbishop in the 1820s, but its embodiment in the Irish Church Missions to Roman Catholics belongs to the Famine years of the later 1840s, and Cullen seems to have taken a rather grim pleasure in reports that converts were most numerous in the province of his great ecclesiastical rival John MacHale, Archbishop of Tuam, 'the Lion of the Fold of Judah', as O'Connell had called him, and 'Patriarch of the West'. MacHale was an old-fashioned militant Irish nationalist and differed from Cullen by protecting some of the more revolutionary or Fenian-minded clergy like Father Patrick Lavelle.[13] MacHale's opposition to the state-supported National Schools allegedly left some of his flock illiterate. Cullen saw in the Protestant converts in the west the consequences of MacHale's policies. It would perhaps be truer to see them in the setting of the pre-Tridentine folk-Catholicism of western Ireland, so that the Irish Church Missions can be interpreted as a last valiant attempt by Protestant clergy to become the instruments of modernisation. The general Catholic hostility to the Protestant converts apparently made many of them emigrate, and while the 1861 census showed a fall in the Catholic population, this was also a consequence of emigration, and it was clear that the conversions of the Second Reformation had made no significant difference to the overwhelming preponderance of Catholics over Protestants in Ireland.

Miller had drawn attention to the different, 'premodern' character of much Irish folk religion, and Larkin's picture was if anything reinforced by Sean Connolly's depiction of Catholicism before the Famine. Connolly described a body of religious practices which existed without benefit of clergy outside the chapel, and which was centred on prayers in the home and on the 'pattern' or pilgrimage to a local holy site or well in a still sacred landscape where the faithful would gather for prayers and feasting which sometimes degenerated into drunkenness and faction-fighting with other families or villages, to the scandal of middle-class Catholics and the clergy. Irish weddings and wakes were also often rough affairs, attended by drunkenness and ritualised obscenities. There were popular celebrations to do with the agricultural year, on St Bridget's day, St Patrick's day, May Day and August harvest in which pre-Christian folklore had been loosely Christianised without benefit of the clergy. Miller suggested that this horticultural magic was proved a failure by the Famine and that this failure enhanced the alternative religious culture of the chapel. Connolly made much of the lack of discipline among the priesthood themselves before 1840, as their reform was necessary to achieve a higher level of practice among their people. He described an anticlericalism which peaked in the 1780s and 1790s and still lingered in places in the early 1840s, largely caused by the charges of the clergy for the rites of passage, baptisms, marriages and burials.[14]

This thesis has its fascinating aspects. It roots the exceptional fidelity of modern Irish Catholicism not in its distinctive history before 1800 but in a nineteenth-century movement of Ultramontane piety which transformed the Catholic Church in Ireland as in France, where, superficially, at least, it seems to have been comparatively ineffective. It also links the Irish Catholic experience, at least by implication, with a wider religious revival in Victorian Britain and with the movements of nineteenth-century Protestant Evangelical pietism to which it was consciously opposed. On certain points, it has been refined rather than refuted. Professor Corish has suggested that 'the untidy Irish system, with its strong emphasis on the home, proved more durable than the tidy continental system of parish catechesis centred on the church',[15] or as Sean Connolly glosses this with John Bossy's argument[16] that 'in the long run Irish Catholicism was to benefit from the failure of the church authorities to bring popular religion entirely within the confines of the new structures prescribed at Trent'.[17] In other words, the Irish Church was strong in so far as its native tradition was extra- or pre-Tridentine.

On the other hand, Desmond Keenan has argued that the Church was a good deal more orderly, and the clergy were a good deal more disciplined, than Larkin and Miller had implied; that the nineteenth-century Irish Catholic Church was, in spirit and in its formal organisation, thoroughly Tridentine; and that the great church building boom in Ireland occurred before 1850, so that church building after 1850 was largely an enrichment or improvement or enlargement of already existing churches. Some of the devotional themes described by Larkin were already common before 1850 in the towns in the east and in the chapels belonging to the religious orders. The adoption by the clergy of a distinctive clerical dress goes back to the 1820s and to the reforms of Dr Thomas Doyle, the celebrated bishop of Kildare. Annual clerical retreats also began in the 1820s,[18] while the borrowing of the Anglicised Catholics of the east from English Catholic devotional works also has a long history.[19] This may make the 'Devotional Revolution' more of an 'evolution'. Thus Thomas McGrath wishes to replace Larkin's 'Devotional Revolution' with a 'Tridentine Evolution', beginning in the sixteenth century rather than occurring over a few decades in the nineteenth century.[20] This difference of opinion is of the sort familiar to historians in other areas of study, between one kind of historian who thinks that a phenomenon happened quickly, and another who thinks that it took place over a very long time.

Yet both the 'revolutionists' and the 'evolutionists' point in the same general direction of change, towards a society which was in both its external ritual behaviour and official interior piety more religious and not less. Indeed, far from noting any tendency to secularisation, both David Miller and Joseph Lee make these religious changes part of the modernisation of Irish society. Lee drew particular attention to Cullen's unflagging concern with the plight of the poor, especially through his support for popular education, while even his church building programme had a similar social purpose: his 'emphasis on the physical primacy of the church buildings concentrated the specialised functions hitherto diffused as status symbols among the private homes of the more affluent members of the community, who suffered with ill-concealed chagrin Cullen's insistence on the equality of Catholics before God'.[21] Lee also drew attention to Cullen's modernity in the sense that 'he basically conceded the autonomy of politics from religion' and the separation of the Church from the state. While he strongly disliked the English Whigs and Liberals, his endorsement of the National Association founded in 1864 to disestablish the Protestant Church of Ireland placed him in practical terms in the liberal camp condemned by Pius IX, Pio Nono, in his Syllabus of Errors.[22] Cullen supported Protestant as well as Catholic politicians; a Protestant who looked kindly on the Church was to be preferred to an indifferent or hostile Catholic. Yet he also professionalised the clergy as spiritual specialists by discouraging their involvement in politics. This portrait of the Liberal Cullen should be borne in mind against the awful picture in Desmond Bowen's study of Cullen as the evil genius who Ultramontanised the Irish Catholic Church, and who thereby bears a heavy responsibility for the re-emergence of sectarian war between Protestant and Catholic in nineteenth-century Ireland.[23] By contrast, to Lee, Cullen was a moderniser despite his anti-Protestantism:

Cullen's clergy did not, of course, preach an explicit gospel of modernisation. Nor should he himself be considered a conscious missionary of modernisation. But his determination to assert the primacy of merit over birth, to mobilise the masses, to emphasise the specialisation of roles within the Church and of the role of the Church itself in society contributed to the creation of systematic sustained participation in institutional religion.

This represented a basic change from the 'peasant revolt' syndrome of previous participatory religious movements, sudden but ephemeral outbursts punctuating general apathy. Some of Cullen's achievements would have distressed him had he appreciated them. Despite his own distaste for exhibitionism his church building programme helped foster the consumer consciousness it was partly intended to curb. The 'Sunday suit' or the 'Sunday shawl' became obligatory, for the rags that had sufficed in many of the pre-famine churches seemed out of place in the fine new buildings. In short, the 'Devotional Revolution' was a very modern thing in the conspicuous consumption of the mass-produced religious artifacts through which it found expression. Lee concluded, perhaps with some overemphasis, that 'Cullen transformed the Irish Church from a Latin-American type institution into one of the most efficiently marshalled Churches in Europe.'[24]

Thus Miller and Lee both suggested that Catholic Ireland took the path to modernisation, through rather than in spite of the Roman Catholic Church, under circumstances peculiarly favourable to Roman Catholicism. This theme is taken further by John White in a recent essay on the appearance in 1879 of the Virgin Mary with St Joseph, St John the Evangelist and the Lamb of God on the external wall of the chapel in the village of Knock in County Mayo. The event has a particular importance as the principal one of its kind in nineteenth-century Ireland. White argues that the apparition was 'not a rearguard action against the forces of modernity: it was itself a force and a manifestation of modernity'. Drawing on the papers which he discovered in the archive of the Sisters of St Joseph of Peace, founded by the strangely protofeminist Sister Mary Francis Clare Cusack, 'the Nun of Kenmare', White points out that the supporters of the apparition included the nationalist T. D. Sullivan, the editor of the *Nation*, and other clergy and laymen who were members of the Land League fighting the Land War for tenant right for Irish farmers, some of them, like Sullivan himself, from prison. The pilgrimage transcended the localism of the normal Irish pilgrimage to attract national and international attention. Those who provided it with publicity and raised money for Sister Mary Francis Clare's projected convent in Knock included the Protestant journalist James Redpath of the *New York Tribune* and the New York Tammany Hall boss 'Honest John' Kelly. Nor was Knock itself immune to rapid social change. The parish priest of Knock, Archdeacon Cavanagh, who promoted the miracle, had seen to the creation of eleven National Schools which were shifting the language of the population from native Irish into English. The apparition was silent, understandably so, as 'the oldest witness, Bridget Trench, had no English, while the youngest, six year old John Curry, was being educated with no Irish'. In Knock itself, Sister Mary Francis Clare 'opened a kindergarten for infants, national schools for boys and girls, and a school to teach industrial and domestic skills to girls bound for emigration, another fact of modern life in Mayo'. The witnesses to aspects of the apparition were not all uneducated labourers but included a schoolteacher and two subconstables from the recently opened barracks of the Royal Irish Constabulary. The schoolteacher organised a fifty-voice choir and introduced the Children of Mary to accompany processions. Pilgrims came from Dublin on the recently constructed railway, while cars for transport from the station were astutely arranged by a former Fenian whose daughter had experienced a miraculous cure. The idea that the apparition was the product of lantern slides was promptly tested and disproved by Dr Francis Lennon, the professor of science at Maynooth, assisted by twenty of the clergy. The shrine suffered from the departure of Sister Mary Francis Clare, who had fallen out with the local bishop, allegedly absconded with the funds for her convent, and subsequently apostatised altogether. In its modern form the pilgrimage has been revived complete with a brand new airport, a not inappropriate conclusion to its history.[25]

The apparition at Knock was compared to Lourdes, but it was also taken as a blessing on the Irish nation, and especially upon its poor; Knock affirmed Catholic Ireland as always faithful where Lourdes condemned the sins of apostate France. This theme was recognised by de Tocqueville: the Irish achieved their human dignity on their knees. Yet as White and James S. Donnelly have pointed out, Knock must be seen in the context of the kind of movement of piety which also produced Lourdes, and the idea of religious revival as a form of modernisation can be overdone. Donnelly demonstrates the survival of a more traditional Irish piety, as pilgrims stripped the cement from the gable wall of the chapel of the apparition, and made large holes in the ground beside it, and carried off the cement and clay and water from the gutters for their miraculous curative properties. The old survived into the new.[26]

Yet whether regarded as 'ancient' or 'modern', Knock was, as the scene of miracle, untypical of Irish Catholicism, which went from strength to strength through the ordinary institutions of the parish church and school. The Church's role in confirming the nation's faith may seem less impressive, however, when it is remembered that the Irish population continued to decline. Thus in speaking of Catholic Ireland in the twentieth century, we are referring to a population of under 5 million people, so that a proper standard for comparison might be with other small areas also noted for high rates of religious practice, like Brittany, the Basque country and Navarre. It could be added that Ireland had a safety valve for anyone not liking the Church's discipline, through a swift passage to America or Australasia; that is to say, Ireland exported any non-practising Catholics to the New World. Against this speculation stand the generally high, if somewhat variable, rates of religious practice among Irish emigrants abroad, as some places seem to have been more conducive to continuing religious practice than others.[27] I have argued that expatriate Irish Catholicism in the United States and in the British Empire preserved a sense of immigrant identity and 'was a vehicle of a local sense of community and of a national identity and of an international consciousness'.[28] Again, the Devotional Revolution in the Irish diaspora in the great new cities of North America and Australasia had to find its holy place in a new urban shrine church, having left behind the sacred landscape of rural Ireland. A full picture of Irish religion would require a consideration of the Irish exiles who lived abroad, among whom lapsing from the faith was a great deal more common than in Ireland.[29]

The nineteenth-century conception of Ireland as a Catholic nation, a pious people, with a body of politicians who were largely bishops *manqués*, was if anything confirmed by the new state which emerged from the Anglo-Irish Treaty of 1921. In the ensuing Civil War between the Catholic supporters and opponents of the Treaty, the Church excommunicated the opponents of the Treaty for whom the new Ireland, a state within the British Empire, and without the six counties of Ulster, was not independent enough. Again, the Irish anti-clerical dog failed to bark. This has been explained by Dermot Keogh in terms of the activities of one section of the clergy who never lost contact with the leading opponent of the Treaty, Eamon de Valera, a curiously clerical kind of layman who brought most of the anti-Treatyites into democratic politics. It was de Valera who welcomed the most extravagantly triumphalist manifestation of the Catholicism of the new Ireland in the Eucharistic Congress of 1932, when street altars were erected in every town and village and a million people gathered in Phoenix Park for the adoration of the Blessed Sacrament.

Yet the new Ireland wore its Catholicism with a difference. De Valera wrote the Church into his new Irish Constitution in 1937. Like Pope Pius XI's Lateran Treaties with Mussolini, this began by invoking the Blessed Trinity, but beyond that it hardly approached the integralist model of Italy or, later, Franco's Spain. In an echo of Napoleon's Concordat with the pope in 1801, the Constitution did not speak of the Catholic Church as 'the one true church'. Instead, it guaranteed 'not to endow any religion', and, like the Napoleonic Concordat, merely acknowledged 'the special position of the Holy Catholic Apostolic and Roman Church as the guardian of the Faith professed by the great majority of the citizens'. Even this rather hyperbolic formula of 'the Holy Catholic Apostolic and Roman Church'[30] was apparently suggested by the Protestant archbishop of

Dublin, George Gregg, who took the phrase straight from the decrees of the Council of Trent, and urged that, on the same principle, the other Irish Churches should also be described in the Constitution in the manner in which they described themselves. Thus the Constitution goes on to recognise 'the Church of Ireland, the Presbyterian Church in Ireland, the Methodist Church in Ireland, the Religious Society of Friends in Ireland (the Quakers), as well as the Jewish Congregations and the other religious denominations existing in Ireland'. At a time when the Jews were undergoing persecution in Germany, the reference to them has a more than merely historical interest. Indeed the Constitution specifically acted to protect these minorities who all together constituted a mere 7 per cent of the population. Even if only out of a keen political sense of the importance of Irish Protestantism and of the very visible ties with Britain, the Constitution represented an extraordinary concession to pluralism which annoyed the cardinal archbishop of Armagh, Joseph MacRory, but the archbishop of Dublin, Edward Byrne, agreed with de Valera, and MacRory was blocked by Byrne and by the papal legate Paschal Robinson in his attempt to get the matter reversed in Rome.[31] In Catholic Ireland, a traditional pluralism prevailed over integral Catholicism.

De Valera's choice of pluralism over integralism was partly the result of a concern not to outrage the Northern Irish Protestants, who complained that 'Home Rule (for Ireland) meant Rome rule'. The corollary of Irish nationalism was a neutral state and not a Catholic one. Certain parts of the Constitution do have a Catholic air, as in its ban upon divorce in article 41; but in the 1930s, the Protestant Churches were no more in favour of divorce than the Catholic Church, a consideration which also applies to the clause in the constitution against blasphemy, which still has its counterpart in English law, as a protection for the Church of England. It is only the departure of the Protestant Churches from the basic moral teachings which they used to share with Rome which has made these clauses seem distinctively Catholic. Again, the elements of Catholic social teaching in the Constitution were not directly offensive to Protestants. The real power of the Church was an informal one, and is therefore more difficult to define. There were some Catholic integralists in Ireland inspired by continental developments, especially among the Jesuits, who wanted a formal Roman Catholic confession in the Constitution. The most flamboyant right-wing integralist was General Eoin O'Duffy, leader of the neo-Fascist Blueshirts, who was an admirer and imitator of Mussolini; it is remarkable how completely de Valera managed to confine their influence in a fervently Catholic country.[32]

Yet the Church's real power in the state was quite considerable, a point made by the ecclesiastical veto of Dr Noel Browne's bill in 1950–1 for free medical treatment for mothers and children. This informal church authority and its more formal expression in legislation against contraceptives – which have not been banned by law in Protestant countries[33] – have proven too integrally Catholic for many modern Irish Catholics, and the Second Vatican Council was a watershed in the gradual undoing of the seemingly indissoluble bonds between the Irish Church and the Irish nation. One can only speak of secularisation in Ireland as beginning in the 1960s. Many Irish Catholics found liturgical change especially unsettling, with the attendant if ill-defined sense that Catholics had accepted the Protestant case in adopting a vernacular liturgy, and that religion was in decline, at a time when the churches were still as full as ever. The most obvious area of change was in sexual mores. The first battle was over contraception, and in 1979 the Fianna Fail leader Charles Haughey described a measure authorising the sale of contraceptives on prescription at chemists as 'an Irish solution to an Irish problem'. At first, there was a reaction against further change. In 1983, opponents of abortion carried a referendum to enshrine an anti-abortion measure in the Irish Constitution.[34] In 1986, another referendum declared against the legalisation of divorce. It is, however, significant that the orthodox side in both referenda owed more to lay activists than to the clergy, and that in 1985 there were thirty-three separate accounts of moving or smiling or speaking statues of the Virgin Mary. Thus the 1980s saw something of a counter-movement, against secularisation, at least in rural areas were the Church was still strong.[35]

That reaction has since produced a counter-reaction, so that divorce was legalised in 1995. This in turn reflects a secularisation of attitudes to marriage and the family especially among 'the young, the unemployed, and housewives working part-time', all growing sectors of the population, together with an educated middle class which no longer buys its religion wholesale.[36] Indeed as far as sexual ethics are concerned, the Irish State is probably in official terms more 'liberal' than either Great Britain or North America. Again, the sections of the population in which belief is strongest, especially the farmers who defined the character of de Valera's Ireland, constitute the classes who are most rapidly declining. There are considerable problems about imparting the faith to a nation which, in part because of clerical opposition to contraception, has the highest percentage of young people in Europe and which, in part because of clerical enthusiasm for education, comprises one of the best-educated nations in Europe. Again, the Church's reputation has suffered a number of major scandals, most notably the one involving Bishop Eamonn Casey of Galway, and others concerning a small number of paedophile clergymen. All this has led to an increasing gulf between the Church and the state, and a blurring of the identities of Irish and Catholic. The change has had some benefits, in giving the Church a new freedom in matters like the 'option for the poor' to challenge the government in Dublin; with its long history of emigration and famine and powerful missionary movement, Ireland is much more conscious than most of Europe of the Third World. The identification of nationalism with Catholicism remains strongest where denominational divisions are still most painful, in Ulster; and for as long as Ulster is still a thorn in Ireland's side, there will be no final healing of the wounds of a thousand years of Irish Catholicism.

NOTES

1. The revelation of Parnell's adultery with Mrs Kitty O'Shea divided Irish Catholic nationalists in 1890–1, and the Church's condemnation of him was unpopular with his remaining supporters. Yet this did little to discredit the Church's authority. In fact, the initial agents of his condemnation were not the Catholics, but their allies the English Liberal Nonconformists, who shamed the Church into denouncing his adultery.

2. David Miller, 'Irish Catholicism and the Great Famine', *Journal of Social History*, 9 (Fall, 1975), 81–98. See also the discussion in Sean Connolly, *Religion and Society in Nineteenth-Century Ireland* (Dundalk, 1985), 48ff.

3. Fr Corish is also the editor of *A History of Irish Catholicism*, 8 vols. (Dublin, 1967–72), and the author of the massive *Maynooth College 1795–1995* (Dublin, 1995).

4. Patrick Corish, *The Irish Catholic Experience: A Historical Survey* (Dublin, 1986), 167. See also on Corish notes 9, 15, 19 and 22 below.

5. 'The wealthiest and most numerous [Catholic] parishes were created in the southeast, in Leinster and east Munster, where in 1800 virtually all the parishes valued at over £150 were located'; L. J. Proudfoot, 'Regionalism and localism: religious change and social protest, c.1700 to c.1900', in B. J. Graham and L. J. Proudfoot, *An Historical Geography of Ireland* (London, 1993), 206.

6. Emmet Larkin, *The Roman Catholic Church and the Creation of the Modern Irish State, 1878–1886* (Philadelphia, 1975); *The Roman Catholic Church and the Plan of Campaign in Ireland 1886–1888* (Cork, 1978); *The Roman Catholic Church in Ireland and the Fall of Parnell 1888–1891* (Liverpool, 1979); *The Making of the Roman Catholic Church in Ireland 1850–1860* (Chapel Hill, NC, 1980); *The Consolidation of the Roman Catholic Church in Ireland 1860–1870* (Dublin, 1987). See my review article, 'Religion in modern Ireland', *The Journal of Ecclesiastical History*, 47 (January 1992), 110–15.

7. Emmet Larkin, 'The Devotional Revolution in Ireland, 1850–75', *The American Historical Review*, 77(3) (1972), 625–52.

8. E. R. Norman, *The Catholic Church and Ireland in the Age of Rebellion 1859–1873* (London, 1965).

9. For a different version of the same point, see Patrick J. Corish, 'The radical face of Paul Cardinal Cullen', in P. J. Corish (ed.), *Radicals, Rebels and Establishments, Historical Studies* 15 (Belfast, 1985), 171–84.

10. Larkin, 'Devotional Revolution', 645.

11. See Ambrose Macaulay, *Dr Russell of Maynooth* (London, 1983), esp. 136–42.

12. Desmond Bowen, *The Protestant Crusade in Ireland 1800–1870* (Dublin, 1978).

13. Gerard Moran, *A Radical Priest in Mayo: Fr Patrick Lavelle: The Rise and Fall of an Irish Nationalist 1825–86* (Dublin, 1994).

14. S. J. Connolly, *Priests and People in Pre-Famine Ireland 1780–1845* (Dublin, 1982).

15. Patrick J. Corish, *The Catholic Community in the Seventeenth and Eighteenth Centuries* (Dublin, 1981), 42.

16. John Bossy, 'The Counter-Reformation and the people of Catholic Ireland, 1596–1641', in T. D. Williams (ed.), *Historical Studies*, 8 (Dublin, 1971), 169.

17. S. J. Connolly, 'Religion and history', *Irish Economic and Social History*, 10 (1983), 80.

18. Desmond J. Keenan, *The Catholic Church in Nineteenth-Century Ireland: A Sociological Study* (Dublin, 1983).

19. Fr Patrick Corish distinguishes between 'what had been a minority culture: the Catholic religious culture of the middle class and the towns' beginning in the seventeenth century, the culture of those who could read and speak English, on the one hand; and the religion of those who were either illiterate and/or spoke Irish on the other. The National Schools which taught English and literacy and Cullen's reorganisation of the Church extended the formerly minority middle-class culture to everyone. Thus Fr Corish says of the Devotional Revolution, 'Some would tell you it took place about 1625. In a place like Bangor Erris in County Mayo it probably took place about 1850 or 1860 when the first English-speaking missions were conducted there.' 'Maynooth Monsignor', *History Ireland*, 4(2) (1996), 19.

20. Thomas G. McGrath, 'The Tridentine evolution of modern Irish Catholicism: a re-examination of the "Devotional Revolution" thesis', in Reamonn O'Muiri, *Irish Church History Today* (Monaghan, *c.* 1991, but no date given), 84–99.

21. Joseph Lee, *The Modernisation of Irish Society 1848–1918* (Dublin, 1973), 45.

22. This is true even though the Vatican supported Cullen's policy of disestablishment of the Protestant Church of Ireland: see Patrick J. Corish, 'Cardinal Cullen and the National Association of Ireland', in *Reactions to Irish Nationalism, With an Introduction by Alan O'Day* (London, 1987), 117–66.

23. Desmond Bowen, *Paul Cardinal Cullen and the Shaping of Modern Irish Catholicism* (Dublin, 1983).

24. Lee, *The Modernisation of Irish Society*, 48, 44.

25. John White, 'The Cusack Papers: new evidence on the Knock apparition', *History Ireland*, 4(4) (1996), 39–43. There has been a subsequent controversy between White and Professor Eugene Hynes over the originality of White's findings in *History Ireland*, 5(1) (1997), 11–13.

26. James S. Donnelly, 'The Marian Shrine of Knock: the first decade', *Eire-Ireland* (1993), 55–99.

27. See, for example, on the various approaches to this subject, the articles on expatriate Irish Catholicism in North America by Owen Dudley Edwards and Hugh McLeod, and by Rory Sweetman on New Zealand, in W. J. Sheils and Diana Wood (eds.), *The Churches, Ireland and the Irish* (Oxford, 1989).

28. Sheridan Gilley, 'The Roman Catholic Church and the nineteenth-century Irish diaspora', *Journal of Ecclesiastical History*, 35(2) (1984), 188–207.

29. For this very large subject, of expatriate Irish Catholicism, see Patrick O'Sullivan (ed.), *Religion and Identity*, vol. V in *The Irish World Wide* (London and New York, 1996).

30. Sidney Z. Ehler and John B. Morrall, *Church and State through the Centuries* (London, 1954), 599.

31. Dermot Keogh, *The Vatican, the Bishops and Irish Politics 1919–39* (Cambridge, 1986).

32. Dermot Keogh and Finín O'Driscoll, 'Ireland', in Tom Buchanan and Martin Conway (eds.), *Political Catholicism in Europe, 1918–1965* (Oxford, 1996), 275–300.

33. Which is not to say that the Protestant Churches have always liked contraception. Thus the Lambeth Conference of 1920 'on the whole condemned the use of contraceptives' and then reversed its position in 1930, cautiously approving them, while indicating that 'The primary and obvious method is complete abstinence from intercourse . . . in a life of discipline and self control.' The greatest of modern Anglican theologians, Charles Gore, 'was quite overcome with grief' at this change of view, and campaigned against it. G. L. Prestige, *The Life of Charles Gore, a Great Englishman* (London, 1935), 515. During the Second World War, the Bishops' War Committee opposed a measure for the supply and explanation of prophylactics for servicemen as 'entirely repulsive' and as 'in conflict with the State as the guardian of public morality, and also in conflict with the right interests of parents, of friends, of many women's organisations, and of many of the men who are the subjects of instruction. In this conflict, the interests of true morality must prevail.' Bishops' War Committee, MS 2488. f. 12v, Lambeth Palace. I owe this reference to Giles Watson.

34. For a sensitive discussion of this whole issue, see J. J. Lee, *Ireland 1912–1985: Politics and Society* (Cambridge, 1989), 650ff. For a crass one, see Tom Inglis, *Moral Monopoly: The Catholic Church in Modern Irish Society* (Dublin, 1987).

35. K. Theodore Hoppen, *Ireland since 1800: Conflict and Conformity* (London, 1989), 244–8.

36. Gerard Francis Rutan, 'The parting of the way: the changing relationship between religion and nationalism in contemporary Ireland', *The European Legacy*, 1(2) (1996), 745.

7

Long-term religious developments in the
Netherlands, *c.* 1750–2000

Peter van Rooden

At first sight the Netherlands could appear to offer a prime example of the
inexorable decline of Christendom, defined as a tight conglomerate of civilisation, territory and ideology. As a political entity, the Dutch Republic arose in the
wake of the Reformation. It duplicated the Reformation's shattering of the unity
of western Christendom within its own polity. The Dutch Republic was notorious for the licence it accorded dissident religious groups. In 1599, Antoine
L'Empereur, an archetypal Calvinist merchant who had been living in exile in
various German cities since Parma's conquest of Antwerp, moved to Utrecht,
in the heart of the Dutch Republic. He did not like what he saw. 'Je voy par deca
peu de discipline par la liberté trop grande, de maniere que rien ne nous advient
que par un juste jugement de Dieu.'[1] His judgement was echoed by visitors
and Reformed ministers throughout the seventeenth and eighteenth centuries.

A linear interpretation of Dutch religious history seems to present itself
with considerable force. In the light of its origin as a mercantile, Protestant
republic, born from a revolt against absolutism, its recent toleration of drugs,
pornography, abortion and euthanasia as well as its staggering dechristianisation
(more than half of the Dutch now declare themselves to belong to no church at
all) causes no surprise.[2]

The main argument of this chapter will rest upon a rejection of such a linear
interpretation of the Dutch religious past. As I have argued elsewhere, it is not
fruitful to interpret the long-term development of Dutch religion as a gradual
process during which an overarching social and political embodiment of Christianity was replaced by a situation in which the existence of Christian groups
depends upon the efforts and commitment of their members.[3] Instead, various kinds of Christendom have succeeded each other: the political and social
practices by which Dutch Christianity as a social phenomenon was created and
sustained have changed drastically and fairly abruptly over time.

The public church

The Dutch Republic was the unforeseen and unintended result of a partially
successful revolt against the centralising policies of the Brussels government

of the Habsburg Netherlands.[4] Political and military vicissitudes had resulted, by 1580, in the emergence of a new and independent political entity in the north. The Dutch Republic introduced the Reformation. The Reformed Church, which had organised itself in the 1550s, and had led an underground existence, became the new public church.

The Dutch Republic's origin in a revolt against centralising, absolutist policies resulted in a devolution of effective power to local elites: the oligarchies of the towns in the heavily urbanised western part; noble or otherwise powerful rural families elsewhere. A second important motive of the revolt had been opposition to the Inquisition and religious persecution. The political elites of the new Republic shared the conviction that no one should be persecuted for his or her religious convictions. Local elites did differ, however, in their toleration of attempts at religious organisation by dissenters. The Reformed Church considered its new role as public church to be its proper status. Yet the Reformed also aspired to be a community of true believers and did not wish to become co-extensive with society. Both civil and spiritual authorities thus refused to gather all subjects of the Republic into a single national church.

This led to a situation which differed from religious settlements elsewhere. The public church of the Dutch Republic had a monopoly on public expressions and manifestations of religion. It was supported by the state, and was financed from public funds. Public office could only be held by those who were not members of another religious group. On the other hand, there were no laws forcing people to attend the services of the public church or even to take part in its rituals. Marriages could legitimately be contracted before the civil magistrate. Baptism was not obligatory, although it seems to have been generally sought. With some misgivings, the church generally baptised all children offered. It accepted as full members only those who were willing to make a public confession of faith and to submit to its discipline.

In the provinces of Holland and Utrecht and in part of Friesland, from a very early date, the authorities allowed the rebuilding of a certain kind of Catholic organisation. It was here, too, that the Mennonites, the peaceful successors to the violent Anabaptists of the 1530s, found most of their adherents, and that the Reformed Church, in various conflicts concerning its confession and public status, formulated its identity most clearly. This is the region people think of when they talk about the tolerant Dutch Republic.

From the very beginning, the civil authorities in this area took an interest in the religious organisations of the Protestant Dissenters and the Catholics.[5] By the last quarter of the seventeenth century, a more or less stable religious structure had sprung into being, the result of a religious policy which was aimed at stabilising the relations between different religious groups. The implementation of these policies was always in the hands of local authorities, but the measures taken show marked similarities. First, local authorities took care to strengthen the position of the laity. In all religious groups in the Republic, among Jews and Lutherans, as among Mennonites and Reformed, the clergy was not involved in the financial administration nor was it allowed to decide on the allocation of money. Second, local authorities always had to approve the appointments of new clergymen of all churches. Third, local authorities oversaw the internal affairs of each religious group and upheld the authority of its lay leadership, although only for as long as the requirements it imposed on its adherents remained within the bounds of a common morality.

This close involvement of the public authorities with the social manifestations of religion implied a certain recognition of all churches as legitimate parts of the social and religious order. It is, in fact, very difficult to distinguish between recognition of a church and the involvement of public authority in its internal affairs. Public authority was most deeply involved in the running of the public, Reformed Church, and the growing recognition of Catholicism as a legitimate part of the religious landscape, for instance, can be monitored by the number of measures taken by public authority to influence its internal working.

Gradually, a hierarchical ordering of the different religious groups emerged. Along with the growth of a religious order of which all churches were considered legitimate parts, Protestant Dissenters and Catholics seemed to have been excluded from a growing number of social and political positions. Religious toleration entailed social discrimination. In the 1620s, a Catholic stonemason working for the city would occasionally be harassed by the authorities while attending a Catholic service. In the eighteenth century, Catholic services were no longer disturbed, but Catholics were passed over for public positions.[6]

This religious policy was an important part of the responsibilities of the civil authorities, part of their upholding of civil order. This civil order, even it was not based on the stark authoritarianism of a centralised, absolutist state, was still clearly hierarchical in nature. The political and social practices of the Dutch Republic localised religion in a visible, hierarchical social order. The public church recognised these practices as Christian, basing itself on an essentially Augustinian view on the relation between political power and religion. In this sense, the Dutch Republic too was a confessional state. On the other hand, the order of the Republic could also be represented as an example of enlightened toleration, because it accepted the presence of Dissenters.

Dissenters and Catholics sometimes resisted their incorporation in this social hierarchy by probing the limits to which they were subjected. Such endeavours lessened in the eighteenth century, as the religious order became ever more stabilised. All religious groups started to take part in the annual public days of prayer, which became in a certain way the main ritual of a civil religion. Some Catholics, especially those in the south of the Republic, with its almost homogeneous Catholic population, pointedly refused to take part in the days of prayer. Catholics in Holland and Utrecht seem to have had no problem with being involved with this religio-political civil ritual.

The Protestant nation

The invasion of French armies in 1795 made possible the fulfilment of an indigenous revolution, which had been aborted some years earlier.[7] The revolution brought an end to the political fragmentation which had characterised the Dutch *ancien régime*. Since then, the Netherlands have been a centralised state with a strong bureaucratic government. The revolution also destroyed the old religious and social order. One of the first important acts of the revolutionary government was to separate church and state. The new nation-state would know only citizens, not various corporate religious groups. It would be a moral community, based on equality before the law rather than on a hierarchical order. The new Kingdom of the Netherlands, established in 1815 after the final defeat of Napoleon, incorporated the former Austrian Netherlands, present-day Belgium. It inherited both the ideal of the nation and the effective central bureaucracy of its revolutionary predecessors, and continued their centralising policies. Both the former public church and Old Dissent (a term which is not used in Dutch church history but which I find useful, for reasons which will become apparent, to characterise the Mennonites, Arminians and Lutherans) received effective organisational structures from the central authorities. Henceforth, they would be dependent not on local elites, but on the central government, as mediated by strong ecclesiastical organisations, staffed by members of the clergy. The ideological differences between the Protestants were reduced. In fact, the former public church together with Old Dissent became an informal national establishment, with the task of furthering the identity of the Dutch nation by teaching and civilising the common people.

In effect, the cultural, social and political practices of the new nation-state located religion in the inner selves of the citizens of the nation. As had been the case with the location of religion during the Republic, theologians justified these practices, now with an appeal to the supposedly individual nature of Protestantism. All Protestant churches considered the Netherlands a moral community of individuals, and saw their own churches as means to further the welfare of this nation by morally informing its citizens.

It is also clear that the various practices entailed by the new location of religion did not, in fact, succeed in creating a homogeneous nation. On the contrary, the new practices, too, resulted in exclusions and led to resistances. The assimilation of Catholics proved to be the most formidable problem. From 1795 on, the nation of moral citizens was very much considered to be Protestant.[8] Attempts by the central government of the post-1815 Netherlands to make the Roman Catholic Church of the former Austrian Netherlands into an institution devoted to nation-building, along the lines of its reorganisation of the former public church of the Dutch Republic, led to the revolt of Belgium in 1830.[9] After the formal separation of Belgium from the Kingdom of the Netherlands in the late 1830s, it became much easier to identify the remaining northern Netherlands with a general Protestantism. Various anti-Catholic organisations sprang up in the 1840s.[10]

Among the Protestants themselves, the new location of religion led to a very strong process of cultural class-formation. The emphasis the new practices put upon education and understanding, style and manners, created a huge distance between the civilised elite and the rude, uncivilised people. When reading through the outcrop of new manuals for the ministry which emerged in the years around 1800, one is struck how all these manuals take for granted the existence of an enormous cultural difference between the minister and his parishioners. He has to transform them in order to elevate them to his own moral and cultural level. The minister is a parent, while his parishioners are children.[11]

This new stress upon civilisation and education as markers of social difference led to forms of resistance which focused upon knowledge. Small groups of lower-class people left the former public church in a steady trickle to set up churches that presented themselves as orthodox Calvinist, as preservers of a knowledge that had been forgotten by their social superiors. I will call them New Dissent. Till 1848 they were persecuted and harassed by the government. Even so, between 1834 and 1889 they grew to 4.2 per cent of the population.[12]

The pillarised society

The unity of this Protestant nation was shattered in the period between 1870 and 1920. Orthodox Protestants, Catholics and Socialists created their own organisational worlds. What came into being was the pillarisation of Dutch society.[13] The particular nature of this system did not consist in the emergence of more or less closed organisational worlds. After all, in these years Catholic and Socialist ghettos emerged in other countries as well. The originality of Dutch pillarisation is to be found in the way in which these mobilisations were successful in contesting the Protestant nature of the nation and actually eclipsed the notion of the nation as the supreme moral community. Ideologically, the ghettos took over the nation. They did so in a literal sense as well. The 'pacification' of 1917 which ended the political struggles between liberals and confessional parties was in reality a clear-cut confessional victory. The pacification rested upon the introduction of universal suffrage and the equal financing by the state of public and private (Catholic and orthodox Protestant) primary schools. The introduction of universal suffrage introduced a period of more than half a century in which Christian political parties polled more than half of the vote. The financial subsidies given to Christian private schools (which were soon

attended by more than half of Dutch children) were followed by similar subsidies for social and cultural Christian organisations. Over time, the subsidies
became ever more generous. The greatest victory of the pillarised system was
the way in which the Dutch broadcasting system was set up. In the case of radio,
as well as later with television, a public broadcasting organisation was lacking.
Radio and television time was divided between various private organisations,
subsidised by the state, although they were closely linked to religio-political
movements.

In social life as well, religious identities became ever more important.
Journals bore a marked confessional character. There were relatively strong
Christian labour unions. It is from the agricultural sector that the usual example of the absurdities to which this system could lead is taken: the famous
co-existence of a Calvinist and a Roman Catholic Goat-Breeders Association.
Such organisations actually did exist. Leisure and sports were to a large extent
confessionally divided as well. Even today, playing table tennis in Leiden and
taking part in the local competition is tantamount to a crash course in religious
geography: organisationally, table tennis is limited to those parts of the countryside around Leiden which have been Catholic since the sixteenth century.

So, during the better part of the twentieth century in the Netherlands, religion
was a more important aspect of social identity than class or region. The Dutch
nation was no longer thought to be composed of individuals. It consisted of
different, yet equal groups, which best served the national interest by preserving
their own distinctive character. The various social and political practices of the
pillarised society still located religion in inner selves, but these selves were
always considered to be members of distinct groups within the nation. What
had happened could be interpreted as an ethnicisation of religion. Religious
identity always involved membership of a group.

There was always resistance to the movement towards pillarisation. Even
those who joined the mobilising drives which made up the dynamic aspect of
pillarisation did not follow all injunctions laid upon them by the clerical and
political leaders of the movements.[14] Principal opponents were mainly to be
found among the liberal and Protestant elite. Theirs was a lost battle. After
1917, even those who desperately wanted to be considered representatives of
the common weal were forced to conceive of themselves as a particular group.

Causes and factors of the shifts between the various regimes

The end of the public church

All explanations of the end of the religious order of the Dutch Republic must
start with political events, because the demise of the public church was closely
linked to the Revolution. In August 1796 extensive discussions took place in the

new National Assembly about the separation of church and state. During these debates, it was quickly agreed upon that the official adoption of the principles of liberty, equality and fraternity in 1795, immediately in the wake of the French invasion, had formally opened political and public office to Dissenters and Catholics. Only a few deputies adopted radical enlightened standpoints. They argued that in the past the collusion between clergy and regents had resulted in despotism, tyranny and bigotry. But even these radical voices argued that the separation of church and state would result in a liberation of true piety. The whole of the National Assembly agreed upon the social relevance of religion. There was no religious or confessional opposition to the Revolution. Moreover, it is difficult to claim that the former public church was oppressed during these revolutionary years. For some years, between 1798 and 1801, it looked as if it would lose all financial support of the government. Recent research has shown that it reacted rather vigorously to this threat, and developed all kinds of local initiatives to raise money.[15] In the end it proved unnecessary to implement these plans. Yet they were only part of the new activities the church embarked upon in these years. In 1796 a missionary society was founded.[16] Various liturgical initiatives were undertaken, the most prominent result being the introduction of a new hymn-book in 1806; till then only psalms had been sung during church services.[17] Church law was codified, the lower organisational level of the church showed a new energy, there was a whole new interest in the efficacy of the ministry, and a vibrant religious press emerged, catering to the needs of an interested laity. All in all, and in marked contrast to the existing church-historical literature, I would not hesitate to speak of a religious revival.

Most of these new initiatives of the church were linked in one way or another with developments in the second half of the eighteenth century. A new version of the Psalter had been adopted in 1776. A spectatorial press, aimed at moralising and civilising the citizen, had been in existence since the 1740s, and a lively societal movement had emerged in the 1770s. Protestant Dissenters played a role in these movements which was of much greater weight than their small numbers warranted. Most of these eighteenth-century initiatives bore a marked moralistic character and were imbued with religion, yet they had not been clerically inspired or under ecclesiastical control.[18]

So how is this link between the enlightened sociability of the late eighteenth century and the religious revival of the early nineteenth century to be understood? The simplest way is to start from the observation that in the eighteenth century religion in its organised form was part of the political and public order. The public church had fiercely combated the Moravians and had suppressed the Dutch versions of the mid-eighteenth-century revivalistic impulses which rocked the Protestant Atlantic world.[19] Its close relation with, and control by, the civil authorities simply left no room for new initiatives. The separation of church and state in the wake of the revolutionary happenings of the

1790s was a liberation not only of religion, but of the church as well, which now could express sentiments and institute changes which rested upon the cultural nationalism which had emerged in the second half of the eighteenth century.

Various reasons can be adduced why this cultural nationalism was accepted by clergy and laity even before the Revolution of 1795. Various shades of pietism had steadily been gaining influence within the public church during the eighteenth century. The pietistic stress on individual faith fitted the attempt on the part of the societal movement to create moral citizens. Pietists depicted the truly converted as the core of the church and of the nation. The eighteenth-century religious order tended to have a similar effect. The logic of the religious policies of the civil authorities was explained in sermons preached during the annual public days of prayer, organised by civil authority and observed by all religious groups. These sermons upheld what is best called a civil religion, and which found the reason for the welfare of the Republic not in the presence of particular religious groups or confessions, but in its tolerant religious order, which made possible the exercise of individual virtue and piety.[20]

A final reason for the general adoption of the new cultural nationalism by the public church has to do with social history. The societal movement was very much an upper-class and upper-middle-class affair. In the last quarter of the eighteenth century the clergy of the Dutch public church adopted the cultural values and manners of this class. A traditional ministry, which in most aspects had resembled the clerical estate of other early modern European societies, with a large clerical proletariat, was at the end of the eighteenth century transformed into a nationally and socially homogeneous profession.[21]

It is, in short, the formation, in the last half of the eighteenth century, of a new and homogeneous cultural and social elite, broader than the traditional political class of regents, but still relatively tiny in numbers, which is the central factor that explains the shift in the location of religion. The formation of this new elite took place by means of enlightened sociability and its print culture. Within this cultural movement, Dissenters, both Mennonites and Arminians, could play an extraordinarily important role, because they had, for reasons which need not detain us here, in the course of the eighteenth century become upper-middle-class groups. Some numbers are perhaps in order. At the end of the eighteenth century, the Dutch Republic had about 2 million inhabitants: 55 per cent of them belonged to the public church, 38 per cent were Catholics, 7 per cent were Jews and Protestant Dissenters, mainly Lutherans. There were some 4000 Arminians (a tiny 0.2 per cent) and 30,000 Mennonites (1.5 per cent). It has been estimated that at the end of the Republic, there were about 2000 *regenten* and some 1500 ministers of the public church. The newly formed cultural elite, the consumers of the new cultural nationalism, consisted of something like 20,000 people.

Shattering the Protestant nation

The Protestant nation of the Dutch liberal elite was destroyed by the emergence of mass politics in the last quarter of the nineteenth century. This, as such, is no surprise. Neither is the role the political organisation of Catholics and Socialists played in this development. Peculiar to the Netherlands is, however, the importance of orthodox Protestant political parties. This importance is twofold. In the first place, orthodox Protestants introduced modern party politics into the Netherlands.[22] In the second place, by forming an alliance with the Catholics they prepared the way for a dominance of Christian Democratic parties which made pillarisation possible and which only ended at the end of the twentieth century.

In searching for explanations of this phenomenon its economic preconditions ought to be pointed out first. During most of the nineteenth century the Netherlands possessed a highly developed market economy, yet industrial development was slow.[23] There was no large industrial proletariat, from which the Socialists could recruit. Early Socialism found its first mass basis among rural labourers in Friesland and Groningen, the two most northern provinces. By the time large-scale industry developed, Catholics and orthodox Protestants already had their organisations, including trade unions, in place and they succeeded in retaining the loyalty of large sections of the working class. The textile industry in Catholic Twente, in the east, fostered a strong Catholic union, as did the mining area in Limburg, in the south. The industrial areas along the rivers north and east of Dordrecht would develop into an orthodox Protestant bulwark.[24]

Politically, the movement of orthodox Protestants was boosted when in the 1870s a new generation of political leaders stumbled upon the possibility of appealing to the people, not only to those who had the vote, but also to those who did not. Various organisational models were tried out, for instance an alliance against the law on public education which was modelled on the British Anti-Corn Law League, and which proved to be a huge success. In 1879 a political party was organised along the same lines, binding its deputies to a party programme. In the 1880s the political leader of the orthodox Protestants experimented with various political issues to mobilise the people, for instance supporting the Boers in their resistance against the British, political anti-Semitism (which he dropped when it did not work), ending the possibility for rich people to buy a replacement for military service, and defending some rights of the new working class. In the elections in 1886, after the first substantial broadening of the electorate since 1848, the orthodox Protestants gained twenty-eight of the hundred seats in Parliament. Together with the Catholics, they could form a government.[25]

The obvious question to pose is amongst which social groups this political movement had success. This is rather hard to answer. Its strength lay mainly in the broad and undefined lower middle class of artisans, shopkeepers and tradesmen. But members of the political and cultural elite played an important role within the party, and they also had substantial working-class support. The orthodox Protestant trade union, Patrimonium, was in the 1870s and 1880s during some years a more important mobilising organisation than the political party itself. This wide class appeal is coupled with a marked geographical pattern. Orthodox Protestantism was strong in only some areas: the southern and eastern countryside of Zuid-Holland, Utrecht, the northern parts of Gelderland, the north-western part of Overijssel, the south-western and north-eastern parts of Friesland. These areas do not bear similar economic characteristics, so it is hard to explain the appeal of the Protestant political movement in economic terms. It seems probable that the orthodox Protestant movement was particularly successful in areas where there was already some kind of pre-existing organisational life among the common people, but the same goes for early Socialism.[26]

By default then, the best explanation of the appeal and success of the orthodox Protestant movement seems to lie in its mobilising aspect. The specific form it took, of opposing the religious values and the educational drive of the liberal state by a claim to have preserved a traditional truth and a wish for private Christian schools, seems to derive from the values and practices of the Protestant nation, which had made religious knowledge the basis of a cultural class-formation.

The end of pillarisation

The strength of pillarisation appeared most impressively after the ravages of World War II. The Germans had dismantled most of the pillarised organisations, and the Resistance and the queen had hoped for a drastic reorientation of Dutch politics. The Socialist Party, in alliance with leading groups within the former public church and some liberals, tried to reorganise itself as a general party of progress. Yet the confessional parties and organisations reasserted themselves without too much effort and won absolute majorities till the late 1960s. The percentage of Dutch children attending confessional schools reached an all-time high in the 1950s. Then, suddenly, this whole world collapsed. Most of the organisations which made up the orthodox Protestant and Catholic pillars have ceased to stress their distinctive confessional identity or have shed it altogether. The Catholic and Socialist trade unions fused. The same happened with the media.

It is only possible to offer tentative explanations for this sudden shift. It is quite clearly connected with the cultural revolution of the 1960s. Although the mobilising movements of orthodox Protestants and Catholics had been genuinely popular, they were also highly patriarchal and ascetic. They stressed the subordinate place of women and frowned upon sexuality and consumption. The 1960s revolt against strict morals, traditional gender roles and patriarchal forms of authority dissolved the popular endorsement of this regime. Moreover, the very successes of the mobilising movements had firmly integrated their adherents into the state and national life, rendering an oppositional stance less and less plausible. Already by the late 1950s, Catholic intellectuals, both lay and clerical, entertained doubts about the value of the closed character of the Catholic movement.[27] Neo-Calvinist theologians in the late 1960s and 1970s undermined the formulation of a strict Calvinist orthodoxy, which for almost a hundred years had been the ideological justification for the separate existence of their church.[28] The highly articulated structures of both the Catholic and the neo-Calvinist churches assured that the self-doubt felt by their leading intellectuals would spread rapidly among their rank and file.

Further important factors seem to have been the enormous expansion of the welfare state, which considerably lessened the power of the leaders of the pillars over their members, and the emergence of an almost complete moral consensus within the Dutch nation, both leading to a common rejection of organisational and symbolical expressions of the existence of different moral communities.

Popular involvement and missionary strategies

Not very much is known about the involvement of the laity with religious life during the *ancien régime*, or about the missionary strategies undertaken by the various religious groups in the Dutch Republic. The impression one gets is that Dissenters and Catholics were much more aggressive than the public church, using laymen and laywomen and working along lines of family, neighbourhood and work. The public church was more or less content with enjoying its recognised status and its public preaching. When it did start to enjoy considerable popular support, in the course of the seventeenth century, it started to worry about the quality of its members and placed greater emphasis on educational requirements. The main role in stabilising the numerical relations between the various religious groups was played by the government. Poor relief played an especially important role here.[29]

The probably rather low levels of attendance during the *ancien régime* were not considered a problem. The public church of the Republic did not feel an urgent need to reach out to the unchurched masses. Most living movements within the church were more concerned with raising standards and setting themselves apart from the merely baptised people, and thus had more to do with keeping people out than with bringing them in. This stress on forming a pure community was in line with the traditions of the church, and was only combated when separatist traditions emerged. The most striking aspect of this absence of a missionary endeavour in the modern sense of the word is a total lack of statistical awareness. The public church did not count its members at any level of its organisation.

The emergence of the modern nation-state changed all this. All Protestant churches became deeply involved with teaching and shaping the citizens of the nation. A general interest in pedagogy emerged, focusing on the need to present messages in such a way that they could be understood. Most of the religious changes taking place in the years around 1800 in matters of preaching, singing and organising catechism can be understood as springing from such a pedagogical awareness. The former public church engaged in a relentless catechetical effort, but also placed a new emphasis on the family as the place where religious instruction ought to take place, as evidenced by a spate of housebooks. In the interest of pedagogy, discussions and polemics within sermons and the catechism were completely wiped out. Lecturing in a simple, civilised way was seen as the best way to inculcate religious belief. Preaching and singing ought to take place in a fairly decorous way. The enormous stress on understanding and knowledge even resulted in a certain domestication of Dutch Catholics and their piety. They gave up those religious activities, like venerating the sacrament or memorial masses, which did not have a pedagogical dimension.

The secessionists of New Dissent were very successful in spreading their message. In the third quarter of the nineteenth century they reached levels of growth of which the British Methodists would not have been ashamed. Family and friends, colleagues and customers were the most important sources of new recruits, with word-of-mouth propaganda by far the most important medium. Their local religious cultures, thoroughly lower class, implied a radical challenge to the national cultural and educational practices of the Dutch state. The members of New Dissent rejected the new evangelical songs, printed books in old-fashioned and hard to read Gothic letters, and loved to use biblical expressions such as those about whoring after strange Gods which the ministers of the public church passed over out of cultural distaste. Whereas the Dutch state treated the common people as minors, in need of education and direction from above, the secessionists created local religious groups, loosely allied to others, with infinite possibilities for conflict and agency. Quarrels and conflicts were endemic within the secessionist churches. Ecclesiastical discipline was, so it seems, mainly exercised against persons who bore ecclesiastical authority. Their continuous internal quarrels ensured that all secessionist churches invested an enormous amount of time and effort into attempts at convincing, in negotiations, talks and visits. It was a system that took the opinions and viewpoints of common people extremely seriously, and thus offered them ample scope for agency. It was also a model of a moral exercise of authority, which was emphatically not predicated upon using existing social or cultural hierarchies to impose re-ligious order.[30] Once they were assimilated to the new mass-political orthodox Protestant movement, however, in 1892, they stopped growing. The new ortho-dox Protestant pillar would reproduce the knowledge-based hierarchies of the modern state within itself.

From the 1870s onwards, formal organisations and a vibrant press became much more important in reaching people. Organisations and mass media were necessary to create the nationwide communities which contested the unity of the Protestant nation. Yet essentially, from the early 1890s onwards, this movement of organising and educating people took place within religious groups whose borders were strictly drawn. Orthodox Protestants and Catholics were more engaged in informing and disciplining their adherents than in converting other people. The losses they suffered they made good by their higher birth-rates. Consequently, during the whole of the twentieth century, religion was the most important part of people's social identity. This social importance of religion made the Netherlands exceptional in two ways.

The first exceptional characteristic of the Netherlands in the twentieth century was the extraordinarily high level of religious practice and discipline among church members. Only Ireland and Poland offer comparable European instances, yet these were economically and socially much less developed societies that strongly identified religion and nationalism.[31] The second ex-ceptional characteristic was the relatively early and fast increase in people who openly claimed not to belong to any church. They grew from 0.3 per cent in the census of 1879 to 14.3 per cent in 1930. Then their numbers more or less stabilised, reaching 18.3 per cent in 1960. Attempts to explain the emergence of this group economically run into the same kind of problem that the emergence of orthodox Protestantism as a social movement presents. There is a marked geographical differentiation. In some areas even in the 1960s almost the en-tire population belonged to a church, whereas in other areas already around 1920 more than half of the people had left it. There is no very clear correlation with economic factors, for instance with either heavy industry or rural poverty. There are, on the other hand, very important correlations with the growth of early Socialism and a general 'left-wing' orientation.[32] In certain districts in Friesland at the end of the nineteenth century, the percentage of people claim-ing not to belong to a church showed marked variations from census to census, declining or growing in line with the political battles between left and right. It is probably best to state that, just as orthodox Protestants and Catholics used religion to mobilise their supporters against the liberal hegemony, the Socialist mobilisation could not escape having religious implications as well, especially among its rank and file, although the leadership of the Socialist Party went out of its way to make clear that it was not an irreligious party.

Conclusion

The Netherlands seem to fit Hugh McLeod's interpretation of European Christianity in his *Religion and the People of Western Europe* as an extreme case.[33] McLeod stated that as nineteenth-century Christianity lost its overarching character and religion ceased to provide a focus of social unity, the churches both gained and lost. Large numbers were alienated from the official church, yet religion also became a major basis for the distinctive identity of specific communities, classes and factions within a divided society. McLeod considered three periods crucial for this involvement of religion with modern social conflict: the years around 1800, with the impact of the French Revolution, the 1870s and 1880s, with the emergence of modern industrial and mass-political strife, and the 1950s and 1960s, when these conflicts slowly abated and traditional communal loyalties were dissolved.

The religious development of the Netherlands fits this chronology rather nicely. But whereas McLeod characterises the conflicts of the period around 1800 as being about religion itself, and those of the 1870s and 1880s as being the result of social and economic strife, that resulted in conflicts in which the churches could not avoid taking sides, in the Netherlands the first period did not result in religious conflict and the conflicts in the second period seem to have pitted religious groups against a cultural and political elite.

It is probably useless to oppose 'religious' and 'social' conflicts, in which religion gets involved. Religion is not a clearly definable aspect of the social world.[34] The vicissitudes of all religions in the modern world seem to rest upon the relation between two fundamental political shifts which take place in all modernising polities. The first is the emergence of the modern nation-state, with its governmental claim to reach all its citizens directly and its nationalist programme to create a moral community of free, equal and related citizens. The practices of the modern nation-state can lead to clashes with religious establishments, when these are closely allied with a traditional political and social order, but the nationalist programme need not involve a conflict with religion as such. The modern state's creation of the citizen can be religiously legitimated by various kinds of religious nationalism. At the end of the eighteenth century, both in the Netherlands and in the United States, political revolutions were supported by former Protestant state churches, which henceforth located religion in the inner selves of the citizens of the nation.

The second major political event with which religion has to contend is the emergence of the consequence of Tocquevillian democracy, meaning modern mass politics, the involvement of the common people within the political process. In the United States only a generation separated the new social location of religion in the inner self of the citizens of the nation from the emergence of modern mass politics. (This is the reason why de Tocqueville himself did not distinguish between both processes.) In these same years, important sections of American Protestantism started to distinguish sharply between education and conversion. These groups did not consider it necessary to create the moral self of the citizens of the nation by means of education. This close link with a specific representation of democratic citizenship seems to have furnished American Christianity with its peculiar flexibility and freedom of tradition. In America the introduction of modern mass politics led to a new conception of the way in which religion shapes inner selves, stressing conversion in favour of education. In the Netherlands, the cultural class-formation which was the consequence of the religious practices of the new nation-state made a much deeper impression, because almost three generations passed before it was challenged by the emergence of modern mass politics. When it finally emerged, modern mass politics was based upon the formation of separate religious communities which attacked a hegemonic religious nationalism by claiming to possess their own kind of knowledge, and which thus replicated the state's practices within their own communities. Religion was not involved with conflicts of another nature, either social or economic, but supplied the identity upon which to found factional communities.

NOTES

1. Letter of Anthoine l'Empereur to H. Isselborgh, 8 August 1602, Bibliotheca Thysiana MS 231, University Library Leiden.
2. The most recent report on secularisation in the Netherlands is to be found in J. W. Becker, J. de Hart and J. Mens, *Secularisatie en alternatieve zingeving in Nederland* (Rijswijk, 1997).
3. Peter van Rooden, *Religieuze regimes: over godsdienst en maatschappij in Nederland, 1570–1990* (Amsterdam, 1996); Peter van Rooden, 'Secularization and dechristianization in the Netherlands', in Hartmut Lehmann (ed.), *Dechristianisierung und Rechristianisierung im neuzeitlichen Europa und in Nordamerika: Bilanz und Perspektiven der Forschung* (Veröffentlichungen des Max-Planck-Instituts für Geschichte 130) (Göttingen, 1997), 131–53.
4. The most recent overview of Dutch religious history is C. Augustijn's article 'Niederlande', in the *Theologische Realenzyklopaedie*, vol. XXIV (Berlin, 1994), 474–502, which offers an extensive bibliography. The most recent overview of the history of the Dutch Republic is Jonathan Israel, *The Dutch Republic: Its Rise, Greatness and Fall* (Oxford, 1995). The interpretation of Dutch religious history offered here rests upon Van Rooden, *Religieuze regimes*.
5. Best worked out by Joke Spaans, *Haarlem na de Reformatie: stedelijke cultuur en kerkelijk leven 1577–1620* (The Hague, 1989); *Armenzorg in Friesland 1500–1800: publieke zorg en particuliere liefdadigheid in zes Friese steden* (Hilversum, 1997).
6. This is a hypothetical combination of two different strands of works: the research into the regulation of the exercise of the Catholic presence (W. P. C. Knuttel, *De toestand der Nederlandsche katholieken ten tijde van de Republiek*, 2 vols. ('s-Gravenhage, 1892–94); P. Polman, *Katholiek Nederland in de achttiende eeuw*,

3 vols. (Hilversum, 1968)) and studies in the Dutch social structure of the eighteenth and nineteenth centuries (J. A. F. de Jongste, *Onrust aan het Spaarne: Haarlem in de jaren 1747–1751* (The Hague, 1984); Jos Leenders, *Benauwde verdraagzaamheid, hachelijk fatsoen: families, standen en kerken te Hoorn in het midden van de negentiende eeuw* (The Hague, 1992)).

7. Main description in English to be found in Simon Schama, *Patriots and Liberators: Revolution in the Netherlands, 1780–1813* (New York, 1977).

8. Theo Clemens, 'De terugdringing van de rooms-katholieken uit de verlicht-protestantse natie', *Bijdragen en Mededelingen betreffende de geschiedenis der Nederlanden*, 110 (1995), 27–39.

9. J. A. Bornewasser, 'The authority of the Dutch state over the churches, 1795–1853', '"Het credo . . . geen reden tot twist". Ter verklaring van een koninklijk falen', and 'Mythical aspects of Dutch anti-Catholicism in the nineteenth century', in J. A. Bornewasser, *Kerkelijk verleden in een wereldlijke context* (Amsterdam, 1989), 98–112, 113–48, 362–75.

10. A. Vroon, *Carel Willem Pape 1788–1872: een Brabants predikant en kerkbestuurder* (Tilburg, 1992); J. P. van den Hout, 'P. Hofstede de Groot als ideoloog van de grootprotestantse beweging (1840–44)', *Documentatieblad voor de Nederlandse-Kerkgeschiedenis na 1800*, 37 (1992), 1–24.

11. Peter van Rooden, 'Ministerial authority and gender in Dutch Protestantism around 1800', in A. Fletcher (ed.), *Gender and the Christian Religion*, Studies in Church History 34 (Oxford, 1998), 301–11.

12. W. Bakker (ed.), *De Afscheiding van 1834 en haar geschiedenis* (Kampen, 1984).

13. Cf. the literature quoted in Van Rooden, *Religieuze regimes*, 169–99.

14. Paul Luykx, 'Andere katholieken, 1920–1960', *Archief voor de Geschiedenis van de Katholieke Kerk in Nederland*, 29 (1987), 52–84.

15. W. H. den Ouden, *Kerk onder patriottenbewind: kerkelijke financiën en de Bataafse Republiek 1795–1801* (Zoetermeer, 1994).

16. J. Boneschansker, *Het Nederlands Zendingsgenootschap in zijn eerste periode: een studie over opwekking in de Bataafse en Franse tijd* (Leeuwarden, 1987); Peter van Rooden, 'Nineteenth-century representations of missionary conversion and the transformation of western Christianity', in Peter van der Veer (ed.), *Conversion to Modernities: The Globalization of Christianity* (New York, 1996), 65–88.

17. Roel A. Bosch, *En nooit meer oude psalmen zingen: zingend geloven in een nieuwe tijd 1760–1810* (Zoetermeer, 1996).

18. Margaret C. Jacob and Wijnand W. Mijnhardt (eds.), *The Dutch Republic in the Eighteenth Century: Decline, Enlightenment and Revolution* (Ithaca and London, 1992).

19. W. Lütjeharms, *Het philadelphisch-oecumenisch streven der Hernhutters in de Nederlanden in de achttiende eeuw* (Zeist, 1935); C. Huisman, *Geloof in beweging: Gerardus Kuypers, pastoor en patriot tussen vroomheid en Verlichting* (Zoetermeer, 1996); Joke Spaans (ed.), *Een golf van beroering: de omstreden religieuze opwekking in Nederland in het midden van de achttiende eeuw* (Hilversum, 2001).

20. Van Rooden, *Religieuze regimes*, 78–120.

21. *Ibid.*, 46–77.

22. Roel Kuiper, 'De weg van het volk. Mobilisering en activering van de anti-revolutionaire beweging, 1878–1888', in Henk te Velde and Hans Verhage (eds.),

De eenheid en de delen: zuilvorming, onderwijs en natievorming in Nederland 1850–1900 (Amsterdam, 1996), 99–120.

23. E. J. Fischer, 'De geschiedschrijving over de 19e-eeuwse industrialisatie', in W. W. Mijnhardt (ed.), *Kantelend geschiedbeeld: Nederlandse historiografie sind 1945* (Utrecht and Antwerp, 1981), 228–55; J. L. van Zanden, 'Dutch economic history of the period 1500–1940: a review of the present state of affairs', *Economic and Social History of the Netherlands*, 1 (1990), 9–25.

24. Th. van Tijn, 'The party structure of Holland and the Outer Provinces in the nineteenth century', in J. S. Bromley and E. H. Kossmann (eds.), *Britain and the Netherlands IV: Metropolis, Dominion and Province* (The Hague, 1971), 176–207; Th. van Tijn, 'De wording van de moderne politieke partij-organisaties in Nederland', in G. A. M. Beekelaar *et al.* (eds.), *Vaderlands verleden in veelvoud: 31 opstellen over de Nederlandse geschiedenis na 1500* (The Hague, 1975), 590–601; H. Daalder, 'Consociationalism, centre and periphery in the Netherlands', in P. Thorsvik (ed.), *Mobilization, Centre–Periphery Structures and Nation-Building* (Oslo and Bergen, 1981), 181–240.

25. G. J. Schutte, 'De ere Gods en de moderne staat. Het antwoord van de Anti-Revolutionaire Partij op de secularisatie en democratisering van Nederland: antithese, soevereiniteit in eigen kring en gemene gratie', *Radix*, 9(2) (1983), 73–104; G. van Roon, 'Politieke conjuncturen en politiek-godsdienstige partijvorming in Nederland', in Th. B. F. M. Brinkel, J. de Bruijn and A. Postma (eds.), *Het kabinet-Mackay: opstellen over de eerste christelijke coalitie (1888–1891)* (Baarn, 1990), 10–41; Kuiper, 'De weg van het volk'.

26. M. Staverman, *Buitenkerkelijkheid in Friesland* (Assen, 1954).

27. Ed Simons and Lodewijk Winkeler, *Het verraad der clercken: intellectuelen en hun rol in de ontwikkelingen van het Nederlands katholicisme na 1945* (Baarn, 1987).

28. G. Dekker, *De stille revolutie: de ontwikkeling van de Gereformeerde Kerken in Nederland tussen 1950 en 1990* (Kampen, 1992).

29. Spaans, *Armenzorg in Friesland*.

30. Hans Knippenberg, *De religieuze kaart van Nederland: omvang en geografische spreiding van de godsdienstige gezindten vanaf de Reformatie tot heden* (Assen and Maastricht, 1992).

31. H. Faber and T. T. ten Have, *Ontkerkelijking en buitenkerkelijkheid in Nederland tot 1960* (Assen, 1970). J. P. Kruyt and W. Goddijn, 'Verzuiling en ontzuiling als sociologisch proces', in A. N. J. den Hollander *et al.* (eds.), *Drift en Koers: een halve eeuw sociale verandering in Nederland* (Assen, 1962), 227–63 contains a wealth of information on the social importance of religion around 1960.

32. J. P. Kruijt, *De onkerkelijkheid in Nederland: haar verbreiding en oorzaken.* Proeve eener sociografische verklaring (Groningen, 1933).

33. Hugh McLeod, *Religion and the People of Western Europe, 1789–1989* (Oxford, 1997).

34. Peter van Rooden, 'Secularization and the trajectory of religion in the West', in Henri Krop, Arie Molendijk and Hent de Vries (eds.), *Post-Theism: Reframing the Judeo-Christian Tradition* (Leuven, 2000), 169–88.

8

The potency of 'Christendom': the example of
the *Darmstädter Wort* (1947)

Martin Greschat

Characteristic of the Christian faith since its beginning is the evidently irre-
movable dialectic between rejection of and the embrace of its environment:
dissolving as well as shaping it, on the one hand relativising and undermining
religious, cultural and social norms and, on the other, infiltrating, stabilising
and pulling them together.[1]

In no way does that apply only to the history of Christianity in late antiquity,
in the middle ages or in the early modern period. Schleiermacher offers an
example of an orientation directed towards modernity, and thus freed from any
strict adherence to structures laid down by the state. On the one side he speaks of
the character of the Christian faith as being 'polemical through and through' –
not only in its stance over against the outside world, but equally 'within its
own boundaries and within its innermost community of saints . . . and indeed
at the same time an ongoing polemicising against all current forms of religion
is laid down as a task which can never be completely fulfilled'. Conversely,
Schleiermacher emphasises the necessity of 'custom' shaped by the 'common
spirit', which is thus 'carried and determined by the shared ethos of the members
of a society'. The possibilities and dangers concealed within this bipolarity will
here be explored not on a theoretical level, but in the light of an important and
justly contested text from recent German church history. Our concern then is
with the so-called '*Darmstädter Wort*' of August 1947.

The political and church context

The year 1947 marks a decisive turning-point in the postwar period. The
tension among the super-powers was now clearly emerging and the Cold War
beginning.[2] By no means was it about Germany alone, not even primarily,
though the Cold War did indeed hit the people there particularly hard. In the
US, during the presidency of Truman (since 1945), those circles finally got to the
helm who for some time already had been very critical, on the grounds of their
Christian conviction, of the Soviet Union. A good example of this development
is John Foster Dulles.[3] In Germany, aversion and hostility to communism and
towards the 'Russians' was the order of the day – this was certainly unsurprising

given the events in the last months of the war and after. Still, the Berlin-born historian Hajo Holborn, who was politically and culturally well connected in the US and in Britain, was astonished on his trip through the occupied Germany in the autumn of 1947: 'I looked in consternation at the intensity of the German hatred of the Russians and tried to explore its roots from different angles. On a purely human level it is the complete "otherness" of the Russians that horrifies every German . . . Horror stories about the Russians are readily believed by the Germans and passed on.'[4]

The leaders of the two big parties, the Christian Democratic Union (CDU) and the Social-Democratic Party of Germany (SPD), were in agreement as to their stark anti-communism. However, the newly constituted CDU, and in Bavaria the Christian-Social Union, undoubtedly had the stronger appeal for the middle class and, in particular, for the church-going population. Though inter-denominational co-operation was never easy, either in 1947 or later,[5] a working together was always achieved on the basis of common Christian-conservative principles and then, increasingly, shared political-ideological convictions. On the Catholic side this co-operation was almost trouble-free. Things were much more complicated on the Protestant side, where more or less all the moods and convictions of those years were reflected. Obviously, however, the question of the relationship of Christianity and the Protestant Church to the political order became in practice and in principle a central issue.

When one looks at the range of political and ecclesiastical statements made in relation to the problems of 1947, it is difficult to make unambiguous general-isations. Certainly, the anti-communist discourse in large circles of the Church in the US, in Catholicism, in the ecumenical movement and also in Germany is evidence of a far-reaching identification of the Christian faith with norms and values that derive from other traditions and backgrounds. Here, Christian faith, Christian life and Christian ethos have grown together into an indissoluble unity. Without question, one can call this a problematic usage and a danger-ous ideologisation of the Christian faith. But there were also very different voices.

Ultimately the question of principle is whether Christian faith is possible, in the sense of being fit for life, without its incarnation, that is its rootedness in cultural, social, political and national peculiarities and traditions, leading inevitably to a variety of forms of Christianity. What matters in this regard is not the discovery of global and general answers. These have anyway to be tested by detailed studies. The importance of the observations made so far lies in the fact that they demonstrate unambiguously the continuous potency of a traditional form of Christendom – contrary to differently directed intentions promoted by theology, the *Zeitgeist* and politics. One of these counter-forces was the theology of Karl Barth, reflected in the *Darmstädter Wort* of 1947. This aimed at not only the negation, but the destruction of 'Christendom'.

The genesis and objective of the '*Wort*'

1. In the 'Opinion of the Fraternal Council [*Bruderrat*] of the Evangelical Church in Germany [EKD] on the political future of our people'[6] the explicit subject was also the relationship between the Church and the political order. In the summer of 1947 Karl Barth had given at various places a paper on 'The Church – the living congregation of the living Lord Jesus Christ'.[7] It was about the reality and the essence of the Church, inclusive of the dangers to its life which forced the Church to seek permanently its renewal through the word of God. On 6 July Barth confronted also the Fraternal Council (the renamed *Reichsbruderrat* that had originated in the Church Struggle of the 'Third Reich') of the EKD with these considerations. The subsequent discussion of Barth's ideas finally focused on the question of German nationalism.[8] Hans-Joachim Iwand, professor of systematic theology at Göttingen and the chairman of the theological board of the Fraternal Council, identified the danger – that had caused him alarm for some time – 'that the Church is used as a refuge for the suppressed nationalism'.[9] Nationalistic and conservative circles from within and without the Church pushed themselves to the foreground and tried to dominate. Iwand expressed his agenda even more pointedly in a letter of early 1948: 'Most important for me was the revocation of the alliance between Christian and conservative.' Iwand judged German conservatism as being without substance and radically discredited by the events of the past. Its only remaining function was that of an impediment and blockage against innovation and life, which Iwand defined as 'socialism' and 'revolution'. Therefore, the 'hyphen between Christian and conservative' was to be rejected. It represented to Iwand the 'law' in distinction to the 'gospel'. In his view, the liberating, innovating power of the gospel came into its own when people recognised that nationalism and conservatism were just repressing and destroying them. In this regard, true Christian faith was in opposition to traditional Christendom. Iwand phrased this insight in the shape of a rhetorical question: 'Are perhaps all our ideas of Christianity, in terms of their sociological side, based on this fragile foundation [i.e. that hyphen]?' If so, it would be even more urgent and necessary to search for and embark on new ways.[10]

The gospel could therefore unfold its full and comprehensive effect only when it was put into practice within the sphere of politics. This is why Iwand emphasised in that discussion: 'It is unacceptable that we are having a two-budget business: here we are Christians, and there nationalists!'[11] And this is the reason why he so passionately advocated a clear political position: 'The BK [Confessing Church] *has* to have a political orientation, we must have a political attitude as Christians, we must say today through the Fraternal Council: We have taken a new path.'

Certainly, Iwand did not wish to identify the gospel with new, better politics. Rather, the true preaching of the gospel would liberate the believer to design new and better political action. But how dangerously easy it was to merge the two approaches is indicated in his demand: 'The Church must be in a position to represent the perverted, bent German character [*Wesen*] in such a way that the true German character [*Wesen*] emerges in the congregation. At stake is the rebirth of the German character [*Wesen*] out of the gospel!'[12] Barth immediately corrected this by referring to his publication *The Christian Community and the Civil Community*:[13] 'Germany should politically find its proper mooring in the Church.' But even here the possibilities open to the Church were totally overestimated – and political realities massively underrated.

The same can be said of the statements made by this circle with regard to the unification of Germany. Iwand declared: 'For the sake of the whole German nation we have to clarify how much of the old structures we have to take down, because the keeping of our German brothers is entrusted to us. The first thing that we as Christians have to think about is not the material question but our *brothers*.'[14] Did the gospel not merge here with the political programme? Did not the old national and conservative values and norms continue here to dominate – contrary to all these denials of Christendom and its traditions, even if these were regarded as radically renewed and transformed in the sense of a visionary, concrete utopia, and even if the brothers now had taken the place of the fatherland?

These ideas, in a restrained but nevertheless recognisable way, influenced the text that Iwand presented to the Council on 7 July. Some were prepared to accept his draft declaration immediately; others insisted on simpler and more concrete formulations.[15] There was agreement that the dig at the CDU should be clearly recognisable. The disagreement related to the question whether or not a plea for Marxism was to be included in the text. A practical consensus was reached on the basis of a position Niemöller had held for some time, according to which every human being is our brother in Christ.[16] Finally the Council decided to prepare redrafts of Iwand's text for the next session. Three of these new versions are known. One was written by Karl Barth, another by Martin Niemöller, and the third was presented by the Kirchlich-Theologische Arbeitsgemeinschaft für Deutschland (Church-Theological Working Group for Germany) that had formed in Bad Boll in October 1946. This group had come together in order to use the heritage of the Church Struggle and, in particular, the Barmen Theological Declaration to benefit the present life of the Church. Phrases and ideas from all the drafts are to be found in the final version of the *Wort*, without, however, modifying the general line of Iwand's text.

On 8 August, after having discussed the document in great detail, the Fraternal Council released the *Darmstädter Wort*.[17] Present at the session, however, were only twelve persons out of the forty-three invited, nine members of the Council and three advisers. From the start therefore one could not possibly talk of a general approval of the Declaration, even within their own ranks.

2. The seven sections of the *Wort* show a clear theological profile. The point of departure (section 1) is the preaching of 'the reconciliation of the world with God in Christ', hence the gospel.[18] The unfolding of the gospel in its full power requires the conversion in a comprehensive sense not only of the individual, but also of the whole nation. This involves a transformation of consciousness, including the understanding of political, historical and social contexts, the re-linquishment of old and attachment to new values. The 'law', interpreted in the light of the 'gospel', is the instructor in this regard. It shows on the one hand where the Christians in Germany went astray, and sets out on the other how they should have righteously thought, lived and acted. Subsequently the sixth section deals with the testimony to the reality of forgiveness 'in the power of the death and the resurrection of Jesus Christ'. This statement, followed (section 7) by a verbatim quotation of the second precept of the Barmen Theological Declaration, is then positively applied to all political and social areas. In this regard, this final section deepens and clarifies what is meant and to be understood by the new existence the Christian and the congregation are to gain from changing their ways.

The centre of attention and debate was of course the concrete statements in sections 2 to 5 on the four mistakes (*Irrwege*) of the Church and the German nation. To be sure, a balanced, and in this regard just, outline of the German history of the nineteenth and twentieth centuries was not on offer. But neither could one claim that those statements were a pure invention. German Protestantism certainly did not act exclusively as the champion of an arrogant German nationalism. Unfortunately, however, there was also in Protestantism no lack of evidence of the 'dream of a particular German mission', the fascination of thinking along the lines of power and empire and, in all of this, the preparedness to commit oneself to a state characterised by internal strength and the demonstration of military power to the outside world.[19] Relatively modest, in contrast, seems to be the admonition that the German nation and the Protestant Church were to accept their 'calling' by using their gifts in fulfilment of a 'service to the common tasks of the nations'.

A similar case is the discussion of the second 'mistake', conservatism, addressed in section 3. As has been highlighted already, the authors attacked the amalgamation and identification of conservative and Christian, the legitimation of the status quo in the name of God and, vice versa, the branding of the attempts at 'reordering humanity's social life' as apostasy from God or rebellion against him. Again, it is not difficult at all to produce tons of evidence proving the correctness of this statement. What matters, therefore, is the reorientation, the new way of thinking and acting, and this requires a permanently alert Christian engagement for a civilisation that stays or becomes truly human.

Section 4 then varies and deepens the critique of the conservative ties of the Church. Addressed again – and this is the third 'mistake' – is the Church's disastrous contribution to 'political, social, and ideological divisiveness'. In this regard as well, numerous examples could be quoted showing the Church thinking and acting in this very way, nationally and internationally. It was only consistent for those claiming to possess the final truth to look for allies in the battle of 'good and evil, light and darkness, the just and the unjust'. They hardly noticed, however, that by tying the Christian faith to a dying concept of society 'the free offer for all of the grace of God' was restricted to the social group of the conservatives that was melting away.

Section 5, marking the fourth 'mistake', namely the sweeping condemnation of Marxism, sounds like a summary and illustration of what has gone before. It goes without saying that a Protestant Church, characterised by nationalism and conservatism, totally rejected it. Again, the evidence for this would be plenty. However, the authors of the *Wort* were primarily interested not in revealing the historical failure of the Protestant Church in relation to the 'cause of the poor and disinherited', but rather in making a reality of the urgent demand and promise to engage with 'the life and social existence of the people in the here and now'. This was precisely the thrust of the whole of the *Darmstädter Wort*. But in none of its sections did it respond to the present in such a direct and angry way as in this partly positive appreciation of Marxist aspirations. Indeed, the highly emotionally charged rejection of Marxism was by no means restricted to Protestant circles. Anticommunism, as indicated earlier, represented for large sections of the German population a pole of negative identification, attracting experience, hearsay, worries and everything they loathed on the political, cultural, social, economic and even religious and ecclesiastical level. The authors of the *Wort* in fact broke a taboo by claiming that it was not just possible but necessary to learn from this Marxism.

The following sixth section has a theological summary: the congregation is offered forgiveness and reconciliation and can and must live out of these. That includes the rejection of all false remedies, particularly the 'catchword: Christianity and Western culture'.

What follows from all this? The last and seventh section has, as was shown, a quote from precept two of the Barmen Theological Declaration and thereby reconnects with the first section. It had now become clear what the gift and the task of the congregation was. Therefore the Christian could not be dominated by 'despair' or even 'faithless indifference', despite all the want and misery that prevailed in Germany. Unacceptable as well were the 'dreams of a better past' or 'speculations of an imminent war'. Instead, what mattered was to become permanently aware of the gift of reconciliation and the new life flowing from this. And this meant, with a view towards the people and the whole society, that 'all and every single one of us' had to strive 'for the building of a better German state', that was 'at the service of justice, welfare, internal peace and the reconciliation of the nations'.

3. At the time, these proposals were mostly met with reservations, frequently even with indignant and emphatic rejection. This is not surprising, as people felt their national and conservative convictions attacked and, therefore, saw the *Wort* as 'a fouling of their own nest' or a 'punch in the face' for faithful Protestant Christians.[20] Several comprehensive theological reactions said the same thing in different words. Walther Künneth for example used the condescending term *Konjunkturtheologie* (a theology following the ups and downs of economic trends): an attempt to gain for the Church not just attention, but 'recognition in the arena of the forces now in power' by 'a purely political confession of guilt' in relation to 'certain mistakes of the past'.[21] In terms of content Künneth criticised the 'unilateral convergence with socialism' and the unjust judgement of German history. Against the first he quoted in a truly sterile way fitting passages of Lutheran doctrine, against the latter he listed, in a way that was both dull and arrogant, numerous corrections. However, he completely ignored the *Wort*'s purpose, which was to achieve, on the basis of the gospel, a comprehensive new start that went beyond the traditional individualist doctrine of justification. Here, all Künneth was able to discern was 'alien motives' and a 'theological gaffe that shows the characteristics of a new Nazi-theology – just the other way round'.

Asmussen argued in a similarly aggressive and brusque vein.[22] He complained that the eschatological dimension was missing, the unambiguous definition of the relationship between faith and works and the clear distinction between law and gospel. His criticism of the historical sections of the *Darmstädter Wort* and, in particular, of its advocacy of Socialism was extreme. Asmussen claimed:

> the parties of the left, and particularly the SPD, right up to the present day, are to blame for the proclamation of class struggle, namely of envy, mass murder, the demonisation of the opponent, the dissolution of human community. The socialist manifesto is a document of intolerance, a precursor of the teachings of Hitler . . . The Fraternal Council cannot possibly approve of but only openly condemn the road to the lack of rights, mass murder and enslavement that the socialist ambition has embarked on since 1789 . . . The totalitarian state is a necessary stop on the Marxist road.

Somewhere else, and a few weeks later, Asmussen wrote: 'The Fraternal Council's vote in favour of socialism has evidently burdened the conscience of thousands of church members. Thousands have now been led to think that it requires a particular political attitude in order to be a Christian according to the New Testament.'[23]

Apart from such distortions and insinuations it has to be said that many readers had considerable difficulties with the unfamiliar and complex theological language of the *Wort*. This objection was frequent, even among intellectuals.[24] As people could – or would – not follow, the theological aim of the Declaration did not get across at all. At most, it was acknowledged that another confession of guilt had been made. That is why the debate focused on the two especially offensive charges: on the one hand, the unbalanced and negative portrayal of German history and, on the other, the much too friendly treatment of socialism.

It does not shed a particularly favourable light on the representatives of Protestantism that, in contradistinction to them, a political daily paper understood very well what was at stake. Under the heading of 'Good Tidings', the *Stuttgarter Zeitung* of 6 September 1947, while also criticising terminological and factual deficiencies, had this to say about the content of the *Darmstädter Wort*: 'These few sentences in their brutal frankness contain a shattering confession; and they seem also to announce the determination of the Church to embark in the future on completely new avenues.'[25] This led to the subsequent question: 'May we then expect that in her position *vis-à-vis* politics or better, in her political attitude, the Church from now on will make a fundamental change, a radical reversal? That would be very fortunate for our nation, an event of unique importance.' Of course, the article quite justifiably went on, this would not mean 'that the Protestant Church and her representatives had now the intention of changing officially, as it were, from the political right to the left. But when the Church, in defence of Christian freedom, now terminates officially her affiliation with political reaction, then she is writing in no uncertain terms a new page of her history and drawing a clear line under the past.'

In this regard, the relativisation and dissolution of the amalgamation of nationalism, conservatism and Protestantism, that dominated in the Church even after 1945, had been convincingly proclaimed. The theological rationale for this process can hardly be argued with. However, the massive programme of leaving the old loyalties and traditions behind and risking a new start was expressed with restraint only in the equally sober and correct 'interpretation' of the *Darmstädter Wort*, written by Hermann Diem.[26] Contrariwise, Iain Wilson emphasised resolutely this trend as the fascinating characteristic of the *Darmstädter Wort*. Wilson was an army chaplain, since 1945 the contact person in the British Occupied Zone to the Protestant churches and, since 1948, consultant for Germany in the Department for Reconstruction of the Ecumenical Council of Churches in Geneva. From there he wrote on 27 March 1948 to the Fraternal Council: 'I want to tell you that in my view, that Statement, despite those faults in its formulation which I believe you yourselves recognise, was and remains the most significant utterance which has been made by the German Church since the end of the war. I would go further, and say that it is one of the most significant statements which has been made by *any* Church in recent years.'[27] All churches in the western world, in terms of their institutions and expressions of life, were deeply rooted in their respective national, cultural and social environment, 'they stake their life upon the continued existence of those social patterns into which they have so closely woven themselves, instead of upon the abiding truth of *God*'. Therefore, what the Fraternal Council had said about the very specific situation of the Church in Germany, meant a calling and a challenge for the Church universal – 'because in varying forms the same situation exists elsewhere'. Those responsible in the Fraternal Council, having so far primarily experienced attacks and hostilities, thanked him emotionally.[28]

Partly on the same line as Wilson's letter was the reaction of Paul Graf Yorck von Wartenburg, the managing director of the *Evangelisches Hilfswerk* (Protestant Aid) in the French Occupied Zone.[29] Yorck called it a 'truly great and serious undertaking' that the Fraternal Council tried 'disentangling the Church from the secular structures and values and liberating her for her calling, to announce the good news to the poor'. However, the Declaration would not really encourage this important and proper intention for it remained too much attached to 'the securities of a bourgeois, state-oriented existence'. Apart from critiquing the unjust verdict on Prussia and Bismarck, Yorck objected in particular to the vague and woolly concept of socialism the *Darmstädter Wort* operated with. He detected very clearly that in reality 'the mere fiction of a new social order' was being presented there. But was it not imperative to X-ray this as well in the light of the gospel – because it was the job of the Church 'to depose the false gods'? Yorck did not take this idea to its conclusion but complained bitterly about the naivety and dishonesty with which Diem and his friends glossed over the realities in the east.

4. With all this the die was cast. Certainly one can and has to reproach the authors of the *Darmstädter Wort* for the fact that their inclusive 'we' lumped together in a rather questionable way the members of the Fraternal Council, the Protestant Christians and the German nation. Here, unmistakably, once again the old, premodern conviction emerges, according to which the cooperation of church and state was useful and beneficial for both sides and, in particular, for the nation. But the *Wort* itself is free from such attachments to various 'hyphens', that is, from the entanglement with Christendom and its values, norms, forces and traditions: not because their realities were denied, but, on the contrary, because all the sincerity, all the pressure and, most of all, the full liberating potency, which is here witnessed to, lie in the departure, in the call to get out of these entanglements.

The strength and attraction of this new way of speaking and preaching derives from the fact that it is not just words and proclamation, but that it gains vividness through the vision of a different, better form of society and a more ideal and humane co-existence of peoples and nations. Without question, the opponents of the Declaration were right in their observation that the idea of socialism had provided the words and colours for this. They were clearly wrong, however, in their conclusion that by socialism was meant what was happening in the USSR or in the Soviet Occupied Zone.

In order to describe the totally different destination for which the church liberated by the gospel had to set out, Karl Barth and his friends spoke of 'socialism' – as a 'fiction', or, put more nicely: as a vision. The decisive question was then indeed: could this vision in any way be related to the reality of socialism as proclaimed in the East? Or, was that just a fiction? And, if there were in the East points of contact for that vision or concrete utopia – in what ways could they be transcended? And, if this transcending turned out to be impossible, what mattered most: the clinging to a vision of socialism – or correcting it, and perhaps even, in the light of lived and suffered realities, abandoning socialism altogether? Put differently, what actually was the relationship between the search of the Christian faith for concreteness, life and *Gestalt*, and the undoubtedly necessary destruction of the false norms and values of Christendom?

It turns out then that the actual touchstone for the possibility the *Darmstädter Wort* envisioned, namely the liberation of the Church from all false ties and strangling traditions, therefore from the realities of 'Christendom', is the question of the relationship between that visionary socialism and its concrete incarnation.

The reactions in Germany's East

The communist strategy aimed at enlisting as many sections of the population as possible. Few people could or would openly oppose the efforts being made for the alleviation of the terrible need, the comprehensive eradication of 'fascism', the realisation of a truly democratic order and the restitution of national unity. However, those who did object, either in principle or because of the methods being used, were soon attacked as 'reactionary' or 'fascist' – and were eliminated, usually not just politically but also physically. This insecurity as to the rule of law and the pressure generated in consequence of this, plus a very common fear, played without question a major role in the postwar Soviet Occupied Zone. On the other hand, the factual influence of the semi-official and official propaganda – by words and deeds – must not be underestimated.

The representatives of the Protestant churches were working hard to prevent their pastors from becoming active in one of the political parties.[30] They committed themselves, courageously and perseveringly, to the political victims.[31] They also defended themselves against the spying on their sermons and their other activities.[32] But public objections to the political conditions in these years came almost exclusively from the East–CDU. Against this background, a session of the Fraternal Council of the EKD was held on 15 and 16 October 1947 in Detmold, with a view to establishing the assessment of the *Darmstädter Wort* by the members coming from the Soviet Occupied Zone.[33] The interpretation of German history met with particularly massive objections in the East. But more significant was the general more or less bitter and also disappointed diagnosis that the authors of the *Darmstädter Wort* obviously had not the faintest idea about the situation in the East. This did hurt. Why had nobody from the Soviet Occupied Zone been consulted before the publication of the Declaration? Kurt Scharf summarised precisely the various emotional and factual objections and accusations:

This *Wort* is a kick in the teeth for those who have been deprived of their rights. After this *Wort*, it seems, we have to state that the Protestant Church in the German West and the German East speaks in totally different languages. We say to ourselves, only those can talk in this way who misjudge absolutely the situation as it exists for us, and who [can] not see or do not wish to see.[34]

Hermann Diem objected to this. The current insistence on the Church's role as 'watchman' *vis-à-vis* the guilt of the victors, in the East in particular, must not lead anyone to forget that the misery of the present was also a consequence of National Socialism. The demonstration of these connections was at the heart of the *Darmstädter Wort*. It also aimed to stop all attempts to escape this reality by referring to abstract, ideological concepts based in an 'unbiblical' Christianity.[35] These explanations once again formulated precisely the intentions of the authors of the *Darmstädter Wort*. However, they were unable to refute the objection made in the East that the Declaration represented a theological position derived and phrased exclusively from a West German vantage point.

On the basis of this theology it was possible to formulate in a grandiose and convincing way what in the situation of the year 1947 was without question imperative, namely the 'no' to the traditions of German Protestantism. But 'custom', the creative ethos generated by the power of the gospel, was in danger of losing its shape in the process. Or, to be more precise, it degenerated into legalism. Because one's own concept was right, the 'brothers in the East' had to take care not to oppose it. Certainly, there was no idealisation of what had passed in the East for socialism. But the Christians in the Soviet Occupied Zone were expected to agree to the insight, that the greater chances for a true and genuine existence of the Church, liberated from all 'Christendom' ideology, lay there, in the East and not in the West.[36]

There is no simple solution to the problem presented here. Part of the Jewish–Christian tradition and of the Reformation's understanding of the gospel is the critical distance to everything that has grown historically, the prophetic calling to overcome this 'Christendom'. But part of this tradition and of this gospel is also the fact that this very impulse has generated, spread and rooted norms, order and values. In this regard 'Christendom' can never be simply the misshapen shell that needs to be broken, dissolved or generally rejected. It goes without saying, at least in Protestantism, that, on the other hand, Christendom must not claim a dignity of its own, separated from the gospel. So, we are confronted by an amalgamation of very diverse traditional ties and cultural blending, and only in theory can they be cleanly differentiated and separated. But this is not what matters most. The essential need is for an approach to the bipolar nature of the Christian faith that is reflected, engages with the situation and, in this way, decides case by case. It is important to take very seriously both sides at the same time: the critique of 'Christendom' and the preservation and the unfolding of the individual and social, political and cultural values that are kept within it.

NOTES

1. This chapter is translated by Werner Ustorf.
2. Very informative is the overview by W. Loth, *Die Teilung der Welt*, 7th edition (Munich, 1989). Important is T. G. Paterson and R. J. McMahon, *The Origins of the Cold War*, 3rd edition (Lexington, MA, 1991).
3. M. G. Toulouse, *The Transformation of John Foster Dulles: From Prophet of Realism to Priest of Nationalism* (Macon, GA, 1985).
4. E. J. Hahn (ed.), 'Hajo Holborn: Bericht zur deutschen Frage, Beobachtungen und Empfehlungen vom Herbst 1947', *Vierteljahreshefte für Zeitgeschichte*, 35 (1987), 135–66.
5. Further discussed by M. Greschat, 'Konfessionelle Spannungen in der Ära Adenauer', in U. v. Hehl (ed.), *Adenauer und die Kirchen* (Bonn, 1999), 193–216; U. v. Hehl, 'Konfessionelle Irritationen in der frühen Bundesrepublik', *Historisch-Politische Mitteilungen*, 6 (1999), 167–87.
6. For the text of the '*Wort* des Bruderrates der Evangelischen Kirche in Deutschland zum politischen Weg unseres Volkes' and of the four draft texts, cf. for example M. Greschat, *Im Zeichen der Schuld* (Neukirchen, 1985), 79–86.
7. Text in K. Barth, *Die lebendige Gemeinde und die freie Gnade* (Munich, 1947), 3–23.
8. Minutes of the meeting in D. Buchhaas-Birkholz (ed.), '*Zum politischen Weg unseres Volkes': politische Leitbilder und Vorstellungen im deutschen Protestantismus 1945–1952* (Düsseldorf, 1989), 77–104.
9. *Ibid.*, 91.
10. To pastor Burdach, Cappenberg; undated. Copy taken from Iwand Papers.
11. Buchhaas-Birkholz, '*Zum politischen Weg unseres Volkes*', 92.
12. *Ibid.*; also the following quotation.

13. Karl Barth, *Christengemeinde und Bürgergemeinde* (Munich, 1946).
14. Buchhaas-Birkholz, *'Zum politischen Weg unseres Volkes'*, 99.
15. For the discussion see *ibid.*, 99–103.
16. *Ibid.*, 100ff.
17. Owing to the objections of *Bruderrat* members in the Soviet Occupied Zone, sections 3 and 5 – as Mochalski wrote to *Präses* Scharf on 11 August – were reformulated in such a way 'that it was no longer possible to extract from them a statement for or against a Weltanschauung' (Archive of the EKHN 62/3663a, also *ibid.* 36/6). This statement is unambiguously wrong.
18. Quotation taken from M. Greschat, *Zeichen der Schuld*, 85ff.
19. Informative in this regard is G. Brakelmann, 'Kirche und Schuld: Das *Darmstädter Wort* von 1947', in Brakelmann, *Kirche in Konflikten ihrer Zeit* (Munich, 1981), 162–87.
20. Quoted in a letter dated 13 September 1947; Archive of the EKHN 36/72.
21. W. Künneth, 'Zum politischen Weg unseres Volkes. Eine theologische Antwort an den Bruderrat der EKiD', *Evangelisch-Lutherische Kirchenzeitung* 1(2/3) (1947).
22. Hans Asmussen, 'Zum politischen Weg unseres Volkes. *Wort* und Antwort', *Evangelisch-Lutherische Kirchenzeitung* 1(1) (1947), 9–11.
23. To the EKD Council, 1 December 1947, 6; EKHN 62/2000b.
24. In this sense, for example, the systematic theologian Prof. Friedrich Delekat complained to Asmussen on 5 September 1947; EKHN 62/3663a.
25. Excerpts in the Archive of the EKHN 62/3663a.
26. Reprinted in *Flugblätter zur Versammlung europäischer Christen*, Darmstadt, 7–9 October 1977, No. 1, 5–18.
27. EKHN 36/7.
28. E.g. the *Kirchenrat* from the Rhinelands, Otto Wehr (14 April 1948), Iwand (20 April), the Westphalian pastor and later *Präses* Ernst Wilm (26 April), also Diem (9 May). I would like to take the opportunity to thank John Conway, Vancouver, for having drawn my attention to these letters.
29. To *Oberkirchenrat* Beckmann, 5 May 1948; EKHN 36/72.
30. See J. J. Seidel, *'Neubeginn' in der Kirche?* (Göttingen, 1989), 293–301.
31. *Ibid.*, 148–54.
32. *Ibid.*, 353–5.
33. The Minutes have been published by D. Buchhaas-Birkholz, *'Zum politischen Weg unseres Volkes'*, 116–32.
34. Minutes, 127.
35. Minutes, 129ff.
36. The commentary, quoted in L. Berthold and E. Diehl (eds.), *Vom kommunistischen Manifest zum Programm des Sozialismus* (Berlin (East), 1964), 18, says in this regard: 'The brothers in the East have a particular task in relation to the Church in the West. The Church in the East is tested in a more genuine way in her existence as a church than the one in the West where she is free and unchallenged from the outside to continue to play, even today, her role as the guardian of occidental culture.'

Part III

9   The dechristianisation of death in modern France

Thomas Kselman

In his landmark work on eighteenth-century Provence, Michel Vovelle argued forcefully that changes in the language of wills suggested that a process of dechristianisation was well under way by the middle years of the eighteenth century.[1] Vovelle based his work on a number of implicit assumptions about the relationship between death and Christianity in France that I would like to use as a starting-point for my discussion. First, and most obviously, Vovelle understood baroque devotional practices in the face of death to be crucial events for measuring the weight of Christianity in the lives of French men and women; indications that they might be less concerned with invoking the help of the clergy and the saints for their souls and those of their loved ones are equated with a lower level of commitment to Christianity in general. Second, Vovelle's work suggests that dechristianisation is a process driven by social and cultural forces that are deeply rooted and irreversible; a decline in the number of bequests for masses and other changes in wills provide an index for measuring this underlying trend. This assumption informs Vovelle's subsequent work as well, and is a dominant theme in his grand survey of death in Europe from the middle ages to the present.[2]

Vovelle's work endures as a monumental achievement, but I would like at the outset to propose some alternative ways of approaching the relationship between death and Christianity that complicate the story that he told so well. First of all, I want to question Vovelle's somewhat ahistorical view of Christianity itself. Despite his sceptical perspective, Vovelle seems generally committed to a view in which Counter-Reformation Roman Catholicism is normative for Christianity. It is possible, however, to imagine other forms of Christianity in which death and the rituals surrounding it do not hold as dominant a position in religious life. If we take a more fluid view of Christianity, the behaviour of people as they approach death might be interpreted as evidence for changes in the way religion is imagined and lived, but not necessarily as 'dechristianisation'.

I would also like to recast the way in which Vovelle uses his evidence, and see changing practices in the face of death as an engine as well as an index for religious change. Writing wills, arranging for funeral rites and designing tombs were not simply acts that reflected some predetermined religious sensibility; they were critical moments that shaped personal religious commitments. On a collective level, debates about the relative authority of family, church and state in managing death and remembering the dead were a crucial instrument in determining the place of Christianity at the deathbed, during the funeral ceremony and in the cemetery. These debates, ambiguous and contested as they were, did not proceed to some predetermined conclusion, but they did provide the French with an opportunity to reflect on the nature and quality of their religious commitments.

Cemeteries as 'lieux de mémoire'

Perhaps the most significant achievement in French historiography over the past two decades is *Les Lieux de mémoire*. This seven-volume collection of essays edited by Pierre Nora proposes that historians rethink the relationship between past and present by focusing on particular entities 'which by dint of human will or the work of time [have] become a symbolic element of the memorial heritage of any community'.[3] Given this agenda, it is surprising that not a single article in the collection deals explicitly with cemeteries, which would seem to provide a paradigmatic example of the ways in which certain places serve to crystallise the past and make it available to the present. Nora's collection covers a few 'places' that imply the contribution of Christianity to French national identity, with essays on the cathedral of Notre Dame, on Reims as the site of royal consecrations, and on the divisions between Catholics and anti-clericals.[4] On the whole, however, 'lieux chrétiens' have been neglected by Nora, with no attention paid, for example, to the system of shrines that has played such an important role in defining local, regional and national identities.[5] My assumption in this chapter is that cemeteries provide a particularly fruitful site for considering the relationship of Christianity to French national identity, and for measuring the extent to which this identity can be understood as 'dechristianised'.

The Parisian cemetery of Père Lachaise is a prominent example of a carefully constructed 'lieu de mémoire' which the French have used as a way of recalling and integrating their complicated past. Strollers through Père Lachaise might not call it a Christian cemetery, but neither could they deny the important place that Christian symbols play, in view of the large areas of nineteenth-century tombs decorated with prominent crosses. But many tombs evoke themes which suggest other ways through which life is remembered and granted meaning. Abélard and Héloise are commemorated through a neo-gothic chapel that suggests the power of romantic love.[6] Prominent socialists are buried near the 'mur des fédérés', where thousands of Communards were executed and buried in a mass grave in 1871, a site which still draws a large crowd every May.[7] The victims of the concentration camps of the 1940s have their monuments as well.

Popular culture is represented by the tombs of Edith Piaf and Jim Morrison, whose tomb has become a shrine for rock-and-roll cultists. It is hard to imagine any other place in France where so many diverse memories are so intensely concentrated.

Père Lachaise became a popular site for Parisians and foreign visitors soon after it was opened in 1804. The sense of devotion to the dead in a quiet pastoral setting encouraged at Père Lachaise became a model emulated elsewhere in France. Towns and villages carefully maintained burial grounds, many of them newly created in the course of the nineteenth century, as a focus for family traditions and communal memories. As Philippe Ariès indicated in his landmark work, the visit to the cemetery became a characteristic ritual for the French in the nineteenth and twentieth centuries.[8] Ariès, however, never establishes a clear position on the relationship between the new cult of the dead and Christianity in France, though in general he seems to accept that some form of dechristianisation has occurred. In commenting on the cross displayed at cemeteries throughout France, for example, Ariès concludes that it is 'more or less detached from its historical Christian meaning, [and] is vaguely recognized as a symbol of hope and protection. People are attached to it without knowing why, but they are attached to it all the same. It evokes not the next world but something else, something mysterious, profound, and inexpressible, of which we are only dimly aware.'[9] Ariès, like Vovelle, sets a high standard for Christianity, one which I want to question in the course of this chapter. His own wavering language, in which the cross is 'more or less detached' from its Christian meaning, suggests a certain hesitancy in his judgement. But Ariès' comment suggests also that the status and significance of Christianity in the cemetery might be an issue that can help us grapple with the deeply held but ultimately mysterious religious commitments of the French.

The eighteenth century and the Revolution

During the middle years of the eighteenth century dramatic changes in the location and design of cemeteries were actively debated by members of the Parlement of Paris, and of the Académie Royale de l'Architecture.[10] By 1765 investigators primarily concerned about public health were able to persuade the Parlement to issue a decree requiring all cemeteries to be moved outside of Paris and severely restricting burials in churches. The Cemetery of the Innocents, the largest burial ground in Paris, was closed in 1780, and the bones of its dead were transferred to the old stone quarries under Paris, the Catacombs that can still be visited through an entrance at the Place Denfert-Rochereau. Richard Etlin's study of the plans for new cemeteries drafted by artists and architects of the late eighteenth century suggests that the projected sites would be spiritually as well as physically separated from their Christian predecessors. It is virtually impossible to find a single Christian symbol in the designs of Etienne-Louis Boullée or his colleagues, who were instead preoccupied with pyramids, classical arches and obelisks.

Etlin, following Vovelle, uses the term 'dechristianisation' to describe the 'mental revolution' of the mid-eighteenth century that he understands to be 'a turning point in one thousand years of Western history'.[11] But there is a hint of equivocation in his analysis, for the word is always placed in quotation marks, and surrounded with qualifying phrases. Etlin's discomfort is warranted, for his evidence is restricted for the most part to texts and plans developed by an educated elite whose ideas may or may not have been generally representative. He notes only briefly the substantial resistance to the plans of the reformers by Parisian curés, who complained that the Parlement was treating Parisians 'like Huguenots. They are sending us to the garbage dump.'[12] This comment adds a religious context to the debates over cemetery reform, for the curés were undoubtedly conscious of the religious bias of the Parlementaires, who had been engaged in a long and public campaign to defend Jansenism, an austere and Augustinian form of Christianity whose influence in France extended from the seventeenth well into the nineteenth century.[13] The quarrel over cemeteries may have been informed partly by a dispute between those Catholics who were anxious to preserve their churchyards as an essential element of baroque piety, and others who sought a more restrained approach to death and burial, one associated with the Protestant reform and with Jansenism. Enlightenment values, including religious scepticism and a preference for neoclassical decorations, clearly influenced some of the artists charged with imagining the shape and style of the new suburban cemeteries. But there were Christians involved in the reform movement as well, a point which should lead us to see the displacement of cemeteries as a complex issue that is not fully and fairly characterised if we see it only as a movement towards dechristianisation.

The revolutionary crisis that began in 1789 generated the most dramatic religious conflicts in France since the Reformation. However one views the previous period, it seems fair to apply the term dechristianisation to some of the actions taken during the 1790s and to their consequences as well. The Catholic cult of the dead was a principal target of the dechristianisers who spread out from Paris in 1793, as most clearly illustrated by the work of Joseph Fouché, representative-on-mission from the Convention to the Nièvre. In an attempt to destroy what he understood to be religious fanaticism, Fouché issued a decree on funeral practices that required all local cemeteries to raise a statue representing sleep, destroy all other symbols, and place at their entrances signs announcing that 'Death is an eternal sleep'.[14]

Reforms such as those introduced by Fouché were adopted elsewhere in France as well, and were frequently accompanied by other violent acts directed against the clergy and the icons of Catholicism.[15] But the aggressive campaign of dechristianisation provoked responses in defence of Christianity and its symbols. In the churchyard of the village of Concoret, in Anjou, revolutionaries replaced a large crucifix with a liberty tree, only to see it cut down by Chouan rebels.[16] Women played a leading role at times in such demonstrations, which were instrumental in leading Robespierre to condemn the actions of Fouché and his colleagues.[17] Robespierre's attempts to formulate an alternative civil religion met, however, with little success, for only a militant minority was drawn to the Cult of the Supreme Being and to the religion of Theophilanthropy promoted by the Directory. By the end of the 1790s politicians in the Council of Five Hundred had become concerned that the assault on Christianity and the failure of the new religions was producing a desacralised and demoralised population. Focusing particularly on the cult of the dead, critics were appalled by the neglect with which the dead were treated, and called for dignified funeral services and well-maintained cemeteries. Dechristianisation thus became associated not only with attacks directed particularly against Christian symbol and ritual, but with a more general assault on the sacred atmosphere surrounding the dead believed essential for social order. Politicians such as the former priest Jacques-Michel Coupé and P. B. F. Bontoux were not necessarily anxious to restore Catholicism, but the movement to resacralise the cult of the dead, co-incidental with Napoleon's efforts to negotiate a Concordat with the papacy, opened the way for the rechristianisation of the cemetery which occurred in the nineteenth century.

The French Revolution clearly had a major impact on the status of Christianity in France. The process of 'stripping the altars', to borrow a phrase from Eamon Duffy, broke traditional relations between priests and people and produced a generation more inclined to independence and scepticism.[18] But there were limits beyond which most people were not willing to go, and one of these seems to have been a Christian setting for death and burial. Catholicism was a source of conflict and violence during the revolutionary decade of the 1790s, but while at least some French were willing to move quickly to destroy the Church's control of the cult of the dead most seemed to understand the Christian symbols and rituals employed by the Church as essential elements in creating a sacred atmosphere around the corpse and the community.

From churchyard to cemetery

The religious peace that followed the Concordat provided a general setting for the rechristianisation of the cemetery during the nineteenth century. This process is especially remarkable in that it occurred not only in the older churchyards, but in new cemeteries purchased and developed by communes. This shift from churchyard to cemetery was based on the Napoleonic legislation that made the eighteenth-century effort to remove the dead from cities into a national mandate.

The decree of 23 prairial, year XII (1804) prohibited burial in churches, and required that cemeteries be relocated at least 35 metres outside of town. The law also eliminated the common graves of the old regime, and required that each individual have his or her own particular space. For the rest of the nineteenth century, French cities and villages struggled to comply with this law which resulted in a shift of the dead from parish churchyard to communal cemetery. The cemeteries that developed became a central element in the nineteenth-century cult of the dead, and relied heavily on Christian symbol and ritual, though these were no longer granted a monopoly, and were at times the source of considerable conflict.[19]

Père Lachaise, first opened in 1804, provided a model for other cities, which sought to re-create its pastoral spirit, generated by curved and landscaped walkways designed to provide a peaceful setting for the dead and those who mourned them. Illustrations from the first few years of its operation, however, suggest that Christianity was not a dominant motif in the tombs and epitaphs of the first who were buried there.[20] It is also worth noting that the cemetery as a whole was never consecrated by any priest, minister or rabbi. The practice developed for individual sites to be blessed, but the cemetery as a whole retained its secular character, a trait which was to make it exceptional in the history of the French cemetery. The Catholic writer M. de Saint-Victor commented on the secular character of Père Lachaise in 1825, when he complained that many of the inscriptions 'expressed religious indifference . . . and, looking carefully, even professions of faith in materialism and atheism'. Saint-Victor, thinking back perhaps to the Revolution, feared a time would come when the few crosses that marked Christian graves would be eliminated.[21] Catholic anxieties were not without foundation. When the famous actor François Talma died in 1826 he refused to see the archbishop of Paris, and received a civil burial, the first in a long series of public ceremonies that were both religiously and politically subversive. His funeral procession to Père Lachaise drew thousands into the streets, who were apparently not offended that his monument was completely free of any Christian reference.[22]

Although the cross was a contested symbol at times, Saint-Victor's concerns were in fact exaggerated.[23] In the year that his piece on Père Lachaise appeared, a chapel surmounted by a cross was opened at the end of the main thoroughfare leading into the cemetery.[24] By the middle of the century observers at Père Lachaise and elsewhere were describing rows of crosses as the standard decorations marking individual graves, establishing a style that would later be adapted for the dead who returned from the battlefields of World War I.[25] Cities that purchased and developed new cemeteries generally arranged to have them opened with a formal blessing by the Catholic clergy, a rite that helped give them a proprietary sense over the communal burial ground similar to what they felt about the older churchyards. When the city of Angers was about to open its new suburban cemetery in the autumn of 1847 the mayor sought the blessing of the local bishop, who was willing to co-operate on two conditions: land had to be set aside outside of the consecrated area for the burial of stillborn children and Protestants, and a large cross on a pedestal would have to be installed.[26]

Burial in consecrated land was taken seriously by the French, as can be observed in the conflicts that arose when the clergy tried to exclude non-Catholics from what they regarded as a Catholic cemetery. Although most people accepted the last rites that certified their Catholic identity and gave them access to the consecrated ground, a number of scandals in the first half of the century drew attention to the ambiguous status of the cemetery, christianised through the blessing of the Catholic clergy, but also communal property to which all citizens, regardless of their religion, could make a claim.[27]

Conflicts developed over differing interpretations of the law of 1804, which called for separate areas for Catholics, Protestants and Jews, assuming that everyone would fall into one of the standard confessional categories. The law was silent, however, on how to resolve conflicts that arose when the Catholic clergy refused to bury someone in consecrated ground despite the insistence of their family that they deserved such treatment. In taking this position the clergy were seeking to exclude not only children who died before baptism, but public sinners and notorious anti-clericals, even if they had been baptised. When such a refusal occurred, bitter quarrels would break out between the clergy and the families of the deceased, who resisted any attempt to let their loved ones be relegated to shamed and isolated corners. Families would sometimes organise their own services, breaking into churches to say prayers over the dead. Mayors, charged by the law with assuring respect for the dead, would sometimes be enlisted to lead a service, and to oversee the burial in consecrated ground. Commenting on such improvised rituals, the historian Maurice Agulhon disparaged their religious significance, and insisted on the agnosticism and religious indifference of the participants.[28] But it seems fairer to relate the insistence on a christianised cult of the dead to the attitudes we saw displayed during the French Revolution. Just as dechristianisation was rejected when it culminated in a desacralised disposal of the dead, resacralisation was imaginable primarily through the familiar Catholic rites administered by the clergy.

The clergy were sensitive to the attractions of Catholic burial, which explains why they were willing to use it at times as a threat to bring the indifferent back into the Church. But such minatory behaviour was resented, and contributed to a confusing condition in which resentment towards the Catholic clergy could co-exist with dependence on them as the ministers whose use of Christian symbol and ritual was needed to consecrate death and burial. The ambiguous status of Christianity in the cult of the dead around the middle of the century can be illustrated by considering Courbet's famous masterpiece *The Burial at Ornans*, displayed in Dijon and Paris in 1850–51. Most critics at the time and subsequently have interpreted this scene of a country funeral procession gathered around an empty grave as devoid of any transcendent religious feeling. Art history textbooks uniformly present it as the paradigmatic example of 'realist' art which rejected the spiritual consolations available in romantic depictions of death, such as Monsiau's *Devotion of Monseigneur Belsunce*, presented at the salon of 1819. The figures in Monsiau's painting are linked in a moment of religious fervour, with the dying consoled by the vision of the crucifix which pierces the horizon, and by the presence of the clergy. In Courbet's painting, according to Linda Nochlin '[t]he psychological and pictorial dissociation of the figures from each other' indicate that for him 'the transcendent meaning of funerals in general is completely unimportant'.[29] Such a point could be made, however, only by evoking unfulfilled conventional expectations about the religious mood believed to be characteristic of a funeral. Courbet relies on the crucifix that pierces the horizon and the priest who officiates at the grave to recall Christian hopes, but simultaneously deflates these by the emotional distance that separates the mourners from the ritual, for none of those present focus their attention on either the crucifix or the priest.[30]

Pierre-Joseph Proudhon, in reacting to Courbet's painting, illustrates precisely the ambivalent status of Christianity in the cemetery, and in French culture more generally. For Proudhon insists on the one hand on the need to sacralise death: 'If something must remain sacred, for the believer as well as for the unbeliever, it is the last moments, the will, the solemn farewells, the funeral, the tomb.' Proudhon insists, on the other hand, that the French 'have lost the religion of the dead; we no longer understand this sublime poetry with which Christianity surrounded it; we have lost faith in prayers, and we mock the next life'. This loss of faith has made the standard rituals meaningless: 'Why the funerals? Why the burials? What do these marble tombs, these crosses, these inscriptions, these crowns of flowers mean? Wouldn't it be enough for you that a cart, ordered by the police, would take the body and lead it to . . . the garbage dump?'[31] But during the Revolution the French had experimented with the desacralised disrespect that Proudhon mockingly suggested as appropriate, and clearly preferred the tombs, crosses and flowers that he judged to be meaningless. Courbet's painting and Proudhon's commentary suggest the continuing importance of a Christian framework for death, doubts about its significance, and regrets about the apparent gap that had developed between an idealised ritual characterised by belief and fervour and the practice of ordinary Christians, unable to measure up to this high standard. The anxieties of the unbelievers Courbet and Proudhon echo those expressed by the Catholic clergy, similarly concerned that the Christian rituals were losing their power, even as people continued to rely on them for managing the passage from life to death.

In the first half of the nineteenth century the clergy fought against what they perceived as an erosion of belief by continuing to insist on the segregation of Catholics and non-Catholics in cemeteries. This policy was intended to force the dying and their families either to commit themselves definitively to Catholicism, or face burial in a shamed and unconsecrated quarter of the cemetery usually preserved for suicides. During the second half of the century, however, the ambivalence about Catholic ritual evident in *The Burial at Ornans* was also manifested in the behaviour of a dissident minority who refused to accept what they regarded as abusive treatment by the clergy. A series of scandals, well covered by the anti-clerical press, provided the impetus for a debate over the cemetery which lasted throughout the 1870s, and forms part of the general climate of political and religious conflict that characterised the decade. The scandals in question frequently involved mixed marriages between Protestants and Catholics, with the clergy attempting to force husbands and wives who had shared their lives to accept separate burial sites. Protestants and militant freethinkers were increasingly determined to resist such pressure, and insisted on their right to a place of their choice in the communal cemetery, many of which were new sites, no longer adjacent to Catholic churches, purchased and developed with communal funds. Catholic polemicists struck back, with the vituperative Monseigneur Gaume condemning those who would allow unbelievers to be buried next to the faithful. 'You believe that all men, including yourselves, are nothing but living dirt, soulless creatures, with no higher destiny than to gratify your appetites. You cannot have a conscience, for there is no conscience in a heap of dirt.'[32] But such an attack clearly missed the mark, for though there were some militant freethinkers among the dissidents, there were also Protestants and spiritualists who believed in a soul and an after-life. Even more thoroughgoing unbelievers had, by the end of the century, developed moral philosophies that belie the caricature presented by Gaume.

The transfer of power to a republican majority in the late 1870s provided the occasion for pushing through legislation that had been floating around for ten years. Despite an acrimonious debate, article 15 of the law of 1804 was abrogated in 1881, ending the right of the Catholic Church to exercise the substantial power it had exercised in the communal cemetery. The civil funeral and entombment of Victor Hugo in 1885 was a culminating event in the emergence of an alternative to Catholicism as the source of a sacred atmosphere for the cult of the dead. His services drew over one million Parisians to what may have been the largest demonstration in nineteenth-century France.[33] In the twenty years following Hugo's funeral the politicians of the Third Republic continued to dismantle the Catholic hegemony over the cult of the dead. In 1887 the French legislature passed a law designed to protect the right of an individual to receive a civil burial, even when his or her family requested a Catholic service. In 1904 the French funeral industry was secularised when management of the service was transferred from parish councils to communal authorities.[34] Taken together, these laws reveal an important shift in the French cult of the dead in the closing decades of the nineteenth century.

There can be no doubt that the cultural authority of the Church had waned, but the laws passed during the Third Republic by no means re-enacted the aggressive campaign of Fouché and his colleagues during the French Revolution. The French were left free to choose a Catholic service and a tomb marked by Christian symbols, and most continued to do so.[35] If we were to compare a cemetery from the old regime, in which mass graves with no individual marker were the norm, with a cemetery from the end of the nineteenth century, in which crosses would be the predominant motif, displayed in some form over most of the graves, we would be hard pressed to conclude that death had been dechristianised, even in the midst of the anti-clerical passions of the Third Republic. Following the shock of the Revolution, cemeteries had become sites where families gathered to reflect on and pray for their deceased, creating a cult of the dead unique to the nineteenth century. Crowds were particularly large on 1 and 2 November, the feasts of All Saints and All Souls traditionally used by the Catholic Church to recall the dead.[36] Even Socialist papers at the turn of the century were forced to acknowledge the popularity of visits to the cemetery on these days, though they emphasised the devotion paid to their own saints.[37] By the end of the century a minority was willing to forego Christian rituals and symbols, but even in the reputedly dechristianised Paris over 70 per cent of the population still insisted on a Catholic funeral in 1900.[38] The Catholic clergy were understandably distressed by republican legislation that eliminated their control of cemeteries, and the debates generated between clericals and anti-clericals over a range of issues, including the cult of the dead, certainly led some away from both Catholicism and Christianity. But many of the French in the early twentieth century seemed to make a distinction between these two, and their cemeteries suggest that, regardless of any hostility directed against the clergy, Christianity continued to provide a consoling atmosphere for most families as they reflected on their dead.

World War I and the twentieth century

The contemplative mood in the cemetery, generally though not invariably in the midst of Christian symbols, was the result of decisions and distinctions made in the course of the nineteenth century. As passed on to the twentieth century, the cult of the dead proved to be a potent force in the face of the catastrophic bloodletting that occurred in France between 1914 and 1918. Historians who look for dramatic breaks in cultural history have generally identified World War I as a crucial turning-point in the creation of 'modernity', understood as a sceptical frame of mind which dissolves traditional certainties about politics, art and religion. If the Enlightenment, the Revolution and the laic legislation of the Third Republic did not 'dechristianise' death, perhaps this process was at work in the trenches and battlefields of World War I. But if we follow the research of Annette Becker and Jay Winter, the carnage of the war produced not so much a modernist impulse as a reversion to principles and beliefs inherited from the past.[39] The cult of the dead as it emerged from the war, and as displayed in cemeteries and memorial monuments, found an important place for Christianity, though not one that allowed it to monopolise the work of consolation.

The military cemetery at Douaumont offers striking evidence for the importance of the cross as part of the repertoire of symbols that 'were retrieved from the past to help people mourn'.[40] Thousands of crosses, arranged in neat lines as in military formation, decorate the individual graves of the vast majority of soldiers. The cross was also the symbol of choice for many of those 300,000 dead soldiers who were transferred back to cemeteries in their home towns, a move made in part to bring them closer to their parish churches.[41] What is more surprising, however, is the deep involvement of the Catholic bishops in the creation of three of the four national necropolises at Douaumont, Lorette and Dormans.[42] As Annette Becker has argued, the architecture and ornamentation of these sites embodies a central theme of Christianity, that of sacrifice and resurrection, represented through scenes of the passion of Christ and the suffering of Mary.[43] But this emphasis did not efface the wartime ecumenical spirit, as exemplified in the interdenominational chapel at Hartmanwillerkopf, which includes Protestant and Jewish altars as well as a Catholic one. In the commemorative ceremonies as well, Catholic clergy seem to have taken care to be inclusive. According to the abbé Bergey, speaking at the opening of the ossuary of Douaumont in 1932, 'We ask no longer, "Art thou republican, monarchist, socialist, Israelite, free-thinker, or Catholic?" But simply: "Art thou French?" '[44]

Abel Gance's epic film on World War I, *J'Accuse*, is an even more telling illustration of the power of Christian symbol and belief to shape the experience of mourning, for Gance was an artist rather than a minister, responding more to deep-rooted cultural motifs than to specific doctrines and practices. The closing sequence of his film reflects the power of Christianity to represent feelings of hope and redemption without implying any particular doctrinal commitments. In Gance's story the poet-hero Jean Diaz dreams of himself in a graveyard of crosses, out of which the dead rise in order to return to their villages. The civilians are converted by this vision, not to religious practice, but to lives of rectitude and fidelity. Gance closes his film with a scene of Christ on the Cross, a reference to the equation of the suffering soldier with the passion of Christ that was commonplace both during and after the war.[45]

The cemeteries of France, as they developed in the nineteenth century, became a kind of training ground, a contentious terrain at times, but one on which and through which the French eventually worked out an understanding of death that accommodated Christian belief and symbol with a devotion to family, village and nation. This ability of the cemetery to serve as a 'lieu de mémoire' which synthesised and expressed the multiple loyalties of the French was already in place before 1914, and established the context for the military cemeteries and memorial monuments that addressed the sacrifices and trauma of World War I. If we follow the history of the cult of the dead into the present we can find some anxiety about a falling off in the devotion to the dead, as tombs are abandoned, and visits to the family grave seem to be in decline. But other evidence suggests that although the cult of the dead continues to undergo change, we still need to be cautious in making judgements about 'dechristianisation'.

Throughout most of the last two centuries rural Brittany has been among the regions most devoted to orthodox Catholicism. But social changes, including a shift from polyculture to cash crops, the mechanisation of production and the decline of neighbourly mutual aid, have contributed to the secularisation of Breton culture. According to the anthropologist Ellen Badone, who spent fifteen months in the villages of Plouguerneau and La Feuillée in the mid-1980s, Bretons are involved in a 'gradual transition from a religious view of the world to one based on naturalistic, empirical science'.[46] This overall process, which has led to dramatically lower levels of regular religious practice, has had particular effects on the cult of the dead, which had traditionally been an intense and central part of Breton culture. At the traditional *veillée*, for example, neighbours and friends used to watch over the body of the deceased throughout the night. Since the mid-1970s, however, the wake has been shortened, with people leaving at one or two in the morning, just after refreshments have been served.[47]

Despite unambiguous evidence of an erosion of Catholic practice, Badone insists at the same time on strong patterns of continuity with the past. Civil burials are rare, anniversary masses are still commonly requested to commemorate the dead, and crosses still dominate the cemeteries. Badone's conclusion suggests that the people of contemporary Brittany are negotiating a change similar to that which occurred elsewhere in France during the nineteenth century. 'Despite the opposition to the church voiced by many *rouges*, the clergy continues to provide the only acceptable ritual mediation of the passage from the community of the living to that of the dead.'[48] Yves Lambert may be correct to conclude that 'Dieu change en Bretagne', but despite these changes Bretons, like the French in general, continue generally to insist on a Christian setting for death and burial.

Badone recounts at one point the story of Michel Quiviger, a Communist municipal councillor in the Monts d'Arrée. Although he had officiated at civil burials himself, Quiviger asked for and received a Catholic funeral, a choice which provoked extensive comment from both Catholics and Communists. In the end, Quiviger seems to have decided that only the 'symbolic power of the Catholic Mass' was able 'to elevate death from the natural to the cultural realm'.[49] Quiviger's funeral resembles in some ways the much grander ceremonies which marked the death and burial of François Mitterand in January 1996, which I will use as the final illustration of the complex relationship that has emerged between death and Christianity in modern France.

As the first Socialist president in French history, François Mitterand might have been expected to honour the tradition of the French left and forego a Catholic funeral and burial service. After all, he had the precedent of Victor Hugo's civil burial a hundred years before, an event used by the anti-clericals of the Third Republic to help forge a dignified alternative to the Catholic ritual of death and burial.[50] But as a number of recent biographies have made clear, Mitterand never entirely escaped the pious Catholic milieu of his origins, a tradition to which he showed himself faithful in arranging both a private mass for his family in his home at Jarnac, and a public mass attended by foreign dignitaries in Paris at the cathedral of Notre Dame.[51] It was typical of Mitterand to have balanced this reversion to his Catholic past with a separate ceremony of remembrance for his associates on the political left, held appropriately at the Place de la Bastille.

The only official words spoken at the Notre Dame service were those of the archbishop of Paris Cardinal Lustiger, who delivered a remarkable homily in which he drew heavily on the words of Mitterand himself.[52] Lustiger recalled that Mitterand had kept a portrait of St Francis of Assisi in his library, and quoted him as critical of the 'spiritual dryness' of the contemporary age. For Lustiger, Mitterand's funeral was the occasion for recalling the 'secret place where the life of a man crystallises, and from which flow the most contradictory desires and ambitions'. In contemporary civilisation this essential mystery at the heart of every life tends to be forgotten, and instead people turn to 'appearances and . . . vain words imposed by the artifice of communication which becomes a substitute for life'. Lustiger concluded by recalling that Mitterand had claimed to believe in the 'communion of saints', and prayed that he find with them 'the help, forgiveness, and courage to open his eyes on the invisible'.

The Catholic setting for Mitterand's funeral and Lustiger's attempt to associate the president with a Catholic culture and world-view contrast sharply with the events surrounding Hugo's death, and illustrate how much has changed since the end of the nineteenth century, when the militant programme of republican 'laïcité' would have made such collaboration unthinkable. René Rémond's comment that 'laïcité n'est plus ce qu'elle était'[53] would seem borne out by Mitterand's death, which became a vehicle for the reconciliation of the two Frances that fought so bitterly throughout the nineteenth century. But we need to be cautious in interpreting this event, which can bear multiple meanings that would lead to very different conclusions about the status of Christianity in France. Is it the case, as Robert Solé proposes, that on such occasions Notre-Dame 'n'est plus catholique, mais oecumenique, et même universelle'?[54] Is it a sign, as Lustiger suggests, that the French and others in the contemporary west feel a need for spiritual consolations that are not available from the secular material culture that is pervasive in France and elsewhere? Or does it perhaps indicate that Catholicism has now been absorbed into a French civil religion in which Catholic and Republican 'lieux de mémoire' are mixed indiscriminately in a stew of nationalistic nostalgia which provides a kind of compensation for the decline of France as a world power?[55] However we interpret Mitterand's funeral, the carefully orchestrated use of Catholic ritual and the extensive coverage in the media suggest that for Mitterand personally and the French in general Christianity is still understood to have an important role to play in negotiating the passage from life to death.

Throughout this chapter I have been arguing implicitly for a generous standard in establishing Christian identity and have suggested caution in making judgements about the process of dechristianisation. Recent surveys indicate that, despite signs of eroding belief, a clear majority of the French still identify themselves as Catholic.[56] The evidence of the cemetery, past and present, suggests a profound though ambiguous attachment to Christian symbols, which has been maintained despite intermittent and occasionally intense conflict with the institutional church and the clergy. The crosses in French cemeteries exemplify what the American historian Colleen McDannell has termed 'material Christianity', which she distinguishes from a religiosity centred on texts and doctrines.[57] McDannell points to the tendency of some American scholars to disparage such religion, which is expressed through artifacts, and is generally not articulated in any systematic manner. Theological scepticism about 'material Christianity' may be less common in France, where the Catholic sacramental system has traditionally mingled matter and spirit, but there are echoes of similar sentiments none the less in the work of historians as diverse as Vovelle and Ariès. From the perspective of 'material Christianity' as defined by McDannell, theologians and ministers concerned with evangelisation might wish to consider the possibility that the continued insistence on Catholic identity and Christian symbols represents an authentic form of Christianity. Ariès touches the core of the issue when he writes that the cross in the cemetery 'evokes ... something mysterious, profound, and inexpressible, of which we are only dimly aware'. But these meanings, which he grasps for without being able to define, are certainly based on the ability of the cross to express feelings of grief and hope, sacrifice and redemption. This reservoir of religious and Christian sentiment may be inchoate, but it merits further reflection by both scholars and ministers concerned with Christianity and dechristianisation.

NOTES

1. Michel Vovelle, *Piété baroque et déchristianisation en Provence au XVIIIe siècle* (Paris, 1978).
2. Michel Vovelle, *La Mort et l'occident de 1300 à nos jours* (Paris, 1983). For example, in commenting on folk practices imbued with Christian themes that endure despite low levels of orthodox practice, Vovelle writes that 'Derrière le compromis se profilent les réalités d'une déchristianisation réelle, qui n'épargne pas la société traditionnelle en voie de mutation, même si les apparences de stabilité subsistent plus que dans les villes' (*ibid.* 573–4). For a comparison of the work of Vovelle with that of Philippe Ariès see Thomas Kselman, 'Death in historical perspective', *Sociological Forum*, 2 (1987), 591–7.
3. Pierre Nora, 'From lieux de mémoire to realms of memory', in Pierre Nora and Lawrence Kritzman (eds.), *Realms of Memory*, vol. I (New York, 1996), xvii.
4. Jacques Le Goff, 'Reims, ville du sacre'; Claude Langlois, 'Catholiques et laics', in Pierre Nora (ed.), *Les Lieux de mémoire*, vol. III (Paris, 1992), 141–84.
5. Mary Lee Nolan and Sidney Nolan, *Christian Pilgrimage in Modern Western Europe* (Chapel Hill, NC, 1989); Thomas Kselman, *Miracles and Prophecies in Nineteenth-Century France* (New Brunswick, NJ, 1983), 25–36; Ruth Harris, *Lourdes: Body and Spirit in the Secular Age* (New York, 1999).
6. Charlotte Charrier, *Héloise dans l'histoire et dans la légende* (Paris, 1933), 342–63, 493–545.
7. Madeleine Rebérioux, 'Le mur des fédérés', in Pierre Nora (ed.), *Les Lieux de mémoire*, vol. I, *La République* (Paris, 1984), 619–49.
8. Philippe Ariès, *The Hour of Our Death* (New York, 1981), 516–55. See also Françoise Zonabend, 'Les morts et les vivants: le cimetière de Minot et Chatillonnais', *Etudes Rurales*, 52 (1973), 7–23; Roger Bertrand and Michel Vovelle, *La Ville des morts: essai sur l'imaginaire d'après les cimetières provençaux* (Paris, 1983), esp. 112–13, where the authors indicate that from the early nineteenth century to the present between 80 and 90 per cent of the tombs include a cross in some form.
9. Ariès, *Hour of Our Death*, 276.
10. Richard Etlin, *The Architecture of Death: The Transformation of the Cemetery in Eighteenth-Century Paris* (Cambridge, MA, 1984); Ariès, *Hour of Our Death*, 479–506.
11. Etlin, *Architecture of Death*, ix, 16.
12. Ariès, *Hour of Our Death*, 489.
13. Dale Van Kley, *The Religious Origins of the French Revolution: From Calvin to the Civil Constitution, 1560–1791* (New Haven, CT, 1996). Ariès (*Hour of Our Death*, 498) is surely wrong when he characterises the parliamentarians responsible for the decree of 1765 as 'enlightened and radical'.
14. Nicole Bossut, 'Aux origines de la déchristianisation dans la Nièvre', *Annales Historiques de la Révolution Française*, 264 (1986), 181–202.
15. Michel Vovelle, *La Révolution contre l'église: de la raison à l'Etre Suprème* (Paris, 1988).
16. Joseph Le Calonnec, 'Les sépultures des catholiques pendant la Révolution', *Impacts*, 3 (1993), 41.
17. Vovelle, *Revolution contre l'église*, 230–55; Suzanne Desan, *Reclaiming the Sacred: Lay Religion and Popular Politics in Revolutionary France* (Ithaca, NY, 1990).

18. Eamon Duffy, *The Stripping of the Altars: Traditional Religion in England, 1400–1580* (New Haven, CT, 1992).

19. Thomas Kselman, *Death and the Afterlife in Modern France* (Princeton, NJ, 1993). Much of the material I draw on here has been reformulated and compressed from chapters 3 and 5 of this study. For case studies see Philippe Boutry, *Prêtres et paroisses au pays du Curé d'Ars* (Paris, 1986), 153–81; Madeleine Lasserre, 'La loi et les morts: la difficile création du cimetière général de Tours au XIXe siècle', *Annales de Bretagne et des Pays de l'Ouest*, 98 (1991), 303–12; Michel Bée, 'Les cimetières de Calvados en 1804', in M. Bée *et al.*, *Mentalités religieuses dans la France de l'ouest aux XIXe et XXe siècles* (Caen, 1976), 9–34; Marcel Launay, 'Le cimetière comme élément de la nouvelle sensibilité funèbre au XIXe siècle: un exemple nantais', *Bulletin de la Société Archéologique et Historique de Nantes et de Loire-Atlantique*, 119 (1983), 179–90.

20. Etlin, *Architecture of Death*, 345–54.

21. M. de Saint-Victor, 'Sur la cimetière du Père Lachaise', *L'Ami de la Religion*, 43 (1825), 360–1.

22. Avner Ben-Amos, *Funerals, Politics, and Memory in Modern France, 1789–1996* (New York, 2000), 114.

23. Michael Phayer, 'Politics and popular religion: the cult of the cross in France, 1815–1840', *Journal of Social History*, 11 (1978), 346–65; Kselman, *Death and the Afterlife*, 65–7.

24. Etlin, *Architecture of Death*, 328–30.

25. Francis Head, *A Faggot of French Sticks or, Paris in 1851* (New York, 1852), 455; for similar descriptions see Alphonse Esquiros, 'Les cimetières de Paris', *Revue de Paris* (Feb.–March 1844), 261–6.

26. Archives Municipales, 37 M 42, file on Cimetière de l'Est. See also Lassere, 'La loi et les morts', 310.

27. Thomas Kselman, 'Funeral conflicts in nineteenth-century France', *Comparative Studies in Society and History*, 30 (1988), 312–32.

28. Maurice Agulhon, *La République au village* (Paris, 1970), 183.

29. Linda Nochlin, 'Innovation and tradition in Courbet's *Burial at Ornans*', in *Essays in Honor of Walter Friedlander* (New York, 1965), 119–26.

30. For a fuller discussion of this painting and additional references, see Kselman, *Death and the Afterlife*, 291–302.

31. *Du Principe de l'art et de sa destination sociale*, in *Œuvres complètes*, ed. C. Bouglé and H. Moysset (Paris, 1939), vol. XV, 175.

32. Jean-Joseph Gaume, *The Christian Cemetery in the Nineteenth Century, or the Last War Cry of the Communists*, trans. Rev. R. Brennan (New York, 1874), 73.

33. Avner Ben-Amos, 'Les funérailles de Victor Hugo', in Nora (ed.), *Les Lieux de mémoire*, vol. I, 473–522.

34. For these reforms see Kselman, *Death and the Afterlife*, 107–10, 273–87, and Jacqueline Lalouette, *La Libre Pensée en France, 1848–1940* (Paris, 1997), 307–15, 333–67.

35. Michel Lagrée makes a similar point in 'Exilés dans leur patrie (1880–1920)', in François Lebrun (ed.), *Histoire des Catholiques en France* (Paris, 1980), 373.

36. Kselman, *Death and the Afterlife*, 200.

37. *L'Humanité*, 2 Nov. 1904, 2 describes the flowers left at the 'mur des fédérés' and at the tombs of Blanqui, Zola and Waldeck-Rousseau, among others.
38. Fernand Boulard, 'La "déchristianisation" de Paris. L'évolution du non-conformisme', *Archives de Sociologie des Religions*, 31 (1971), 78–9.
39. Annette Becker, 'From death to memory: the national ossuaries in France after the Great War', *History and Memory*, 5 (1993), 32–49; Becker, 'Les dévotions des soldats catholiques pendant la Grande Guerre', in Nadine-Josette Chaline (ed.), *Chrétiens dans la première guerre mondiale* (Paris, 1993), 15–34; Becker, *Les Monuments aux morts: patrimoine et mémoire de la Grande Guerre* (Paris, 1988); Jay Winter, *Sites of Memory, Sites of Mourning: The Great War in European Cultural History* (New York, 1995).
40. Winter, *Sites of Memory*, 224. See the photograph of Douaumont in Becker, *Monuments aux morts*, 33.
41. Winter, *Sites of Memory*, 26. In Angers the crosses over the graves of the World War I dead include a military motif, with the top of the cross embellished to make it resemble the hilt of a sword. Kselman, *Death and the Afterlife*, 214.
42. Becker, 'From death to memory', 40.
43. *Ibid.*, 34, 41, 45–6.
44. *Ibid.*, 43–4. On the ecumenical spirit of the war see also Nadine-Josette Chaline, 'Les aumôniers catholiques dans l'armée française', and Michel Lagrée, 'Ces chers protestants', in Chaline (ed.), *Chrétiens dans la première guerre mondiale*, 95–120 (esp. 107), 133–52. For the collaboration of Catholic and secular intellectuals see Martha Hanna, *The Mobilization of the Intellect: French Scholars and Writers during the Great War* (Cambridge, MA, 1996).
45. Winter, *Sites of Memory*, 15–17, 133–7; Becker, *Monuments aux morts*, 93–102; Jean-Pierre Blin, 'Le vitrail commémoratif de la Grande Guerre: les catholiques françaises et le culte du souvenir', in Chaline (ed.), *Chrétiens dans la première guerre mondiale*, 167–96.
46. Ellen Badone, *The Appointed Hour: Death, Worldview, and Social Change in Brittany* (Berkeley, CA, 1989). See also Yves Lambert, *Dieu change en Bretagne* (Paris, 1985).
47. Badone, *The Appointed Hour*, 72, 214.
48. *Ibid.*, 241.
49. *Ibid.*, 211.
50. For a more extended comparison of these funerals see Thomas Kselman, 'Religion as an enduring theme in French culture', in Frank Brinkhuis and Sascha Talmor (eds.), *Memory, History and Critique: European Identity at the Millennium*, Proceedings of the 6th International ISSEI Conference at the University for Humanist Studies, Utrecht, the Netherlands, 1996 (Cambridge, MA, 1997).
51. Pierre Pean, *Une Jeunesse française: François Mitterand, 1934–1947* (Paris, 1994); Catherine Nay, *The Black and the Red: François Mitterand and the Story of an Ambition* (San Diego, CA, 1987); Robert Solé, 'La République à Notre Dame', *Le Monde*, 13 January 1996.
52. Cardinal Lustiger, 'Le respect du mystère de son existence', *Le Monde*, 12 January 1996.
53. René Rémond, *Le Catholicisme français et la société politique* (Paris, 1995), 175–97.

54. 'La République à Notre Dame'.
55. Steven Englund, 'The ghost of nation past', *The Journal of Modern History*, 64 (1992), 299–320.
56. *Le Monde*, 12 May 1994 reports that 67 per cent of the French still identify themselves as Catholic, compared to 23 per cent who say they are without religion.
57. Colleen McDannell, *Material Christianity: Religion and Popular Culture in America* (New Haven, CT, 1995).

10 The impact of technology on Catholicism in France (1850–1950)

Michel Lagrée

Who is to be believed? The French philosopher Henri Bergson, in one of his last major works at the beginning of the 1930s, composed an emphatic eulogy on mechanisation, at the very time when the spread of Taylorism and the industrial depression were leading many intellectuals to call it into question. He made no hesitation in concluding that 'Spiritualism leads to mechanisation.'[1] He meant by this that technical progress, by liberating humanity for the first time in its history, from the obsessive 'fear of not feeding its hunger', allowed it, by escaping from a constrained and inevitable asceticism, to reach finally genuine spiritual experience. Conversely, throughout France in the 1950s, the chaplains of the rural Catholic 'Action Group' were raising the alarm as agricultural mechanisation reached the French countryside. They may have read Bergson during their studies at the seminary, but their view was totally the opposite.[2] In their opinion the 'technical mentality' went towards accelerating the breakdown of traditional parish civilisation.

Comparing the fields of religion and technology inevitably leads to the following type of contradiction: some hope to find in technical progress a starting-point for a new type of evangelisation, while on the contrary others see in it a fearful dissolution of ancient Christian civilisation. The issue is too vast for an overview to be easily taken. We shall start from a precise point in time and space: France during the century which runs from 1850 to 1950. It is therefore a place in which the culture is predominantly Catholic which will be studied, and French Protestantism will be deliberately ignored.[3] This place of Catholic culture will be studied from the middle of the nineteenth century, when industrialisation was taking off, with a perceptible advance in Great Britain, but also in neighbouring Belgium, until the middle of the twentieth century, when the combined effects of 'technoscience' and postwar economic growth created, this time in line with the rest of western Europe, a new acceleration of change. Clearly one must be cautious before extrapolating on issues relating specifically to France, as much from the point of view of technological progress as of the religious context. First the religious effects of technological change will be measured, before determining in the context of this volume the answers put forward by the key religious players. In both cases, the impossibility of a single-stranded conclusion will be confirmed: it is rather a tension, or indeed a dialectical contradiction, that technological change introduces into the religious domain.

The effects of technical change on religion

Two forms, or degrees, must be marked out when examining the effects of technical change on religion. First-degree effects, that is to say those with a direct impact on religious acts and rituals, have not always received the attention they deserve: these should therefore be distinguished from the more commonly recognised 'technical mentality' which can be seen as emanating from second-degree effects. A sufficiently detailed study which takes into account certain details of secondary appearance in fact leads one to see the impact of technical innovation on the religious experience itself, even in the act of worship and the liturgy. Some innovations are clearly beneficial, in that they bring, as they do to other human activities, a material ease which is the very principle behind technical innovation. Others are problematic, as technical innovation goes against the fabric of symbols which defines a ritualistic religion such as Catholicism.[4]

Modern techniques, especially for the general public, are embodied in means of communication, in both senses of the term: the physical displacement of people and the conveying of messages. On the first point historians and sociologists specialising in religion agree that in the domain of Catholicism the act which has best survived present-day erosion is the pilgrimage, even if it is has been considerably transformed. Forms of overland transport first of all (railways, coaches and cars), and then air transport, have contributed to a sharp focusing of the places visited for pilgrimages. While numerous local pilgrimages passed into a state of disuse from the middle of the nineteenth century, the great shrines, particularly those devoted to the Virgin Mary, attracted growing crowds.[5] At Sainte-Anne d'Auray, the railways and passenger trucks, familiar to the area since 1914–18, unloaded 200,000 people per year at the beginning of the 1920s;[6] after 1960, the airport at Tarbes-Lourdes became the major provincial means of access by air. However, ease of transport caused one essential aspect of pilgrimage of the past to disappear: the journey. Whereas before, the pilgrimage began as one stepped outside one's front door, and the route itself was part of the *univers consacré*,[7] from then on it began when stepping off the train.

Conversely, the clergy welcomed the disappearance of profane temptations, distractions and licentiousness – particularly among the young – which were traditionally associated with the pilgrim's journey: a pilgrim's train with its schedules to be respected and its hymns sung in the carriages took something from both military transport and the religious service.[8]

In either a spectacular or surreptitious way technical innovation modified the way in which the religious message was both transmitted and received. This was the case for organs used to accompany the religious service. From the 1880s electricity considerably overcame transmission problems in large organ cases;[9] and above all allowed a certain democratisation of the instrument, enabling it to be operated in churches which until that time had been without one. Around 1930 some people even thought that the electric organ would become commonplace in churches,[10] but the Roman authorities, when consulted, objected on several occasions to an instrument with such strong connotations – exactly like its pneumatic ancestor to begin with – of the corrupt pleasures of entertainment.[11] Even more spectacular was the association of the microphone and loudspeaker which was to transform the practical conditions of preaching. This first became obvious for open-air events at which those who experienced the technology soon became dependent upon it, and so the need for electric address systems was rapid and irreversible. Inside the churches, the pulpit was a sort of balcony above the congregation, representing the hierarchical and vertical superiority of the priest.[12] The microphone which lay preachers also came to use after the church council reforms meant a *rapprochement*, while chrome instruments and the mass of wires around the altar may have somewhat trivialised the event.

The benefits reaped by French Catholicism from the use of means of communication and the media need not be emphasised.[13] This was first of all the case for printing on all scales; at one extreme the abbé Migne's Montrouge printing houses were among the largest industrial presses at the time of 1850; while at the other extreme, the huge number of diocesan printers often made up a key element of the profession in provincial towns. At the same time the periodical or daily press was developing. After the French episcopate's bitter experience with *L'Univers*, an Ultramontane war machine against the Gallican bishops,[14] *La Croix* and its local editions moved towards the concept of the *bon journal* around the end of the nineteenth century, but did not reach a sufficient readership in comparison with other national publications. In the provinces, only western Brittany with *L'Ouest-Eclair* founded in 1899 and going on to become *Ouest-France* in 1944, today's foremost national daily paper in terms of circulation, represented a real success in this field. The spread of Catholic magazines starting with the *Pèlerin* was more satisfactory. The remnants of this are still highly visible with the success of the periodicals edited by the Catholic publishing houses, even if they display a respectable neutrality aimed at two key 'targets': the elderly on the one hand, and children and young people on the other. The development of radio was gladly accepted by Catholic opinion because of its favourable view of its two pious inventors, the Frenchman Branly and the Italian Marconi. Challenged at first by the Roman authorities,[15] the broadcasting of services was finally accepted in the 1950s, meeting a clear need on the part of those housebound in all sorts of ways: the disabled, mothers of young children, etc. Nevertheless, as with television later on, the rise of radio was the cause of repeated protest. On the one hand religious broadcasts were always judged to be too self-effacing, and on the other hand there were complaints about the immorality of numerous irreverent programmes. Audiovisual media, however, gave the Roman authorities an unexpected means of communication. The use of radio took off under Pius XI, allowing everyone to receive the *urbi et orbi* blessing, along with the indulgence.[16] Pius XII brought radio messages almost up to the status of encyclicals, ignoring borders in the middle of the Second World War. On the evening of 6 June 1954, as part of one of the first Eurovision programmes, he addressed television viewers in Italian, French, German and Dutch.[17] He was thus giving a new meaning to Pentecost, and initiating a practice which was to be perfected by his successors: the importance of television in John Paul II's papal work is a perfect example of this.

When put to effective use for pastoral work, modern technology could, however, prove embarrassing when it came into competition or even conflict with the realities of religious symbolism, in particular those of the scriptures: liturgical services, in their framework, setting, acts and words are strongly marked by references to the scriptures. And this stood in clear opposition to the changes at work in the world outside religion. Whether it was a matter of altar cloths or even the sacred clothes and albs of those celebrating the mass, it was linen, or hemp in extreme circumstances, which had to be used, and from 1819 Pope Pius VII stood in the way of the new fabric cotton. But right throughout the nineteenth century the calls to order had to be increased, in the face of the irresistible economic and psychological pressure working in favour of the textile which symbolised the Industrial Revolution. Now this was incompatible with the minutely detailed instructions given to Aaron and his sons (Leviticus 16:4; Exodus 28:5 and 42) or with the symbolism of Revelation 19:8. Linen was the product of domestic spinning and weaving, that is to say 'honest sedentary work', which was considered greatly superior to 'the best product obtained through the science of mechanics';[18] its piety and whiteness were obtained 'by hard work and repeated soaking; in the same way that work and mortification achieved and perfected the saintliness of the priest's attire'.[19] If nowadays we still evoke in a broad archaeological perspective the linen ritual dress of the ancient Egyptians and Romans, compared with that of the Jews, it is always with the belief that only pre-industrial material has the authenticity which makes it suitable for its purpose.[20]

It should be remembered that the instructions given to the great priest Aaron concerned not only liturgical clothes, but also building materials for the shrine: the arch, the altar, the framework, etc. (Exodus 25 and 26). Industrial technology began to supply materials which were literally without precedent, the first of

which was reinforced concrete. The first example of the use of reinforced concrete for a religious building in France was Saint-Jean de Montmartre church
(1894–1904), which was soon followed by other more prestigious projects:
Oran cathedral (1908) and particularly Notre-Dame du Raincy by the Perret
brothers (1922), which was a real manifesto in favour of the new material. It
is noticeable, however, that architects, and even more so their sponsors, did
not use it for long and even when they did it was with a relative timidity. It
was as if concrete would have seemed unworthy of its function. It was disliked
because of its utilitarian appearance with its overly strong connotations of large
buildings used for industrial purposes. As with cotton, it was difficult to take to
'a rebel material created by intelligence and shaped with a tool'.[21] Rome had
made no mistake in this respect and had decreed in 1909 that a church built from
cement could only be consecrated if it had been embedded with natural stone
in the places where the bishop undertook the anointing with holy oil.[22] This is
a powerful symbolism which came to strengthen the tradition of Gallo-Roman
building work.[23] Stone was the symbol of Jesus Christ as the foundation of the
church (Luke 20:17; I Corinthians 10:4). Now, the very time that industry was
providing new materials coincided with the rediscovery of the medieval liturgy
and the growth in liturgical symbolism, as the following lines from Durand de
Mende's 'rationale' illustrate:[24]

On this base the foundation of the apostles and prophets has been placed: the walls are
the Jews and the gentiles, the four corners of the world called to the faith, the stones, of
different sizes and smoothness, represent the faithful with their various merits; finally the
cement which binds them together, is charity, through which the members of Christian
society become one in heaven, in purgatory and on earth.[25]

It took the *Mediator Dei* encyclical of 1948 to bring about the idea that 'modern
works when well harmonised with to-day's materials should not all be despised
and rejected out of prejudice'.

    Even more heated debates arose concerning the introduction of new sources
of light into churches, as this touched on one of the fundamental forms of
symbolism. It is well known that close links exist between the spiritual and
theological importance of light (*lumen de lumine*) and its physical reality in the
place of worship, through the various forms of lighting. Technical innovation
emerged in three forms. The first concerned the oil lamp having to burn permanently in front of the holy sacrament according to the ancient order recalled
by the council of Trent. The renewed taste for allegorisation provoked numerous mystical commentaries on this lamp in the nineteenth century: the flame
symbolised Christ, light of the world, the heat his love, the consumption the
sacrifice of Calvary and of the altar, as well as the vigilance of the church.[26]
Cardinal Landriot reminded everyone that the oil extracted from the olive represented the perfection of the holy spirit: oil from the lamps of wise virgins

or oil penetrating substances it touches is like the holy spirit entering into just souls.[27] Olive oil, however, fell into competition, because of its high price, with other vegetable oils on the market, which were reluctantly allowed by Rome in 1864, under the control of the bishops. Petrol was even accepted, but only as a very last resort. While the petrol lamp swept through homes, for some people it held 'great diabolical significance; since the events of May 1871 petrol has become, particularly in France, an object of horror'.[28] During the First World War the difficulties in getting supplies and the rise in prices favoured petrol more and more, as well as electric lamps, which were provisionally accepted and only in extreme cases (*ultimo loco*) from 1916 onwards. This went against a whole series of earlier decisions forbidding the placing of gas or electric lamps on the altar.[29] There ensued a significant loss in symbolism of the altar lamp, about which the following was written: 'the vulgar appearance it has been given for a number of years in too many churches takes away its charm and poetry. It is no more than a "pigeon" lamp with nothing to distinguish it from those seen in our kitchens.'[30] The acceptance granted in 1916 was reiterated in March 1942, still as a temporary measure and with regard to the wartime circumstances (*praesenti hello perdurante*);[31] it was repealed in the decree of 18 August 1949. This was something which did not prevent electric lighting from being maintained to the present day, as can be seen in many churches, 'for reasons of cleanliness and convenience as much as economy'.[32] The influence of the common material culture finally proved the strongest.

Similar problems emerged with liturgical candles as a result of progress in chemistry and the industrialisation of the practical and cheap stearic candle from the 1830s onwards. The stearic candle passed quickly from homes to the altars of humble churches to such an extent that candlemakers in Marseilles alerted Rome in 1839 and the rules were strictly recalled in 1843 and reiterated in 1878.[33] Once again modern industry was clashing with the liturgical system of symbols. Candles which are consumed, likened to Christians carrying out good works,[34] had to be made from beeswax, as laid down in the prayer of the Easter candle blessing (*Exultet*) or the prayers of the purification of the Virgin. 'Ancient scholars' saw a parallel with the virginity of bees, the purity of the substance 'drawn from the finest sugar of the flowers' and the 'conception of the saviour in Mary's chaste breast'. On the other hand, stearin, extracted from animal fat, has something squalid about it, 'a symbol of the flesh and earthly instincts'.[35] However, economic pressure led to a growth in the use of stearin, either in the additional candles above the number required for the liturgy, or in carefully prepared quantities with wax.[36]

Finally to everybody's relief and acknowledging a fraud which was no doubt widespread, in December 1904 the Congregation of Rites relaxed the rules considerably. Only the Easter candle and at least two liturgical candles had to be made from wax, or contain at least a major amount of it.

The third form of liturgical light is the actual lighting of churches. It was particularly in America, with its great love of modernity, that there was an immediate temptation to introduce modern lighting, such as gas and electricity, as soon as they were available, but reservations remained strong over in the old continent. Rome totally forbade gas lighting for altars.[37] Once again symbolism was the cause:

Everything has a meaning in the church. Gas would not have one. To give it a place the paving and tomb stones would have to be broken, the pillars cut, the corners clipped from the chapters and prominence given to profane devices . . . A gas lit church looks like a cafe, a wise peasant said to me one day. The sense of religion was alive in him and he understood that anything without a special mark, an ecclesiastical mark, had to be kept away from the church.[38]

Towards the end of the century electricity became an even greater rival to gas lighting. Rome gave its views on three occasions,[39] recalling two fundamental principles: electricity was forbidden on altars, but allowed for lighting naves providing it was only used in a functional way, *ad depellendas tenebras*, with moderate power and giving no theatrical effect. Electricity in fact suffered from having been used in its early days, at the time of arc lamps and autonomous generators, in places of pleasure such as the opera and theatres. The very clear 'no' given to the bishop of Los Angeles in 1908 regarding the propriety of strings of lights around statues or in the altar vases served as a marvellous illustration of the refusal of a baroque use of electric lighting, the very one which was flaunted in the streets and shops, that is to say the outside and profane world. The numerous liberties taken with this prohibition, as can be seen today in very many churches, can be added to the long list of popular revolts against ecclesiastic instruction.[40] The austere measures imposed for lighting were less and less understood by the faithful who were perfectly well accustomed to artificial light. But this development undoubtedly cost a loss in meaning. In pre-industrial civilisation, which was careful not to waste light, churches at nightfall were shadowy places full of mystery, about which Barbey d'Aurevilly has left us a striking evocation.[41] At that time the liturgical value of light, even without pouring in the esotericism of the allegorists, was immediate, which is no longer the case today.

If today natural candles have replaced spring mounted devices and electric candelabras on the altars in a move back towards simplicity, they often shine surrounded by more and more sophisticated electric lighting which opposes their subtle and flickering glow in the supreme flood from projectors and fluorescent tubes. Could this be a metaphor for the position of religion in the face of technology?

Seen from this angle the question leads to the secondary effects of technical change, that is to say, on religious awareness in general. These effects are contradictory: if we go back to Max Weber's categories they can be seen to contribute as much to the re-enchantment of the world as to its disenchantment. It is often by means of technology that the spirit of the supernatural and of wonder is introduced into the world today. This is clear from the flowery rhetoric which inevitably accompanied the great technological breakthroughs while they maintained an element of novelty, before being assigned to routine: the railways around 1840–50, electricity around 1880–90, the conquest of space around 1950–60, and the Internet of today. The *mirabilia* of modern times were those of technology, Louis Figuier affirmed.[42] Metaphors came spontaneously. Factories were compared to cathedrals, 'temples' were raised to industry, and the great exhibitions were like a new form of pilgrimage. Electricity became a sort of magic fairy, infinitely allegorised by publicity posters. For their part, the preachers were not fooled by it, using it as an apologetic argument:

Electricity is a force which is, at present, totally unknown to us, even if we can see the visible effects or phenomena it produces. We therefore address the positivist in these terms, regarding electricity: how can it be! you believe in this force because you can see its effects, yet you do not believe in the universal cause, of which you yourself and everything around you are the effects! . . . Electricity is no more known to you, nor visible to your eyes, as a cause or force than God . . . Be logical therefore.[43]

The harnessing of nuclear energy was like a blow in the very heart of the structure of matter; with the background of the Cold War and the race for strategic supremacy arousing apocalyptic fears.[44] These were to have repercussions later on when they rebounded on its civil applications.

The almost religious aspect surrounding new techniques often rested on the mystery and secrecy reserved for the initiated only. The exclusivity of the secrets of manufacture and implementation could lead to a sort of esotericism. Before the iron and steel industry became truly scientific by incorporating laboratory chemistry methods around the end of the nineteenth century, discoveries made by trial and error were jealously guarded. Visitors to the Krupp factories around 1860 came away with the description of a very cut-off universe which seemed removed from the rest of the world. All things being equal, the very first computer scientists of the 1940s and 1950s could be compared to a real 'caste', jealously defending their position as initiates. The initial resistance of this group to the introduction of an adapted vocabulary which was more accessible to the uninitiated and which replaced the highly obscure 'technical jargon' cannot be explained only on economic grounds. Moreover, the slowness in developing this vocabulary can be attributed to the almost religious attachment, known as 'théologie de la programmation' (the creed of information technology) displayed by these specialists.[45] The division between these initiates and the general public must have aided the spread of irrational fears, owing as much to the possibility of a generalised social control by machines as to that of the replacement of workers by automatic systems. Conversely, the democratisation of microchip technology and the creation of user-friendly interfaces was presented as the access route for the great majority to a 'numerical Nirvana'.[46] In this lies what seems to be a recurring theme, a sort of spontaneous religion based on technology. The philosophy of Saint-Simon gave a good illustration of this at the beginning of our period; and the current debate about 'cyberspace' is full of echoes of this.[47]

However, the action of technical change in the opposite direction, that is to say in the direction of Weberian disenchantment (*Weltentzauberung*) was regularly denounced by Catholic clerics, calling it 'the technical spirit' or 'technical mentality'. The majority of French priests, spread out for the most part in rural areas, with few in the towns, and even fewer in the industrial suburbs, remained for a long time out of touch with manufacturing realities and their religious effects, which have been covered on numerous occasions and which will not be examined here.[48] It was when mechanisation reached their familiar world made up of countryfolk that it revealed all of its consequences to them. It should be remembered that the French countryside, particularly the regions of traditional Christian practices such as western Brittany or areas south of the Loire, were affected quite a bit later than the Anglo-Saxon countries and Germany. The feeling of change was all the greater, coinciding as it did with the intense debate on pastoral care led by the clergy from the 1940s. As a result of its negative effects on the need for agricultural manpower and the attractive development of urban employment, mechanisation was given as the principal cause of the exodus of countryfolk to the towns, which were judged to be full of dangers for morals and religious practice, as well as the accompanying devitalisation of rural parishes.[49] Mechanisation tended to free agricultural workers from natural constraints which had formerly been so burdensome. Nature, it was said, was omnipresent in traditional culture, its events forming the path to God. Life, death, storms, sun, etc. led to the conclusion that 'there is someone up above'. Machines and chemical products led to the pursuit of efficiency at all costs: 'It's good because it produces, it works hard, it brings in a profit.' This efficiency was now merely the product of rationalism. 'Holy water is replaced by DDT.'[50] The fatalism of earlier times was opposed by an almost limitless optimism, with progress constituting an irreversible and infinite course: 'One day or another we will get there . . . we can make anything now.'[51] Machinery aroused a real interest, if not a fascination, feeding in particular all the conversations of the impatient young, who took a different view from their more cautious elders, especially women. Let us add at this point that forcing countryfolk to equip themselves with technical or even scientific knowledge contributed to the reduction in the traditional superiority of the priest and cleric as regards the *rusticus*.

By introducing more capital into agricultural work, modern technology ended up as a race to pay off debts. While the countryfolk of earlier times were prepared to hoard their money, they now threw themselves into endless investments at the cost of getting into debts which would drastically change their relationship with both money and the future. There was an increase in inquiries into the abusive practice of Sunday working, which had been traditionally tolerated when bad weather threatened, but could not be when it was caused by the need to pay for combine-harvesters which tended to blot out the Sunday landmark during the summer months.[52] 'I know of farms where they work day and night using tractors fitted with lights, and where the wife herself drives the machine.'[53] Paradoxically, while machines were created to lighten the workload, they in fact created new constraints, in particular for family manpower which was called upon more and more, and caused the disappearance of salaried agricultural workers, and the decline of co-operative spirit.[54] The conclusion was evident: technology 'exalted for itself and taken away from the context of all around it, becomes harmful and disrupts the existing order rather than actually improving it'.[55]

Technical change – a blessing or a curse?

During the great exhibition of 1855 in Paris a fairly bitter polemic arose between the democratic and anti-clerical newspaper *Le Siècle* and *L'Univers*, the instrument of the Ultramontane Catholics.[56] Broadly speaking, *Le Siècle* accused the Ultramontane Catholics of an anti-industrial and anti-technological obscurantism, and of wanting to take France back to the middle ages. The fact that *L'Univers* replied on two fronts, first against *Le Siècle* and second against clearly favourable leanings towards industry displayed at the same time by *Le Correspondant* and *L'Ami de la Religion*, publications of liberal Catholicism, distinctly illustrated the existence of two Catholic attitudes towards technical change. On reflection, these two attitudes had deep-rooted theological backgrounds stemming from Christian antiquity, and had repercussions which can still be felt today.[57]

Louis Veuillot, the uncontested leader of the Ultramontanes, was a tireless denigrator of modernity in all its forms: political, moral, literary, etc., but it was probably his strong views against the technical innovations of the Industrial Revolution which struck the greatest number of the public. Using the paradigm of 'La Science' and his imaginary hero Coquelet, struck dumb with admiration whenever he comes across technological 'miracles', Veuillot attacked his sworn enemy, the liberal and Voltairean bourgeoisie. He asserted that he had more dread of the destruction wrought by the 'blinkered polytechnic' than the attacks by small groups of anti-clericals: in fact, he believed that by proclaiming the demiurgic power of the industrial man, 'decent people' would end up believing that the creator was no longer God but the French Academy. He admired the eternal Italy, which had been miraculously saved from the stains and contamination of the northern countries thanks to the wisdom of the papal government. In an almost obsessional fashion, two types of object came in for his anger, those which exactly embodied the new industrial age for the public: steam engine transport and the electric telegraph. The railways were accused of ending travel carried out at the traditional walking pace, and in particular at a pilgrim's pace, going from 'church tower to church tower', with the time to pray and enjoy the rapture of the countryside. Modern man, hurried and rushed, deprived himself of the time for contemplation and the encounter with God. 'We're stuck on the locomotive. Oh no! I couldn't possibly condone this violent machine! I shall never like its smoke, its wailing, its brutal course across the torn earth. I shall never be happy to look at the uniform automatons who serve the monsters.' The railways meant being shut away, the tyranny of the timetable, and the disappearance of the sociability that went with the stagecoaches and post houses:[58] the traveller was reduced to the level of a parcel and number, which, for Veuillot, constituted the best metaphor for his hated democracy.[59] Of course, the steamboat undeniably eased the bishops' journey to Rome[60] – and Veuillot's journey too, but he saw it only as an ugly engine, 'long, black and having neither masts, sails nor ropes. – Its rigging, as brutal as it is, is made of iron chains. In this modern mechanisation all we see are iron teeth and iron chains', as opposed to the sailing ships of earlier times, 'Whose sails filled out in the breeze like breasts swollen with milk'.[61] Even though the first words transmitted by the electric telegraph between Washington and Baltimore in 1844 were 'The Words of God', Veuillot remembered only the commercial and police uses for this invention:

Coquelet adds: Imagine an eloquent priest: he preaches on the same day in three or four towns. His speech, taken down in shorthand, sent by telegraph and then immediately multiplied by photography, rings out over the four corners of the earth . . . And you reject that? Your view on this matter is that your thoughts travel at the speed of lightning. Only the stock exchange and the police travel this way. Freedom is hung from these posts.[62]

It is true that the state's monopoly on telecommunications in France following the ruling of 1837 had unfortunate connotations in a dictatorial regime such as the Second Empire. And Veuillot, *laudator temporis acti*, exalted the ancient 'sacred telegraph', whether it was the apparitions of angels in the Bible or, more prosaically, the call of church bells, which was perfectly clear to all, particularly the poor and uneducated, to whom God's message had first been addressed.[63] This was enough for *Le Siècle* to imagine, under the title 'A funeral pyre for the industrialists', a Veuillot-style parody in which the court of the inquisition judged and condemned the representatives from the different sectors of technical innovation.[64] It was fair enough, given the success of *L'Univers* and

Veuillot's books among the lower clergy, but it dismissed a whole current of opposing Catholic opinion, which was active in the ecclesiastical *establishment* and which was evident from the numerous declarations by the bishops: in their mandates and pastoral letters, and above all in lending their presence to the blessing of ships, railway lines and urban developments.[65] Many prelates under the July Monarchy and the Second Empire never stopped praising the new technologies. 'The religious spirit and non-progressive spirit' should not be confused; it was no longer the time of Veuillot's beloved medieval mysteries but the time of modern society.[66] High in the pulpit of Notre-Dame, Fr Felix solemnly challenged the notion that Christianity was 'industry's curse' or even 'anathema to material progress'.[67] Although close to Ultramontane ideas, abbé Moigno developed a busy career as a scientific and technical populariser, imitating Figuier and Flammarion.[68] A new theme was flourishing: nineteenth-century man was beginning to exploit the treasures hidden by God since the time of creation. In a certain sense it was a new type of miracle.[69] Monseigneur Plantier, the bishop of Nîmes, marvelled before the new mechanisms created by man: although without eyes or hands they seemed equipped with a vision and subtlety to facilitate manufacturing: 'it could be said that a single soul runs through all these parts'.[70] Monseigneur Landriot (La Rochelle) was not far from thinking that, unlike at the time of creation, God was in some way stepping aside a little to give man the lead role.[71] It was the blessings of the railways which gave the bishops the chance to use rhetoric which was poles apart from that used by Veuillot:[72]

The railway is, in the material order of things, the image and complement of intelligence. Intelligence acts as steam in the order of ideas, and while the vulgar drags its feet along the torturous paths of dialectic subtlety, intelligence travels in leaps and, having arrived at the pinnacle, sees everything with a single glance. This is just like the railway: while the poor coachman still struggles with his mount's harness, as soon as the carriage leaves it arrives . . . In earlier times, intelligence may have dared, but its arm moved slowly; today its lever has a type of power which seems to transport it to several places at once: it has something of God's power which does everything at the same time: *creavit omnia simul.*[73]

Moreover, the occasion of the blessing allowed for the evocation of danger, which was always present despite the engineers' talent, and which only divine protection could keep at bay. Even though the ideas of Saint-Simon had been opposed in their time as expressions of a truly secular religion aspiring to overthrow the Christian metaphysics, many of its economic and technical premises had been preserved, albeit in adapted forms. Many bishops saw in the railways the promise of economic growth, of the distribution of cheap goods for all, of the bringing together of nations, of peace. In these early years of the railways, before the mass rural exodus to the towns, and before the massive spread of the irreligious popular press, in the opposite direction into the provinces, the prelates did not see any threat to the faith or morality in the new means of transport. On the contrary, they believed they would facilitate the spread of the evangelical message.

In their eyes it was the same for the electric telegraph, which was, moreover, closely linked in general to the railway line:

May the electric spark, on its invisible wing, instantly transfer thought from one end of the universe to the other: may steam be harnessed to our chariots to give them the speed of lightning; angels of peace will use these discoveries to bring the good news of salvation right into the furthest regions and to work for consummation of great Catholic unity.[74]

In an era so clearly fascinated with allegories a new form of exegesis was appearing. This was the search for biblical quotations containing some sort of prophetic announcement of the realities of the new age, which could then be thrown into the blessings. In its accuracy Leviathan's evocation (Job 41:4–26) seemed to Monseigneur Planner to describe locomotives and steam engines 'in advance'. Whether Veuillot liked it or not, speed of transport was recommended in Ecclesiastes (32:10–11) for the same reason that Monseigneur Landriot was in favour of it.[75] Psalms 104 (3 and 4) and 18 (8–13) were readily invoked, particularly for these 'messages on the wind' produced by the telegraph.

Although these two waves of religious thought, one hostile and the other in favour of technical innovations, are especially evident around the middle of the nineteenth century their lineage is ancient and they have their successors to the present day. Since the times of pagan antiquity in the heart of cynical stoic philosophy there was a tendency to value natural things at the expense of the technical artifact. Certain church elders, influenced by stoicism,[76] inherited these prejudices. Tertullian thus denounced the dyeing of fabrics as falsified and in some way 'adulterous':

God does not like what he has not produced himself. Do you think he could not have ordered the flocks to be born purple or sky blue? If he has not done so it is because he did not want it like that; one does not have the right to make what God did not want. That which has not come from God, the creator of nature, is therefore not good by nature. It should be understood, therefore, that these things come from the devil, the falsifier of nature.

In the same way Saint Ambrose went on to denounce human *industria*, that is, any effort made to obtain artificially anything other than that found in nature. Innocent III was saddened that 'substance became an accident and nature was changed into art' and people acted 'as if man's artifice surpassed the creator's art'.[77] This was very similar to the arguments against Coquelet and 'Science' put forward by Veuillot, who would have been brought up on the Church Fathers. Traces of this attitude can even be seen in certain nineteenth-century inventors, who were so careful to imitate nature to the letter.[78]

In the stoicism of antiquity, however, there existed an opposing tradition which valued technical activity. Panetius of Rhodes (first century BCE) placed the 'brutish nature' of providence in opposition to a 'second nature' created by the hands of man. His pupil Posidonios of Apamea wrote a lot on technology, and Cicero, Posidonios' disciple, popularised this eulogy on man transforming the universe.[79] Cicero was used by Christian authors, and in particular for commenting on the book of Genesis (1:28). St Augustine's apology for the role of providence in man's God-given capacity to transform the world rationally provides us with the source of numerous bishops' speeches in the nineteenth century:

What marvels has human industry not achieved in the fabric of clothes, in the construction of buildings? What progress in agriculture and navigation? So much imagination, so much perfection in these vases of every shape, in this multitude of statues and paintings. . . . And then there are so many types of poisons, weapons and machines invented by man against man, so many remedies and forms of aid created to defend and separate human life.[80]

The privilege given to the *ars* – in which Tertullian denounced the *artifex*, valuing man's competence and skill – resulted in medieval developments in the mechanical arts (Hugues de Saint-Victor, Saint Bonaventure). Saint Thomas went one step further by breaking with the tradition of Plato and Aristotle regarding the creation: human action is an imitation, or indeed part of God's creative activity. This shaped the nineteenth-century bishops' declarations regarding the 'miracles' carried out by man with divine authorisation.

It would be useful to examine in detail the way in which these two attitudes have persisted to the present day, but we shall have to settle for a broad sketch concentrating on just a few of the milestones. It is true that once the first Industrial Revolution was over there was less discussion of innovation, owing to the fact that most people were fairly accustomed to it. This phenomenon was accentuated by the decline in public blessings, at least in France.[81] The religious tendency towards 'technophilosophy' was again illustrated at the turn of the nineteenth century by Ernest Hello, who, turning upside down the usual views on the Enlightenment, not without paradox, could almost see the technical miracles of the nineteenth century as a sort of revenge on the incredulity of the eighteenth century:

Imagine how those of the eighteenth century would have laughed if somebody had told them about a railway. Imagine how rational men would have got together, enjoyed jokes and taken satisfaction from mocking it! Imagine the tranquillity of their irony and the entirely good faith with which they would have scoffed at the madmen, the same madmen who would have said: it will be. And what about the mountains, the eighteenth-century philosopher would have objected with the insolent pleasure of self-satisfaction. We shall go through them, the madman would have replied. I can hear the roar of laughter, the mad laughter of the philosopher.[82]

As for photography, about which Veuillot held such a poor view – despite his friendship with Nadar[83] – for Hello it was wholly appropriate for the era of the busy man, enabling him to extract his memories 'from the authority of time and death'. Even better was the behaviour of the photographic plate, which required total cleanliness, while the invisible image that had to be *revealed* in the meditative obscurity evoked human conscience itself.

It was around the 1950s that a Catholic discussion on technology re-emerged in force at a time coinciding with the arrival of 'technoscience' and the reign of a pope with encyclopedic curiosity, Pius XII. The latter gave his views on the subject whenever he could, and this was immediately echoed throughout the Catholic world. For example he made the most of the congresses held in Rome by professionals from various sectors, who were in turn, and with great eclecticism, gratified by a short speech. One day it would be linen and hemp producers[84] then on another day metal casters,[85] and on another radiologists.[86] The official designation of patron saints for new industries provided other opportunities: Saint Gabriel, who had already been promised as patron of radio and television in 1951 (as it was he who announced the redemption to mankind), was called to give a special blessing for the signals division of the Italian army.[87] This curiosity rubbed off on the French clergy and could be seen to grow in the magazines written for them, such as *L'Ami du Clergé*, and in the well-informed popularised articles on science and technology. The death of Pius XII brought this phase of optimism to a relatively sharp halt. Paul VI came back to more traditional views on issues relating to science and technology, particularly taking up the theme of the discrepancy between technological advances and the moral development of humanity.[88] The shift in interests was confirmed during John Paul II's papacy, when priority was given to reflections on technology which concentrated heavily on ethics: on the one hand nuclear weapons, and on the other and more especially, medical techniques affecting procreation, bringing the old question of nature and artifact back to the fore.

There is a link here with the other tendency, which can be qualified as ascetic/ecological, and which continued to be expressed throughout the period. There is no need to limit oneself to the well-known anti-modern commentators such as Huysmans and Bloy. For example, here is Henry du Roure, a known *silloniste*, who went explicitly against the views of his time on the subject of electricity '*Electric*! A hard, dry, abrupt, cramped word like the thing it expresses . . . All this is more serious than one might think, and the sociologists ought to study carefully the social utility of candles and the destructive power of modern inventions. With its stoves, heaters and electricity, sacrilegious progress has put out the flame.' As there is no longer a hearth in the proper sense, du Roure continued, the family is breaking down. Years ago, when night had fallen, children experienced the fear of the supernatural and the world beyond, whereas now the electric switch has made them 'omnipotent dispensers of day and night, and the whole of their little person is full of un-bearable self-importance'.[89] There was a decisive shift later on, linked to the influence of Hindu mysticism, with Lanza del Vasto and the community of the Ark. This heralded the flourishing, which was especially evident in the 1970s, of new Christian communities with an emphasis on returning to nature, the only guarantee of truth, including the religious one.[90] This leads on to the religious element in the huge ecology movement, whose history clearly goes beyond the scope of this study. For his part, Jacques Ellul, the prolific writer of original essays, developed a concise and well-argued critique of the 'technical system', which he saw as a sort of mechanistic totalitarianism, using its own logic to escape from human control to a greater or lesser extent.[91] It would be useful to study how this viewpoint, which came from the Protestant domain and was probably better understood in Anglo-Saxon countries, was received in French Catholic circles.

As a conclusion to this short and somewhat selective study let us accept that the issue of relationships between technological evolution and religion during the last two centuries has been relatively unexamined.[92] It is quite a different matter for the connected but distinct matters which have provoked numerous works: religion and science, religion and social structures in the industrial world.[93] In the fairly thin body of historical studies linking *homo faber* and *homo religiosus* the most detailed concern the high periods of antiquity and the middle ages.[94] As regards the modern and contemporary era, this relative timidity on the part of historians – and theologians for that matter – can be attributed in the first instance to the autonomy of the two disciplines, taking into account the high degree of specialisation that the history of technology requires in this day and age. Historians of technology pay hardly any attention to religion[95] while historians of religion pay equally little attention to technology.

We therefore risk arriving at too simplistic conclusions as to the effect of technical transformations on religious behaviour – and vice versa. Does the Promethean character of contemporary activities go only and inevitably in the direction of a decline in religion's influence in general, in Christianity in particu-lar, and towards an irresistible rise in spontaneous materialism? It is easy to state that, in many cases, whether it is a matter of towns or the countryside, religious detachment preceded the most radical technical changes. We can see clearly that some cultural zones in southern Europe (the south of the Iberian peninsula, for example), long known for having maintained an obvious technological ar-chaism, are marked by a precocious emancipation from ecclesiastical influence and by a taste for advanced ideas. Conversely, a society like America's, deeply marked by the unbridled pursuit of technical progress, is among those which have remained the most 'religious' to the present day. Many sociological studies show equally that today's various forms of fundamentalism have a following among engineers and technicians from the newest domains, while the heritage of critical examination of the Enlightenment is stronger among the intellectuals who work in the more traditional social or literary fields. Technology is not inevitably the main agent of the world's disenchantment.

NOTES

1. *Les Deux Sources de la morale et de la religion*, in Bergson's *Œuvres* (Paris, 1963), 1238.

2. Examples can be found in the *Cahiers du clergé rural*, in an overview of the pastoral day in the diocese of Séez (1958, no. 201), and another of the Quercy area, diocese of Mantauban 211 (1959).

3. In his 'Ideology and technology. Reactions to modern technology in the Netherlands, 1850–1920', *European History Quarterly*, 22(3) (1992), 383–414, Dick Van Lente gives a far more detailed account of the situation in the Netherlands, based on various denominations.The same applies to Judaism, perhaps even to a greater extent. See *Dictionnaire encyclopédique du Judaïsme*, French trans. of *Encyclopaedia Judaica*, ed. Geoffrey Wigoder (Paris, 1996), 420–2 for the Jewish law (Halakhah) regarding technical modernity.

4. Only in the most recent period have they sporadically been reactivated, in a way which makes the separation of the religious and patrimonial dimensions difficult.

5. Cf. Pierre Nora (ed.), *Les Lieux de mémoire*, 7 vols. (Paris, 1984–92).

6. To a lesser extent, the distribution of baby-carriages from the 1900s made the family pilgrimage considerably easier and should not be omitted: the 'gender history' of pilgrimage remains to be undertaken.

7. The paradigm being represented by the 'Chemins de Saint-Jacques' (de Compostelle). See Alphonse Dupront's *Du sacré: croisades et pèlerinages, images et langages* (Paris, 1987); Jean Chelini and Henri Branthomme, *Les Chemins de Dieu: histoire des pèlerinages chrétiens des origines à nos jours* (Paris, 1982), on the traditional aspects of pilgrimage.

8. In Guingamp (Côtes d'Armor), for the pilgrimage of Notre-Dame de Bon Secours, the railway timetables have shortened the pilgrims' stay and 'the Breton jigs used as a form of relaxation to pass the time during a whole day of waiting have practically disappeared' (*La Semaine Religieuse de Saint-Brieuc*, 25 August 1887).

9. 'Les nouvelles orgues', *Les Etudes Religieuses*, 14 (1891), 146–54.

10. Abbé D. Duret, *Mobilier, vases, objets et vêtements liturgiques* (Paris, 1932) p. 344.

11. Decisions by the Holy Congregation of Rites, 5 Dec. 1938 and 4 Sept. 1939. An advertisement published in *L'Ami du Clergé* asked: 'If the Hammond organ was not an organ, what would the 3000 churches that have one do with it?' (1 October 1939).

12. P. Bruneau, 'The lineaments of an archaeology of Catholicism in the 19th and 20th century', *RAMAGE, Revue Archéologique Moderne et d'Archéologie Générale*, 4 (1986), 141.

13. On the problem of religious communication in general, see Maria-Cristina Carnicella, 'Communication', in René Latourelle and Rina Fisichella (eds.), *Dictionnaire de théologie fondamentale* (Montreal and Paris, 1992).

14. Austin Gough, *Paris and Rome: The Gallican Church and the Ultramontane Campaign, 1848–1853* (Oxford, 1986).

15. The Rescript of the Holy Office of 22 May 1928 mentions an abuse, practised without its consent. On the other hand, while expounding on the value of mass as a 'social and public act of worship', *L'Ami du Clergé* (21 April 1949) compares two periods. 'In the old days [the person far away] would have picked up their prayer-book, read the Lord's Prayer, knelt on the ringing of the bell announcing the elevation . . . From now on, he can pick up his prayer-book and switch on his radio, to tune his own prayer to that of the community more easily', in Decree of the holy penitentiary, 15 June 1939 (*Acta Apostilicae Sedis*, 31 (1939), 277). See Marc Agostino, *Le Pape Pie XI et l'opinion, 1922–1939* (Rome, 1991), on Pius XI's communication policy.
16. See Agostino, *Le Pape Pie XI*.
17. *La Documentation catholique*, 1954, cols. 897–99.
18. *L'Ami de la Religion*, 22 November 1855 (about the Great Exhibition).
19. Abbé J. F. d'Ezerville, *Traité pratique de la tenue des sacristies, des églises et de tout le mobilier liturgique* (Paris, 1886) 40.
20. Jean Aubert, *Des Eglises pour nos assemblées* (Paris, 1982), 51.
21. René Gobiliot, *Architecture moderne et contemporaine* (Paris, 1933), 180. This comment is close to that made by the abbé Duret about iron, wrought by the hammer on an anvil to make entrance gates, as opposed to products shaped and machined: 'the marks left by the tool on the metal bear witness to the worker's efforts and are a sign of probity. The file and the vice are the instruments of the locksmith and fitter' (*Mobilier, Vases*, 340).
22. That is to say the frame, ready to receive the twelve crosses of consecration and the stiles of the main door. Rescript of the Congregation of Rites, 12 November 1909, to the archbishop of Port-au-Prince.
23. Wooden churches could not be consecrated, only blessed (Rescript of the Congregation of Rites to the archbishop of San Salvador, 11 April 1902; cf. *Nouvelle Revue Théologique*, 34 (1902), 406–7). The same applied to iron buildings (Canon 1165, chapter 4 of the 1917 Codex).
24. After being somewhat ignored during the seventeenth and eighteenth centuries, the works of the great liturgist from Languedoc became popular again in the nineteenth century, from Dom Guéranger to Huysmans (see *Guillaume Durand, Evêque de Mende, v.* 1230–96, Texts collected by Pierre-Marie Gy (Paris, 1992)).
25. Abbé F.-J. Penn, *Petit rational liturgique* (Verdun and Paris, 1872), 5.
26. *L'Ami du Clergé*, 19 June 1903 (Supplement).
27. *Sermons à des religieuses*, by Mgr Landriot (Paris, 1881), 525–6.
28. D'Ezerville, *Traité pratique*, 171.
29. Congregation of Rites, 23 February 1916. The fact that Canon 1271 of the 1917 Codex makes no mention of the electric lamp was interpreted as a proof of the purely transient aspect of tolerance. In 1923, the total cost of maintenance of an olive oil lamp was valued at 200 francs, whereas a low-voltage lamp 'costs little or hardly anything at all' (*L'Ami du Clergé*, 25 October 1923).
30. *Prêtre et Apôtre*, October 1921.
31. *Acta Apostolicae Sedis*, 34 (1942), 112.
32. *Catholicisme, hier, aujourd'hui, demain*, vol. VI (Paris, 1967), col. 1749.
33. The missionaries from Oceania were the only ones to be allowed to use whale blubber.
34. A. Lerosey, *Histoire et symbolisme dans la liturgie* (Paris, 1890).

35. D'Ezerville, *Traité pratique*, 181. The *Mélanges Théologiques* (5th series (1851–52), 111) readily use scientific arguments: 'Vitality is a strength which cannot be found in laboratories and which produces effects chemists will never achieve. How many isomerous compounds, made up of the same ingredients and in the same proportions, but which are still so different in aspect and property, do we know? No amount of handling, modelling, amalgamation with other substances could make animal produced stearin into a piece of wax.'

36. Cf. *L'Ami du Clergé*, 11 August 1881.

37. Refusal put to the bishop of Newark (8 March 1879), and again on 16 May 1902.

38. D'Ezerville, *Traité pratique*, quoting the *Traité d'archéologie* of the abbé Pierret.

39. Congregation of Rites, 4 June 1893, decree of 22 November 1907 (*De luce electrica*), of 24 June 1914 (*De lucis electricae usus in ecclesiis*).

40. The ordinance of cardinal vicar of Rome (*Osservatore Romano*, 19 March 1932) clearly lists the branded abuses: luminaries 'shaped into gloires, halos, diadems, rays, hearts, flowers, roses or other similar figurines', 'stands recreating the architectural profile of the church or altar, or in the shapes of stars or other similar figurines'.

41. 'At an atheists' diner', in *Les Diaboliques* (Paris, 1966), 172–3.

42. See, in the same vein, Louis Figuier's *Les Merveilles de la science, ou description populaire des inventions modernes*, 3 vols. (Paris, n.d.).

43. Bergie et Lenoir, *Dictionnaire de théologie appropriée au mouvement intellectuel de la seconde moitié du XIXe siècle* (Paris, 1876), vol. IV.

44. Cf. *L'Ami du Clergé*, 5 June 1947, 30 September 1949, 5 February and 6 March 1952, 9 April, 5 November and 3 December 1953, 3 June 1954.

45. Philippe Breton, *Une Histoire de l'informatique* (Paris, 1990), p. 182.

46. Steven Levy, *La Saga Macintosh* (Paris, 1994), 19. The title of the work by J. Chposky and T. Leonsis is also significant: *Blue Magic: The People, Power and Politics behind the IBM Personal Computer* (New York and London, 1989).

47. Christian Huitema, *Et Dieu créa l'Internet* (Paris, 1995).

48. See classical studies: François-André Isambert, *Christianisme et classe ouvrière* (Tournai, 1961). Pierre Pierrard, *L'Eglise et les ouvriers en France, 1840–1960* (Paris, 1984), is more concerned with socio-economic realities than with the effects of technology on the mind, which are latent in Ralph Gibson's *A Social History of French Catholicism* (London and New York, 1989).

49. This process has been studied in depth in numerous monographs, collected in the *Cahiers du clergé rural*.

50. *Cahiers du clergé rural* (1958), 201.

51. *Ibid.* (1959), 454.

52. *Ibid.* (1958), 199 and *L'Ami du Clergé*, 9 June 1960.

53. *Cahiers du clergé rural* (1947), 301.

54. 'Will agriculture suffer from the plague that has infected industry for half a century: man being enslaved by the very machine he created to lighten his load?' (*L'Ami du Clergé*, 11 June 1959).

55. Speech at the first international congress of engineers (*Osservatore Romano*, 11 October 1953).

56. Cf. Michel Lagrée, *La Bénédiction de Prométhée: religion et technologies (XIXe–XXe siècles)* (Paris, 1999).

57. *Le Parfum de Rome*, in Louis Veuillot, *Œuvres complètes*, vol. IX (Paris, 1926), 14.

58. *Ça et là*, 4th edition (Paris, 1860), 85–6.
59. The utopian socialist Constantin Pecqueur saw it as an extraordinary instrument of equality between the different social classes, cf. Wolfgang Schivelbusch, *Histoire des voyages en train* (Paris, 1990), 75–6.
60. *L'Ami de la Religion, 2* May 1846.
61. *Parfum de Rome*, 42.
62. *Ibid.*
63. Cf. Alain Corbin, *Les Cloches de la terre: paysage sonore et culture sensible dans les campagnes au 19e siècle* (Paris, 1994).
64. *Le Siècle*, 24 November 1854.
65. The follower of Saint-Simon, Michel Chevalier, as early as 1841 had already drawn attention to this corpus (*Le Journal des Débats*, 20 September 1841).
66. E. Bonnier, in *L'Ami de la Religion*, 5 April 1860.
67. Lent of 1856, cf. *Le Progrès par le christianisme: conférences de Notre-Dame de Paris*, vol. I (Paris, 1859), 223–6.
68. On Moigno, see Pietro Redonti, 'Physique et apologétique: le *Cosmos* de l'abbé Moigno et de Marc Seguin', *History and Technology*, 6 (1988), 203; Michel Lagrée, 'L'Abbé Moigno, vulgarisateur scientifique (1804–1884)', in *Christianisme et science*, series of texts compiled by the Association française d'histoire religieuse contemporaine (Lyons and Paris, 1989), 167–82.
69. The fact that man had taken 6000 years to turn water into steam when it had been there since creation should be seen by man as a source not of pride, but of humility (*Le Progrès par le christianisme*, vol. XLVI, 64).
70. Letter for Lent, 1860, in *Instructions, lettres pastorales et mandements de Monseigneur Plantier, évêque de Nîmes*, vol. I (Nîmes, 1867), 121–2.
71. The same idea is expressed by Mgr Giraud, bishop of Cambrai: 'Simply because He no longer shows himself directly to us, at least not in the ordinary course of his providence, by suddenly and abruptly suspending the laws he has given to the universe, let us not jump to the conclusion that he takes no part in the thoughts and actions of man' (*Discours pour l'inauguration de la fontaine centrale de Bailleul*, June 1844).
72. Cf. Paul Droulers, 'Christianisme et évolution technologique: les premiers chemins de fer', *Histoire, Economie, Société*, 1 (1983), 119–32.
73. Mgr Landriot, speech on the inauguration of the La Rochelle railway (Sept. 1857) in *Œuvres*, vol. I, 289.
74. Inauguration of the Perigueux railway by Cardinal Donnet (*L'Ami de la Religion*, 30 July 1857).
75. The blessing of the La Rochelle railway, Landriot, *Œuvres*.
76. Michel Spanneut, *Le Stoïcisme des Pères de d'Eglise: de Clément de Rome à Clément d'Alexandrie* (Paris, 1957).
77. Robert Bultot, 'Les sources païennes de l'opposition entre "naturel" et "artificiel" en milieu chrétien', in Jacqueline Hamesse and Colette Muraille-Samara (eds.), *Le Travail au moyen âge* (Louvain la Neuve, 1990), 101–3.
78. Michel Lagrée, 'Religion and technological innovation: the steamboat in 1840s France', *History and Technology*, 12 (1995), 327–59.
79. *De natura Deorum*, 2.60.
80. *De civitate Dei*, 22.24.

81. This study should be broadened to include other areas of Catholic religion, from Italy to Quebec.
82. *L'Homme: la vie, la science, l'art* (Paris, 1903), p. 164.
83. Bénoit Leroux, *Louis Veuillot: un homme, un combat* (Paris, 1984), 143–7.
84. *L'Osservatore Romano*, 4–5 October 1954.
85. *Acta Apostolicae Sedis*, 48 (1954), 584–7.
86. *L'Ami du Clergé*, 19 August 1954.
87. *L'Ami du Clergé*, 6 April 1956. We know that the communication server used at present by the French episcopate has been placed under the protection of the archangel Gabriel.
88. George Minois, *L'Eglise et la science: histoire d'un malentendu*, vol. II, *De Galilée à Jean-Paul II* (Paris, 1991).
89. Quoted by Emile Poulat, 'Histoire des mentalités et histoire de l'électricité', in *L'Electricité dans l'histoire: problèmes et méthodes* (Paris, 1985), 143.
90. Danièle Léger and Bertrand Hervieu, *Des Communautés pour les temps difficiles: néo-ruraux ou nouveaux moines* (Paris, 1983).
91. *La Technique ou l'enjeu du siècle* (Paris, 1990), reprint of a work published in 1960; *Le Système technicien* (Paris, 1977); *Le Bluff technologique* (Paris, 1988).
92. Cursive, non-detailed works: Paul Bourgy, *Les Chrétiens face aux techniques* (Brussels and Paris, 1958), Charles-Alfred Courson, *Science, Technology and the Christian* (New York, 1961). More philosophical: Frederick Ferré (ed.), *Technology and Religion: Research in Philosophy and Technology 10* (Greenwich, 1990).
93. Cf. Owen Chadwick, *The Secularization of the European Mind in the Nineteenth Century* (Cambridge, 1993).
94. Ernst Benz, 'I fondamenti Cristiani delle technica occidentale', in E. C. Astelli (ed.), *Tecnica a casistica* (Rome, 1964), 241–63; Lynn White Jr., *Medieval Religion and Technology: Collected Essays* (Los Angeles, 1978); George Ovitt Jr., 'The cultural context of western technology: early Christian attitudes toward manual labor', *Technology and Culture*, 27(3) (1986), 477–500.
95. François Russo makes some suggestions on the link between technology and culture in *Introduction à l'histoire des techniques* (Paris, 1986), chapter 3. See also Patrice Flichy, *L'Innovation technique* (Paris, 1995), 186ff.

11   Semantic structures of religious change in modern Germany

Lucian Hölscher

There can be little doubt that religious life has changed within recent centuries in western Europe. But how to describe and how to define this change is highly controversial. The relationship between the object of historiography and the methods to get hold of it is at stake. In this situation the so-called 'linguistic turn' indicates a new awareness of the concepts used for the description of historical change. In the 1960s and 1970s it was a widely accepted strategy of historians to adopt some kind of theoretical model from other disciplines, mainly from political and social sciences, and to apply it to past societies. But this strategy seems less acceptable today, and it is not difficult to see the reasons for the growing reluctance among historians to go on in the same way as before: there has been a long discussion about the usefulness of the master-concepts of social sciences such as 'modernisation' and 'social differentiation', which I do not want to go into here. Today we may sharpen and modify them in order to accommodate them to new experiences and new needs of scientific research. But in any case we have to accept the fact that the concepts which serve to describe historical change are part of this change themselves. It seems to become more and more obvious that the scientific language can no longer be excluded from being the object of historical investigation and reserved to systematic constructions. It is my conviction that we have to treat the parameters of historical description themselves as changing concepts of changing perspectives on history, that each of them can be related to some specific historical situation and historical interest.

The concept of 'secularisation'

I would like to demonstrate this in analysing the use of the concept 'secularisation' in historical research. Nobody will deny that for many decades this concept seemed to most scholars appropriate and useful in describing the changes in religious culture in modern societies.[1] First used by the so-called 'secularist movement', a society of freethinkers founded by George Holyoake in the mid-nineteenth century, the concept came to be more widely used in both England and France around 1900 in a broader sense. Whereas the secularists had used it in the programmatic sense of a necessary development towards a society of enlightened ideas, with the elimination of religious prejudices and the spread of good knowledge, from the beginning of the twentieth century onwards it was mostly used in the broader sense of a historical trend towards a 'secular' society, including many different developments: first the separation of state and church on the level of a common government, of school administration, of support for the poor, etc.; second, the diminishing attendance of church-members at public worship and the decline of private worship, of prayers, reading biblical and other religious writings, etc.; third, the renunciation of religious explanations for natural phenomena, of Christian cosmology; fourth, the diminishing use of religious symbols in public and private life: of the religious oath, the religious formulas used when people met or said goodbye – formulas like 'God save you', 'Grüß Gott', 'A Dieu', etc.

In the twentieth century the concept of 'secularisation' seemed to be useful to bind all these trends together into one big historical movement. For its dissemination among historians, sociologists and other learned persons before and after the First World War, it was very important that influential theories made it the cornerstone of their concept of modernity: Max Weber used it to describe a very ambiguous historical trend of modern society towards rationalisation and – the other side of the coin – what he called the *Entzauberung*, the disenchantment of the modern world. Ernst Troeltsch, his theological friend, was more optimistic, when in the secularisation of modern society he recognised the dominating influence of the Protestant Reformation with its concepts of individual liberty, of active Christian practice in social institutions, etc.

But very early we find at least two different strategies of historical argumentation, both combined with the concept of 'secularisation'. Starting from the positive origins of the concept, a small group of liberal Protestants used the term for the idea of bringing together the opposing concepts of God and world, of church and society, of the holy and the mundane. Mostly among Protestant German theologians the vision of a religiously inspired secular society was articulated, which was based not on the church as institutional framework but on the religious conscience of the Christians themselves. However, after the First World War the term 'secularisation' was also used in a rather pessimistic sense by most Catholic authorities and the more orthodox wing of Protestantism. In their view the influence of religion was constantly diminishing in modern society. In a strange alliance of orthodox churchmen and secular scholars this view was adopted by many historians and sociologists as well. They disagreed in their moral judgement of the trend but agreed on its direction.

However, the apocalyptic and the progressive concepts of 'secularisation' had one thing in common. They both took it for granted that history moves to one final goal, the 'eschaton' of biblical prophecy. It is exactly this implication which makes the concept so problematic today. In recent years, the hypothesis of a final goal in history has been opposed by many historians and sociologists of religion. They have argued that historical development differs in different countries. For example, church membership has increased in the United States within the last decades, whereas in western Europe it has fallen to a new minimum. There is no common trend to be seen. And even in one country the various trends of religious life cannot be bound together to one universal trend or development: we find periods of increasing and decreasing church attendance, of hostility and co-operation between church and civil authorities, of religious inspiration and anti-religious rationality, and sometimes we even find them at the same time in different parts of society. And what is more, we find different criteria of what is religious at different times and places. Therefore, what is a decreasing level of religiosity for some observers may be seen as an increasing level by others.

This shows the problems of adapting the concept of 'secularisation' to our present situation and to our knowledge of the past. Today the fact that in the past the concept has been successfully used for the interpretation of historical change in the religious culture of the last centuries probably tells us more about the mentality of those who used it than about the past itself. This is the first step towards historicising the concept; the second would be to ask which other concepts were used in earlier periods of history to interpret long-term religious change. But since I have already done this in another paper[2] I can be brief in the present context. Within the last 250 years one can distinguish between at least four periods – not so much of religious change in the traditional sense of objective structures in society, but rather of different ways of conceptualising this change. In sketching these periods I mostly rely on the situation in Germany, which may sometimes differ from that in other European countries; but in general the periodisation was the same in most parts of Europe.

1. Up to the first half of the eighteenth century people had no long-term vision of historical change at all, since the world was expected to come to an end very soon and the sins of men could be easily ascribed to the activity of the devil which, according to the Bible, would be most intense in the period immediately before the Last Judgement.

2. But in the later part of the eighteenth century this pessimistic perspective was radically overthrown. In the period of Enlightenment most educated people in Europe believed in religious progress. Today, they argued, the religious ideas of a growing number of men were more enlightened than a century ago; why should they not be even more enlightened and widespread (especially among the lower classes of society) after another hundred years? Religion was more or less identified with morals and rational thinking.

3. After the French Revolution this optimism broke down, giving place to almost the opposite perspective. People now became aware that church services and other religious obligations had lost much attraction within the

'enlightened' century, that now open contempt for church authorities and doctrines had become more and more frequent. The German concept *Kirchlichkeit*
which was invented around 1800 probably describes best the new perspective on religious life. In this concept religious practice was much identified
with church attendance and loyalty to the church authorities. The decreasing readiness to follow this ideal was called *Entkirchlichung*. It produced a
pessimistic view on the future of Christianity which dominated the following
century, especially among the clergy and orthodox members of all Christian
churches.

4. However, already in the second half of the nineteenth century a new model
began to win attraction mainly among liberals. It tended to define the future
of Christianity neither as pure decline nor as pure progress, but rather as a
dialectical process of both decline and progress. The most appropriate term for
this concept which dominated historical discourse from about the turn of the
century onwards was, as I have pointed out already, 'secularisation'. Different
from the concept of *Entkirchlichung*, it analysed religious culture in the broader
context of state and society and described its change in terms of both loss and
profit.

What can we learn from this story of conceptual change for the methodology
of historical investigations in general? It is a characteristic assumption of the
history of mentalities that the past can be seen on two different levels: the level
of 'objective' reconstruction (which in fact is our present perspective in terms
of mentality) and the level of 'subjective' perception by contemporaries (which
is a mental fact in terms of 'objective' history). Our example shows, on the
one side, how differently religious change could be conceptualised in different
periods of history. It demonstrates that changes of religious concepts are closely
linked with the changes of religious culture. Each of them can be seen as the
'expression' of the other. But it would be too simple to restrict each of our
concepts of religious change only to that period in which it dominated in public
discourse. As we are used to extending our own concepts (like 'secularisation')
to periods without knowledge of these concepts, so other concepts of earlier
periods can be extended to other periods as well. That means, for example,
that the concept of *Entkirchlichung* (vanishing attendance at church services
and loyalty to church authorities) can be applied to our own time as well as
the concept of 'secularisation'. There is no historical privilege for one concept,
except as a result of our own rational choice.

The semantic analysis of religious concepts

This is true for other fields of religious culture as well. What follows is the
first sketch of a greater project of historical research dealing with the changing meaning of religious concepts from the eighteenth century onwards. The

purpose of such a project is: first to make clear the differences between the current meaning of religious concepts and the ways in which the same terms were used in the past; second to understand these concepts as mental realities of past religious cultures, as basic parameters for the change of religious attitudes as well as of ecclesiastical structures. I think that in doing so we have an opportunity to take these concepts much more seriously than we usually do.[3]

As far as I can see, investigations into the changing meaning of religious concepts have been much neglected in theology and historiography so far.[4] To most theologians it even seems to be a kind of sacrilege to concede that religious concepts are constantly changing. This is true for Protestants as well as for Catholics. Protestant theologians probably would allow that Luther, Zwingli and Calvin had found new religious concepts for their new teachings, and some of them would even concede that important modern philosophers and professors of theology, like Immanuel Kant, Friedrich Schleiermacher or Karl Barth, had imported new religious concepts – if not defined the old ones in a better way, adequate to the understanding of their time. But in studying the history of modern religion I get the impression that they do not realise the profound impact of changing religious terms on the religious consciousness of modern societies; and that this change affects not only religion itself, but also the way of living in the modern world as a whole.

Of course, the dogmatic differences between the Christian denominations are often represented in different terms. But what strikes me more is the existence of a common feature of religious change, which is not confined to one Christian church or school of theology, but involves all Christian churches with all their different theological schools. To stress my point even more: I get the impression that a certain change of religiosity is basic to all Christian churches, and if it is not one religious pattern, it is at least a certain structure of opposite positions which we find in almost all denominations. To put it in other words: I do not deny the profound differences of religious belief and lifestyle in various Christian (and non-Christian) groups, but I think that there is something like a common change of religious culture 'beyond' or 'behind' the constitutional and dogmatic framework of the churches.

I shall demonstrate this by analysing the conceptual change of some religious terms and notions, which to me seem to be vital for the religious orientation of bourgeois society from the eighteenth century onwards. Since it is a huge project, I shall do this on the small basis of encyclopedias only. Encyclopedias usually register the change of meaning only with some temporal delay, but on the other hand they do, as I hope, represent a broader use of terms than we find in most other historical sources. It is true that in my material there is to be found a strong bias towards Protestant sources, and – what is even worse – to the German idiom. Therefore the following sketch can be no more than the hypothetical basis of further comparative investigations, which in years to come may work out the common and different features of various religious cultures within Europe.

'Religion'

To start with the concept of 'religion' itself, it is well known that there is no definition of the term which is generally accepted. Different religious groups have established different religious cultures; different theological schools defined the term in different ways. Hence it may be a practical hypothesis to take the term 'religion' for whatever people declare it to be. At least for the purpose of historical research this is a helpful hypothesis, because even contradictory definitions tell us a lot about the mentality of religious groups and their relationship to one another. But following the line of changing religious discourses in encyclopedias from the eighteenth century onwards, we find some common semantic patterns beyond the difference of religious confessions and organisations.

In the encyclopedias of the mid-eighteenth century the term 'religion' was still defined in a very traditional way. It is partly 'knowledge of God', partly 'service and reverence to God' (*Erkenntnis, Dienst und Verehrung Gottes*) (Walch (1740), 2146).[5] In this respect no difference can be found either between the Christian denominations or between the European languages (Furetière (1690), Art. religion; *Encyclopædia Britannica* 3 (1771), 533; *Encyclopédie* 28 (1782), 248). Many religious controversies of the time go back to the traditional distinction between 'natural' and 'revealed religion' (*natürliche* and *Offenbarungs-Religion*) (Walch (1740), 2146; Zedler 31 (1742), 443ff; Pierer 17 (1835), 656). It gives a starting-point for two kinds of religion, which in the modern religious culture tend to oppose one another: for the theology of the Enlightenment and its modern successors there was but one religion, which was seen to be more or less identical with the true principles of morals (Mellin 5 (1802), 114; Krünitz 122 (1813), 527; Krug 3 (1828), 451). This natural religion was said to be common to all mankind, a kind of human predisposition – as normal to human beings as hunger and thirst. On the other side there were the religions of the churches, the positive or revealed religions, which were based on historical constitutions and dogmas. Some religious parties differed in preferring natural or revealed religion, but normally people were inclined to combine or reject both of them.

But the inclination to natural or revealed religion also changed with time: whereas the religious culture of the Enlightenment was based mainly on natural religion, by the turn to the nineteenth century we find a new esteem for revealed religion in all Christian churches. This is true not only for religious orthodoxy, but also for its liberal opponents, because parallel to the restoration of traditional religious concepts we also find an increasing emancipation of bourgeois morality from what was called 'natural religion' before. This can be demonstrated by the fact that, in the nineteenth century, for an increasing part of 'secular' society it was possible to hold up high moral standards without being 'religious' in the sense which the word tended to assume within the discourse of the churches – some secularists even started to quit church membership – and vice versa. It was a commonplace for the enlightened critics of religion from the eighteenth century onwards that 'religious' people were sometimes known to be very immoral in their behaviour (Krug 1 (1827), 87, *Frömmigkeit*; 3 (1828), 465, *Religiös*). It may be that for parts of the nineteenth century this conceptual differentiation of religion and morals was stronger in France and Germany than in England, but in general, I think, it was quite the same historical tendency in all European countries, which makes a strong distinction between modern and premodern religion.

'Religiosity'

Closely linked with the change of meaning of 'religion' is the birth of another religious concept in the late eighteenth century: the concept of 'religiosity', 'subjective' or 'private' religion (Mellin 5 (1802), 114; Krünitz 122 (1813), 527; Krug 3 (1828), 451; Pierer 17 (1835), 656). It leads us to one of the most typical features of modern religious culture: the now established distinction between the religion of the church and the religion of the individual. In premodern societies there is no comparable distinction to be found between 'objective' and 'subjective', or between 'public' and 'private' religion.[6] By many Protestant theologians (especially those with a Pietist background) it was even acknowledged that the two – public and private religion – could be in disharmony, and what is more, in case of dissent, they taught that it was more important to follow one's own convictions than to obey the dogmas of the church.

At the time of the Enlightenment it seems to have been important that religiosity was to be seen as a common characteristic of all mankind, not of one church or religion in particular. Therefore 'religiosity' was almost identical with morality; or as the Brockhaus Encyclopedia of 1820 put it: 'Religion and religiosity relate to one another as morality to reason, as conscientiousness to consciousness, as the fruit to the blossom; religious sentiment is moral sentiment, related to the eternal and the divine' (*Die Religiosität verhält sich zur Religion, wie die Moralität zur Vernunft, wie die Gesinnung der Gewissenhaftigkeit zum Gewissen, wie die Frucht zur Blüte; religiöses Gefühl ist das moralische Gefühl auf das Ewige und Göttliche bezogen*) (Brockhaus 8 (1820),180; cf. also Krug 1 (1827), 87). It is true that the enlightened position cannot stand for modern religion as a whole, but up to our days the moral – or immoral – dimension of religion is one of its most vital features. Moral values like veracity, helpfulness and compassion are seen to be almost synonymous with practical religiosity. Since religion has lost its monopoly of cosmological interpretation it is limited to the sphere of history and human society, which is the sphere of morals.

The importance and novelty of this new idea of individual religiosity is underlined by the fact that we find new words emerging in the religious discourse of the eighteenth century: in France and England it was the term 'religiosity' itself (instead of the older 'religiousness') which, although much older as such, by the middle of the eighteenth century took up the new meaning Larousse 6 (1977), 5039; *OED* 13 (1983), 570;[7] Robert 8 (1985), 201), followed by the German variant *Religiosität*, which was adopted from France by the end of the century (Schulz/Basler 3 (1977), 295). At the same time also the new term *Frömmigkeit* emerged, expressing more or less the same quality of religious sentiment.

Let us stay for a moment with this point, because besides expressing a common feature of religion in all modern societies, in the new term *Frömmigkeit* we find something very characteristic for German Protestantism. Up to the eighteenth century there were two religious attitudes defined in Protestantism as well as in Catholicism: one for the clerics, the other for the laity. Whatever was related to the life of the clergy was called 'religiosus' ('religious', 'religiös', 'religieux'). The term stood for a special virtue of clerics. Laymen had to be 'fromm', a word that is best translated as 'brave'. Under the influence of Pietism both religious attitudes melted together at the beginning of the eighteenth century, the word 'fromm' took up the meaning of 'religiös', this now being no longer restricted to the world of the clerics and of the church. Of course, there were other terms of similar sense, like 'pious', 'godly', 'devout'. But the German term 'fromm' is broader in describing a human attitude common to both God and world, Sunday and weekday, the holy and the secular.

The semantic convergence of the originally different concepts of 'religiös' and 'fromm' is a characteristic feature of Protestant culture in Germany.[8] It may be seen as an expression of the long-term convergence of ecclesiastical and civil culture in Protestantism, of what was called 'secularisation' by later theologians. The Catholic Church was well aware of this new type of religious attitude which the Protestants called *Frömmigkeit*. As a consequence it was rejected by Catholic authors as being a new invention of Friedrich Schleiermacher's theology for a long time. But by the twentieth century we find the item *Frömmigkeit* in Catholic German encyclopedias too (*LThK* 4 (1960), 398), demonstrating that the new culture of religious individualism laid hold of Catholicism as much as of Protestantism. In recent years, however, it seems that there is an equivalent transfer of religious attitudes from Catholicism to Protestantism to be found in the concept of 'spirituality', a transfer which has not been explored so far.

'Confession' (*Konfession*) and 'creed' (*Bekenntnis*)

For the historians of conceptual change in history an interesting aspect of non-Romance languages like English and German is that sometimes new ideas and cultural structures go together with the difference of language. One example is the term *Frömmigkeit*. When it was established in late eighteenth-century German it showed much better than the old Romance term *Religiosität* that a new idea or concept of religion was born. The same is true with the German terms *Konfession* and *Bekenntnis*. For the English and French user the term 'confession' refers to activities which people do either at church under the guidance of a father confessor or at high court. But in Germany the term *Konfession* and its German counterpart *Bekenntnis* are used with at least two additional religious meanings today. First they express the religious creed of an individual or a religious group; second they point to the denomination of a Christian church (Brockhaus 1 (1820), 743). It was the Lutheran *Confessio Augustana* of 1530 that introduced both the Latin and the German term into the German language. But by the eighteenth century the concepts began to separate: *Konfession* was used rather for the Christian communions or denominations which were no longer seen as being different 'religions'; whereas *Bekenntnis* was limited to the personal creed of an individual, his 'religiosity' (*RGG* 3 (1959), 1746).

Again, the semantic change of concepts points to a structural change in the religious culture itself: by the eighteenth century the Christian churches were no longer seen as different 'religions' but as different variants (denominations) of one and the same religion. The new concept *Konfession* allowed a definition of a difference of ecclesiastical organisations beneath the *niveau* of different religions. It made it possible to adhere to the idea of the unity of Christianity beyond the difference of Christian denominations (*Konfessionen*). This was essential because in the new era of tolerance the state was defined as being neutral in religious affairs (Rotteck/Welcker 3 (1836), 646). But on the other hand, to belong to a certain Christian denomination (*Konfession*) no longer meant that somebody necessarily shared the public creed of this denomination, as it had done before: beside the public *Konfession* of the churches there were to be found a lot of individual *Bekenntnisse*, i.e. secular 'creeds'. They established something like a private religion or, as it was called later, an individual *Weltanschauung*.

It is not difficult to see how the semantic change of religious concepts reflected – and also promoted (!) – the change of religious attitudes. The concepts of *Konfession* and *Bekenntnis* helped to structure the relationship between different religious groups, between state and churches, between the public religion of the churches and the private religiosity of secular society. For a comparative description of religious cultures in Europe it would be helpful to see how other European languages managed these structural problems of religious life in terms of their own semantic possibilities.

The 'dissenter' (*Dissident*)

Very similar was the semantic structure established by the term 'dissenter' (*Dissident*). Today it is used in the case not only of religious but also of political dissent. But up to the mid-twentieth century it served to define the relationship between competing Christian groups within a Christian state or society. Its emergence is bound to a specific social and political constellation: the co-existence of several Christian groups, which on the one hand are tolerated by the public authorities, but on the other hand are not equal in civil rights (Bluntschli/Brater 3 (1858), 146; *RGG* 2 (1958), 209). As with the concept of *Konfession*, the churches concerned had to treat one another as Christian cousins, well aware that they were not Christian brothers. It is a modern constellation, made possible by the Protestant Reformations, but only in Poland realised during the second half of the sixteenth century.

In German dictionaries we find *Dissidenten* applied to the members of those Protestant groups in Poland (Lutherans, Calvinists and the Bohemian Brothers) which in 1570 agreed to come together and in 1573 fixed the *lex dissidentium*, an agreement of mutual toleration, with the Catholics (Zedler 7 (1734), 1071; Brockhaus 2 (1820), 214; Ersch/Gruber 1.26 (1835), 83). Later it was highly disputed whether the term 'dissident' was properly used for the Protestant minorities only, as the Catholic side maintained, or for both sides, as the Protestants argued (Meyer 7.4 (1846), 877; Wetzer/Welte 3 (1857), 180). But anyway, at least from the early seventeenth century onwards, the one-sided use for the Protestant groups demonstrated the growing weakness of the legal status of the Protestants in Poland. Finally by the middle of the eighteenth century they were excluded from nearly all public positions and from voting to the Diet, and even faced the loss of the civil rights of ordinary citizens. With the intervention of Russia, Prussia and Austria in the 1770s this tendency was reversed, and legal equality re-established. The term *Dissident* now lost, step by step, its political significance and was almost dismissed by the 1830s (Ersch/Gruber 1.26 (1835), 83) – but only to become a much more general concept (Krug Suppl. 1 (1829), 73) in other European countries which participated in the tragic destiny of the threefold divided country.

In Germany up to the revolution of 1848 the status of public churches was reserved to the Lutheran, the Reformed (Calvinist) and the Catholic churches only. By the 1850s the word began to be used as official label for private religious societies, which were tolerated by the constitution but not endowed with the privileges of public churches (such as financial support by the government, school teaching, etc.). But at the same time that state and society were expected to tolerate also the newly called 'dissenters' such as the German Catholics (*Deutsch-Katholiken*), Mennonites, Methodists, Baptists, etc. (Wetzer/Welte 3 (1857), 180), the term lost its former meaning, to distinguish religious groups of a minor legal status in relation to those not recognised by the constitution at all (such as the Baptists and Quakers in Poland). It had become a purely negative specification enclosing even those who quitted church membership without entering another church or chapel. As a consequence, after the First World War, the concept of 'dissent' was very much associated with atheism, because the dissenting Christian groups rejected the term, whereas for free-thinkers it was an acceptable self-denomination (*RGG* 2 (1909), 90; Meyer 3 (1925), 844). This slow erosion of religious substance was the background for an instruction of the Nazi government in 1937 to eliminate the term from public formulas, arguing that leaving the church would not necessarily mean becoming an atheist. For the Nazis the term blocked the possibility of believing in God without being a Christian (Meyer 3 (1937), 133). Although the term *Dissident* was re-established after the Second World War, in official documents it was still ambiguous, as it could have both a positive (being a member of a dissenting religious group) and a purely negative (belonging to no religious group) status in religious discourse (*dtv-Lexikon* 4 (1966), 132).

'Atheism'

With the concept of 'atheism' I come to my last example of the usefulness of semantic analysis in historical perspectives. The concept of 'atheism' is much more complicated than it seems at first glance. Today the meaning of the term is ambiguous: on the one hand it is used to denote those who do not believe in God, but on the other it is also used for a certain form of positive creed or philosophical attitude. Since elaborated theories of atheism such as Nietzsche's nihilism emerged in the nineteenth century, the term can be used in a well-defined sense. This is something new, because as Lucien Febvre demonstrated in his marvellous study of 1942, 'Le problème de l'incroyance au 16ème siècle', at this time the word 'atheism' by no means referred to a well-defined concept, but rather to a vague idea of religious nonconformity. This situation did not change much in the following centuries. But by the eighteenth century we at least find an internal differentiation between a 'theoretical' and a 'practical' atheism established in encyclopedias of that time (Zedler 2 (1732), 2016, 'Atheisterey'; Walch 1 (1740), 134, 'Atheisterey'; *Encyclopédie* (1751); *Encyclopædia Britannica* (1771); Krug 1 (1827), 204; Brockhaus 1 (1833), 474; *RE* 1 (1854), 577). This differentiation had far-reaching consequences. In German dictionaries 'theoretical atheism' now was called *Gottesleugnung* (Grimm 8 (1958), 1281), practical atheism *Gottlosigkeit* ('godlessness') (Zedler

11 (1735), 411; Walch 1 (1740), 1368; Adelung 2 (1807), 763; Campe 2 (1808), 434; Krug 2 (1827), 279; Grimm 8 (1958), 1396ff).

As far as theoretical atheism is concerned, we find numerous variants from the early nineteenth century onwards: 'materialism', 'positivism', 'pantheism', 'naturalism' and 'deism'; later Nietzsche's 'nihilism', Haeckel's 'monism', 'Marxism' and many others (Ersch/Gruber (1821), 172; Krug 1 (1827), 204; *LThK* 1 (1957), 983). We can leave it an open question (highly disputed at the time), how far all these more or less 'religious' philosophies are to be called 'atheism', because for the investigation into the history of religious concepts it is much more important to see how contemporaries drew the line between their concepts of 'religion' and 'atheism'. For the orthodox wing of both Christian churches it was already atheism to believe in God not as a person, but as an idea or as the essence of natural order. (The different concepts of 'God' were reflected in the semantic difference between *Gott* and *Gottheit*, 'god' and 'deity', *dieu et déité*, which had its own, so far undetected history.) On the other side, today we are confronted with modern theologians who teach an 'atheistic creed', preferring the theoretical concept of 'atheism' as a definition of the essence instead of the limits of religion.

Very different from the concept of theoretical atheism was the conceptual structure of practical atheism, that is of 'irreligiosity' or *Gottlosigkeit* ('godlessness') – new terms established by the end of the eighteenth century. In the eighteenthth and nineteenth centuries, for the enlightened and liberal parts of society an irreligious person was primarily defined as a wicked, immoral person. But this did not necessarily imply that he was an atheist in theory too. It was something new in the nineteenth century, that somebody could be an atheist in theory without being irreligious in practice and vice versa. Whereas theoretical atheism was a widespread and often respected philosophy in bourgeois society, people were not yet prepared to tolerate practical atheism, i.e. irreligiosity in society (Krug 5 (1827), 279; Ersch/Gruber 1.76 (1863), 113). Only by the second half of the century did practical atheism, that is, offence to bourgeois morals, begin to be an ideal for the secular avant-garde of intellectuals and artists. Again we find the semantic differentiation of terms reflecting the change of religious attitudes and social values.

The concepts of religious terms were defined on different levels in different periods of history; they changed in use and meaning together with the change of religious attitudes and discourses. 'Superstition', by the age of Enlightenment one of the most important counterparts to religion and reason, was by the second third of the nineteenth century rather seen as a minor, imperfect form of religion. In the superstition of the uneducated classes of society many clerics discovered a basic religiosity which they found to be eroded by the patterns of modern learning and civilisation. More or less the same could be said of the concept of 'myth': in the eighteenth century a counter-concept to religion and history, by the early nineteenth century 'myths' were found to be the outward shape of true religion in early periods of mankind.

I could give a lot of other examples for the long-term semantic change of religious concepts and its significance for the changing structure and organisation of religion in modern societies (concepts like 'church' and 'parish', etc.). But I hope my examples are clear enough to demonstrate two things: first that the semantic change of concepts can be fruitfully related to the changes in mentality and social organisation of modern societies; and second that it will be a very promising project, to work on the common and different features of religious concepts in different times, different countries and different Christian denominations. In this chapter I can give but a foretaste of what could be learned by systematic comparison of religious concepts. But maybe one day we shall be able even to understand the secret links between our own secular view of the modern world and the religious tradition of our ancestors. Then we may find that it was wrong to think of Christian culture in terms of 'decline' as much as it was wrong in earlier periods to hope for an eternal 'progress' of history towards the Kingdom of God.

ENCYCLOPEDIAS AND DICTIONARIES

Johann Christoph Adelung, *Versuch eines vollständigen grammatisch-critischen Wörterbuches der hochdeutschen Mundart*, 2nd edn (Leipzig, 1793–1801).
Johann Caspar Bluntschli and Karl Ludwig Theodor Brater, *Deutsches Staatswörterbuch* (Stuttgart, 1857–70).
Brockhaus, *Allgemeine deutsche Real-Enzyklopädie für die gebildeten Stände*, 5th edn (Leipzig, 1819–20), 8th edn (Leipzig, 1833–37).
Johann Heinrich Campe, *Wörterbuch der deutschen Sprache* (Brunswick, 1807–11).
dtv-Lexikon, Ein Konversationslexikon in 20 Bänden (Munich, 1966).
Encyclopædia Britannica, 1st edn (Edinburgh, 1771).
Encyclopédie, ou Dictionnaire raisonné des sciences, des arts et des métiers, published by M. Diderot *et al.* (Lausanne, 1781–82).
Johann Samuel Ersch and Johann Gottfried Gruber, *Allgemeine Encyclopädie der Wissenschaften und Künste* (Leipzig, 1818–89).
Antoine Furetière, *Dictionnaire universel* (Rotterdam, 1690).
Jakob and Wilhelm Grimm, *Deutsches Wörterbuch* (Leipzig, 1854–1965).
Wilhelm Traugott Krug, *Allgemeines Handwörterbuch der philosophischen Wissenschaften nebst ihrer Literatur und Geschichte* (Leipzig, 1827–29).
Johann Georg Krünitz, *Oeconomische Enzyklopädie oder allgemeines System der Land-, Haus- und Staatswirtschaft* (Berlin, 1773–1858).
Grand Larousse de la langue française (Paris, 1977).
LThK, Lexikon für Theologie und Kirche, 2nd edn (Freiburg, 1957–65).
Georg Samuel Mellin, *Enzyklopädisches Wörterbuch der kritischen Philosophie* (Magdeburg, 1797–).
Meyer, *Das große Conversations-Lexikon für die gebildeten Stände*, 1st edn (Hildburghausen, 1839–52); 7th edn (1924–35); 8th edn (1936–42).

H. A. Pierer, *Universal-Lexikon oder vollständiges enzyklopödishes* (Altenburg, 1835–6).

RE, Real-Encyclopädie für protestantische Theologie und Kirche (Gotha, 1854–68).

RGG, Die Religion in Geschichte und Gegenwart, 1st edn (Tübingen, 1908–13); 3rd edn (Tübingen, 1957–64).

Grand Robert de la langue francaise, 2nd edn (Paris, 1985).

Carl Rotteck and Carl Welcker, *Staats-Lexikon oder Encyclopädie der Staatswissenschaften* (Altona, 1835–43).

Hans Schulz and Otto Basler, *Deutsches Fremdwörterbuch*, 3rd edn (Strasbourg, 1913).

Johann Georg Walch, *Philosophisches Lexikon*, 2nd edn (Leipzig, 1740).

Heinrich Joseph Wetzer and Benedikt Welte, *Kirchen-Lexikon oder Encyclopädie der katholischen Theologie und ihrer Hilfswissenschaften* (Freiburg, 1847–56).

Johann Heinrich Zedler, *Großes vollständiges Universallexikon aller Wissenschaften und Künste* (Leipzig, 1732–50).

NOTES

1. Cf. Hermann Lübbe, *Säkularisierung: Geschichte eines ideenpolitischen Begriffs* (Freiburg, 1965).
2. Lucian Hölscher, 'Secularization and urbanization in the nineteenth century. An interpretative model', in Hugh McLeod (ed.), *European Religion in the Age of Great Cities 1830–1930* (London, 1995), 263–88.
3. For the general theory of conceptual history cf. the articles of Reinhart Koselleck: 'Begriffsgeschichte und Sozialgeschichte', in *Vergangene Zukunft: Zur Semantik geschichtlicher Zeiten* (Frankfurt, 1979), 107–29; 'Sozialgeschichte und Begriffsgeschichte', in Wolfgang Schieder and Volker Sellin (eds.), *Sozialgeschichte in Deutschland* (Göttingen, 1986), vol. I, 89–109, and the 'Introduction' to the encyclopedia *Geschichtliche Grundbegriffe* (Stuttgart, 1972), vol. I, xiii–xxvii.
4. Cf. the great religious encyclopedias in Germany, *Religion in Geschichte und Gegenwart*, *Theologische Realenzyklopädie* and *Lexikon für Theologie und Kirche*.
5. For the full titles see the list of encyclopedias and dictionaries above.
6. The concepts 'public' and 'private' would have pointed rather to the political status of churches – that is to religions which were acknowledged by public authority and those which were not – but not, as it was by the late eighteenth century, to the difference between the official dogmas of church teaching and what the church-members themselves believed in.
7. The term is not to be found in Johnson's *Dictionary of the English Language* (1805).
8. It has to be checked out whether this is true for other Protestant countries as well.

Part IV

12   Master narratives of long-term religious change

Jeffrey Cox

During the last two decades, the theory of secularisation has been the subject of critical discussion by doubters, sceptics and open adversaries.[1] Historians and sociologists who claim no longer to accept the theory, at least in its classic form, have created a valuable body of alternative scholarship.[2] Simon Green is correct in his observation that 'It is the anti-secularisation model which has made most of the running in recent British religious historiography.'[3] But in surveying the debate I remain impressed with the sturdy durability, abiding persuasiveness and rhetorical usefulness of the theory of secularisation. Green also commented that various 'counter-theories . . . taken together . . . are something less than entirely persuasive'.[4] Despite the efforts of doubters, sceptics and adversaries, the most influential general account of religion in modern Europe, and in the modern world, remains the theory of secularisation. Why?

It is important not to underestimate the extent to which secularisation continues to be invoked uncritically. Upon occasion I encounter the assertion that no one believes in secularisation any more. Jay Demerath, an American sociologist of religion, recently put it even more emphatically: 'for a long time there was a notion that society would just become secularised over time, that this was part of modernisation and westernisation, and that religion would disappear due to the legacy of the Enlightenment. I don't know any sociologists of religion worth their salt who really believed that.'[5]

Perhaps there were no sociologists who believed that religion would disappear, but there certainly are many sociologists, not to mention historians, anthropologists, economists, clergy and journalists, who believe that religion in the modern world will survive only in forms that are sectarian and therefore marginal, fundamentalist and menacing, or internally secularised and therefore 'not really religious'. That account of modern history has its own history, as David Martin and Lucian Hölscher have reminded us,[6] but part of the intellectual history of the theory of secularisation is its enduring persuasiveness. The secularisation story retains much of its persuasive force for anyone pondering the situation of religion in the modern world, and it has been reinforced by recent scholarly and public interest in the problem of 'fundamentalism'.[7]

The *New York Times*, for instance, has only three stories about religion. It appears in their columns either as marginal, and therefore unimportant or picturesque, or as a phenomenon which everyone thought was dead but remains surprisingly alive, or as reactive, anti-modern and 'fundamentalist', and therefore a threat to all the values we hold dear. 'Church stifled by good life's roar', reads their headline on religion in Spain, followed by a story of how the words of Spanish bishops are 'drowned out by the roar of discotheques, clinking glasses, fast cars and luxury motor cruisers'.[8] In Turkey, however, it is 'Secular Turks alarmed by resurgence of religion'.[9] More recently, the 'fundamentalist' story has provided a justification for military action against those who can be labelled anti-modern.[10]

You need not read very far in the recent historical literature of modern Europe and the Americas, or indeed most of the world, to find statements just as blunt and old-fashioned as the boldly written assertion of Kingsley Martin that 'Rationalism has argued the church out of existence.'[11] What is more important is the pervasive off-hand invocation of secularisation. Sitting on my desk as I write is the *TLS* of 15 February 2002. On page 12 Jack Goody observes that 'Christians, too, were divided first into the Orthodox and Roman branches . . . and later into the Catholic and Protestant Churches, a division that promoted the gradual secularisation of society and knowledge.' Further along, on page 30, Anne Crowther notes that 'This handsome book offers further insights into Roy Porter's extensive medical history of the "long eighteenth century", this time by using pictorial images to reflect on the secularisation of health and disease.'[12]

In remarking on the continuing, pervasive use of the secularisation story, I do not intend to overlook or downplay the importance of discontent with the theory, as a theory. Even Bryan Wilson concedes that 'If one looks at those who are actively engaged in discussion of the subject . . . the majority are undoubtedly disposed to reject the secularisation thesis.'[13] Secularisation has become an open question during the last two decades. But even those who have ceased to be sure about the process have a habit of returning to it after a period of wandering in the wilderness of uncertainty. As early as the late seventies Peter Burke began his article on religion in *The New Cambridge Modern History* by making fun of the simplicities of the theory, with a tongue-in-cheek 'secularisation may have spread with chemical fertilizer', only to conclude that 'The simple picture with which we started was not radically wrong, but lacking in nuances.'[14] The most instructive case is that of David Martin, whose article 'Towards eliminating the concept of secularisation', published in 1965, is an essential starting-point for any major intellectual effort to develop alternatives to secularisation. His *A General Theory of Secularisation*, published in 1978, does little to eliminate the concept of secularisation, however. Incorporating thoughtful modifications, alterations and variations into the story, it strengthens the theory through its sophisticated handling of history. *A General Theory* is testimony to the sheer usefulness of the secularisation theory, which has great explanatory power precisely because it accounts for so many apparently unconnected changes.

Jay Demerath followed up his bold declaration that no sociologist ever believed in the simple theory of secularisation with a summary of his own work on American urban religion that provides another illustration of the adhesive power of the theory: 'Secularisation is certainly at work in Springfield and has been for 350 years, just as it has been at work in the country. That is not to say you don't get instances of resacralisation. You certainly do, but they are in response to that secularisation. They confirm that secularisation. They're not so much a rebuttal to it, but are linked to it. It's a subtle point, but I think it has to be understood that way.'[15] It is a point sufficiently subtle to raise doubts about the rhetorical utility of the secularisation theory.

One element of Demerath's resacralisation theory, which has been worked out in more detail by Rodney Stark and W. S. Bainbridge,[16] is the attempt to modify a central persuasive feature of the secularisation story, the metaphor of the universal downward slope. Resacralisation changes the slope. Two forces at work in modern history, secularisation and resacralisation, produce a graph that is no longer a downward slope, but a wave. (It is possible to envisage the resacralisation interaction as a dialectic, but the result is difficult to graph.) The resacralisation theory is based on the Durkheimian assumption that there is something natural about the presence of religious sentiment in society, that on a social level religion *is* society.[17]

The Durkheimian approach is a very powerful one. Since first reading Durkheim's *Elementary Forms of the Religious Life* as an undergraduate, I have never been able to contemplate religion without asking, 'religion and what else?' But the argument that all societies are fundamentally religious in one way or another is not one that I find of much use in understanding the course of modern European history. In their neo-Durkheimian 'supply-side reinterpretation' of European religious history, Rodney Stark and Laurence R. Iannaccone propose 'dropping the term secularisation from all theoretical discourse' because 'the observable instances to which to apply it seem lacking'.[18] They are on to an important point when they emphasise the institutional peculiarities of religion in modern European history. But in their determination to 'dispute the claim that any European nation is very secularised',[19] they seriously underestimate the significance of the contrast between popular attitudes towards religion in most European countries and the United States, as well as many other parts of the world. They reinterpret poll evidence about European religious practice and opinion in an attempt to deny outright that the slope points downward. But an unwillingness by most Europeans to declare themselves entirely atheistic, or to abandon irrevocably all hope of life after death, is not persuasive evidence that Berlin and Amsterdam are throbbing with a hidden Durkheimian numinosity.

One of the great stories of modern European history is the emergence of openly declared and publicly sanctioned irreligion and indifference. Popular and elite resistance to religious ideas, to religious mobilisation, to religious institutions, characterise much of modern European history. In large areas of modern Europe, religious men and women who attempt to create new religious institutions or promote religious ideas run into a brick wall of resistance and indifference. That history requires an explanation. Furthermore, if we value fairness, we should allow individuals to be indifferent or irreligious without asserting instead that they are really religious whether they know it or not. On an individual level there is the analogy between Stark and Iannaccone's Durkheimian point of view and Paul Tillich's argument that no one is an atheist since everyone worships something (an argument that I have always found discourteous to atheists).[20]

By the same standard, we should allow people who believe that they are religious to be religious. The 95 per cent of American teenagers who believe in God, and the 91 per cent who pray at least occasionally, are saying something important to pollsters, as are the 29 per cent who claim to have experienced the presence of God.[21] So are the 60 per cent of all Americans who believe that the only assurance of eternal life is personal faith in Jesus Christ, and the 70 per cent who believe in the devil.[22] Like all poll findings in this context, the figures can be knocked down to account for conformism in the face of a pollster. I do not believe the very large poll figures for church attendance in America, any more than I believe the poll results showing surprisingly modest levels of alcohol consumption. If Americans are to be believed, more individuals attend a church or synagogue on any given Sunday than attend all amateur and professional athletic events in the course of an entire year. But the figures for religious participation are notably high when compared to Europe, and the degree of genuine religious piety in the United States should not be dismissed with speculation about the 'internal secularisation' of religious institutions.[23] For a historian, questions of how people view immortality, where they take advice on how to live, and what institutions they support and fund are matters of fundamental importance.

Assertions that Americans are 'not really religious', that American religion is so superficial that it is itself secular, as Bryan Wilson argued in his *Religion in a Secular Society*,[24] are subject to the same objections as the Stark and Iannaccone observations on European religion. There is something about the theory of secularisation that leads repeatedly to a stripping away of the legitimacy of the religious point of view of individuals in the modern world. In America, according to Wilson, 'though religious practice has increased, the vacuousness of popular religious ideas has also increased'.[25] In the words of Roy Wallis and Steve Bruce, men and women with a religious point of view are likely to live in 'society's margins or in its interstices', from which they may emerge into the mainstream 'in times of trauma or major social transformation'.[26] Religion can survive, but only in forms that are secularised, sectarian or fundamentalist. These three categories simply fail to do justice to the diversity of religion in the modern world, or even in modern Europe. The spectrum of modern religious forms cannot be contained within the theoretical boundaries of secularisation theory. Furthermore, invoking the theory does an injustice to individuals, who should be allowed to define their own point of view.

Part of the difficulty with the arguments of Stark and Iannaccone and other resacralisation theorists lies with the global explanatory power of secularisation theory, described rightly by Bryan Wilson as a 'many sided phenomenon'.[27] When they attempt to change the direction of the graph, they find it incorporated into the theory. The all-purpose nature of secularisation theory, by which the major forces at work in the modern world are the cause of decline, allows for a kind of intellectual sleight of hand in meeting objections. Daniel Bell's early resacralisation essay 'The return of the sacred?' met with Bryan Wilson's observation that the returning sacred was not the same phenomenon as the departed religion. Therefore, secularisation remains in place.[28] Callum Brown's persuasive demonstrations that industrialisation and urbanisation cannot have been the primary causes of the decline of religion in England were answered in advance by Alan Gilbert, who identified 'latent' secularisation in the 'manifest' growth of religious denominations during the Industrial Revolution.[29]

Even more important than the promiscuous flexibility of secularisation theory is the persuasive power of the metaphor of the downward slope. When the facts of decline are conceded, the explanatory power of the theory comes into play spontaneously.

Secularisation is an invocatory theory, operating as a kind of stage set in the background of all intellectual effort to understand religion. On many occasions I have addressed audiences who respond to lists of objections to the secularisation theory by agreeing with the specific points of criticism. Yes, the secularisation theory is teleological, Eurocentric, deterministic and deceptively value-laden. Yes, it devalues and marginalises the religious experiences of millions of people in the modern world. Yes, but (comes the query), is it not the case that the overall trend in the modern world is one of decline? It is very difficult to en- visage decline without invoking the metaphor of a universal downward slope with an implicit explanatory cause. Karel Dobbelaere surveys the statistics of recent declines in European church membership, and places them firmly on the slope: 'My conclusion is very straightforward: in Europe, I cannot see that the near future will bring a reversal of the trends described above. Rather, I see a consolidation on the individual level of the secularisation of European society.'[30] Critics like Stark and Iannaccone who attempt to deny that the slope runs downhill invariably run into a triumphant empirical rebuttal.[31] The evi- dence for a decline in the significance of religion in modern European history is overwhelmingly persuasive. In his exchanges with Rodney Stark on Welsh religious history in the *Journal for the Scientific Study of Religion*, Steve Bruce has had much the better of the argument largely because Stark remains trapped in the shadow of the downward slope, a metaphor that invokes the whole theory of secularisation.[32]

Bryan Wilson, who is the best-known defender of the orthodox model of secularisation, has responded to the 'secularisation controversy' with a complacent survey of the facts of decline, those 'items of common knowledge' that 'suggest a process of decline in the social significance of religion'.[33] As a point of logic, it is not clear why the facts of decline should substantiate a particular theory of the causes of decline. But Wilson's error is one not primarily of logic but of rhetoric, a misunderstanding of the rhetorical uses of secularisation theory. He argues that 'secularisation is merely the description, for which empirical evidences can be advanced of a process of social change in which religion loses social significance'.[34] The many-sided theory of secularisation is far more than a description.[35] It is a powerful, all-embracing explanation of religious change in the modern world. As an explanation, it is causal. Furthermore (see Dobbelaere above), it is a prediction. It goes beyond the scope of the normal scientific hypothesis. As Roy Wallis and Steve Bruce concede, 'secularisation is a multi-faceted notion which does not lend itself readily to definitive quantitative test'.[36]

Instead of conceptualising secularisation as merely descriptive, or as a scientific hypothesis to be verified as if conducting a laboratory experiment, it makes more sense to think of secularisation as a story. The practice of history involves comparative story-telling. There are many different kinds of stories, overlapping stories, stories of different levels of generality and even visibility. Historians who make the conventional distinction between narrative history on the one hand and analytical history on the other run the risk of ignoring the narrative nature of analysis, and the explanatory nature of narrative. An analysis is often a story of how a historian has solved a problem. A narrative, far from being a simple arrangement of facts, usually serves some explanatory rhetorical purpose.[37]

Allan Megill outlines a useful classification of the levels of narrative employed by historians.[38] There is the narrative, encompassing not only the familiar chronological ordering of argument usually labelled narrative, but also the story of how the historian has solved a problem. There is the master narrative, the big story that lies behind the narrative, the story that fills in the gaps, as it were. The master narrative is sometimes deployed overtly by the historian, but at other times allowed to stand in the background, making the simple narrative intelligible. Because it is a master narrative, it is often partly hidden from both audience and historian. Finally there is grand narrative, the whole story, the story that God would tell if God could tell a story.[39]

There are several characteristics of Megill's master narrative that come to mind when considering the secularisation theory, or as I will now call it, the secularisation story. The first is that it is partly hidden. It remains in the background to fill in the gaps of the historian's narrative, and to provide implicit explanations where explicit ones cannot be found. It is the master narrative that allows Owen Chadwick to write of secularisation that 'It is often easier to be *sure* that a process is happening than to define precisely what the process contains and how it happens.'[40] The secularisation story can also be invoked for an audience by an image, such as the downward slope on the graph, or by the use of a key word or phrase, such as attaching the word 'only' to a statistic. Only 30 per cent of Spaniards practice their faith, according to *The New York Times*. The word 'dechristianisation', although in many respects both accurate and useful when applied to aspects of modern European history, brings in its train the master narrative of secularisation. It can have that effect despite an author's disclaimers.

The great explanatory power of the secularisation story accounts for its usefulness to such a broad range of people, including many who are not scholars. Secularisation may cause difficulties for those of us who wish to look into religious history in some detail, but invoking the master narrative of secularisation solves the problem of interpreting religion in the modern world for many in the modern European and American professional classes. Bryan Wilson makes this point explicitly and economically:

When . . . one raises this subject with historians, sociologists, economists, or psychologists, one sees how readily those engaged with other aspects of the social system and its culture take secularisation for granted. Their overwhelming tendency . . . is to regard religion as a peripheral phenomenon in contemporary social organisation, and one which, in their studies of the broad contours of social change, productivity, economic growth, or human psychology, they rarely find need to consider. Not infrequently they express some amusement that religion should be given the serious attention which I and others in the sociology of religion devote to it.[41]

Wilson is here appealing to authority: 'these various and numerous social scientists could be overlooking a social force of paramount importance in the operation of those facets of the social system in which they are expert, but I doubt it'.[42]

Frank Turner has outlined the history of this appeal to authority in the struggles among late nineteenth-century British professionals over who has the right to speak with authority within contested spheres of authority.[43] To make this point is not to engage in a reduction of scholarly ideas to class or professional interests. The religious views of professionals vary from time to time and country to country. Although some members of the medical profession were actively secularist in late Victorian England, many doctors are prominent in evangelical

Protestant circles in the United States today. But I have no doubt that Bryan Wilson is right to observe that many social scientists and others in the knowledge industry, especially journalists, take secularisation for granted. David Martin and others based their critique of secularisation in part on an unmasking of its origins in Enlightenment ideology.[44] Some evangelical scholars have complained that the anti-religious bias of the secular academy distorts scholarly discussions of religion.[45] But the uses of the secularisation story today appear to transcend secularist ideology or secularist bias. The secularisation story is a powerful rhetorical device, an explanatory tool with multiple uses. Scholars with an evangelical or other religious point of view resort to it as often as scholars with a secular or 'objective' point of view.[46]

However, Wilson's assertion that social scientists are objectively considering all the alternatives from a disinterested, Olympian point of view, searching for the importance of religion and not finding it, is no more persuasive than accusations of bias or ideology. Social scientists, like historians and other scholars, cannot be questioning all aspects of history and society all the time. They need persuasive, partly hidden master narratives to organise their inquiries. The master narrative of secularisation tells them that religion is not important in the modern world. They need not in any way be hostile to religion in principle, or even irreligious in person, to find the master narrative useful, particularly when a cursory glance at the statistics of religious change in modern Europe will show that religion has, as predicted, declined.

One task of scholarship on modern religious history is the unmasking of the master narrative. We do not always realise how dependent we are on it until it is identified and labelled. But once the secularisation story is unmasked, a third characteristic becomes evident. It is not only partly hidden, and extremely useful, but uncontested. If we set aside celebratory stories of religious triumphalism, the secularisation story is the *only* master narrative of religion in modern history. In some cases it is possible to unmask a master narrative, and discover that it is one of several in contest. The competing master narratives can then be compared directly.

Which is the best story to tell about British history between 1780 and 1840? The growth of working-class consciousness in the face of state oppression and economic exploitation, or capitalist progress and a higher standard of living? Which is the best story to tell about western imperialism? Are all aspects of western culture tainted with the corruption of power, as Edward Said has argued?[47] Or is it possible to write stories of individuals who transcend the boundaries of western power, or to draw up balance sheets on the imperial project? In each of these areas of inquiry there are competing master narratives, acknowledged as such in full or in part by scholars.

When considering the decline of Christendom in modern Europe, however, it is not yet possible to invoke an alternative master narrative. It is possible to write a persuasive critique of the master narrative, and also to write a history of the emergence of the secularisation story. It is also possible to declare the issue open and proceed to write a good book with only an implicit alternative master narrative. But the alternative is never labelled, or identified, or made explicit. It remains implicit, not only partly hidden but altogether hidden. It is not surprising that Sheridan Gilley and W. J. Sheils, editors of the new *History of Religion in Britain*, resort for a summing-up chapter to a secularisation theorist, Alan Gilbert, whose commitment to a linear view of history leaves him unable to imagine an alternative to secularisation other than a 'kind of demodernization which would radically reverse the process of secularisation' and 'might prove catastrophic for civilization as a whole'.[48]

It is difficult to see how civilisation would be threatened, and possible that scholarship would be strengthened, if historians of modern European religion could envisage an alternative master narrative to account for modern religious history. The secularisation story is too complex and many-sided to be 'verified' or 'falsified'; it can only be compared in its persuasiveness to another story, or other stories. As long as secularisation is presented as the only story, one cannot say that it is the best story. Of course, a new master narrative cannot be summoned into existence. Any alternative to the secularisation story, like the secularisation story itself, must emerge from the talks and writings of scholars, theologians, writers, critics and artists, not to mention pastors, priests, nuns, missionaries, and men and women from all walks of life, with religious or irreligious points of view, who are engaged with religion as an historical problem.

Callum Brown has provided a useful starting-point in the form of a list of propositions that constitute his 'revisionist approach to religious change':

The social significance of religion (1) can rise and fall in any social and economic context – pre-industrial, industrial, post-industrial; (2) does not decay automatically or irreversibly with the growth of human knowledge, rationality or technology; (3) does not decay automatically or irreversibly with industrialization or urbanization; (4) is not to be measured by unity of religious belief or uniformity of religious adherence in a given nation/region; (5) can be challenged by fundamental social and economic change, and can suffer short to medium-term decay, but can adapt to the new context and can show significant long-term growth; (6) can change the ways, or the balance of the ways, in which it arises from one social and economic context to another.[49]

The difficulty with drawing up any list of propositions that might constitute elements of an alternative master narrative to the secularisation story is that, by the nature of the intellectual enterprise, they will be less persuasive than the fully formed master narrative. One cannot write a new master narrative from scratch. One can only begin discussions, as Brown has done, and point the way to themes that might emerge in conceptualising an alternative. One theme, evident in Brown's propositions, is the emergence of the possibility of decline. When religion is enforced by state power and force of law, and the only cosmology available is a religious one, then religion cannot decline in the way it has declined in modern European history. There may be broad levels of indifference to religious institutions and ideas, but indifference is never allowed public sanction or even public acknowledgement. The defining characteristic of religion in the modern world is not its decline, but the possibility of its decline. An alternative master narrative will focus on state and legal power and the origins of religious toleration rather than structural differentiation, urbanisation and industrialisation; it will concentrate on the emergence of conflicts over the significance of Newtonian and Darwinian cosmologies, rather than assume that either is in some way intrinsically lethal to religion. There has been enough scholarship on the relationship of science and theology to recognise that scientific views of the world are compatible with religious points of view, and also capable of generating competing irreligious points of view.[50]

The consequences of religious toleration and the emergence of a scientific cosmology have been the creation of alternatives to religion, in the form either of publicly sanctioned indifference or of active opposition to religion. This is compatible with Brown's assumption that decline is a possibility, along with growth. In a new master narrative, decline ceases to be inevitable. It becomes, instead, a topic of historical inquiry.

To the rise and fall of religion in modern history should be added transformation. When measuring the 'declining social significance of religion', one must recognise that the unit being measured has changed its character. The dot on the downward slope does not cease to represent a phenomenon known as religion, but it does represent a different kind of religion. Religion is no longer a sacred canopy, imposed by state power or by the universal force of social opinion. It is a private, voluntary activity, one which occasionally uses social opinion and political force, depending on historical circumstances. The eighteenth- and nineteenth-century European churches contributed to, and participated in, a momentous transition from a 'confessional' religious settlement to a 'voluntarist' religious settlement. Under the early modern 'confessional' religious settlement, the fate of religious institutions was primarily a matter for political and social elites to settle for the benefit of those below them in the social scale. Under the 'voluntarist' religious settlement, public forms of religious institutions are treated as consequences of the conscientious choices of individual believers.[51]

Far from being passive in responding to the emergence of a voluntarist religious settlement, the nineteenth-century churches were extremely aggressive both at home and abroad in a struggle to recruit members, build religious institutions, maintain their influence and create new forms of influence. As a result of that struggle, new religious forms were created that would have been difficult to envisage in the seventeenth century. England was blanketed with parish churches in 1600, a year in which some connection with religious institutions would have been difficult to avoid. England was blanketed with Sunday schools in 1900, a year in which it was very difficult to make it through childhood without some connection with Sunday school. There are important theological and institutional continuities linking the two historical moments, but there are also radical changes in the nature of religion.

Brown's propositions turn the decline of Christendom into a problem, and reflect an implicit alternative master narrative which may be found in the work of sociologists and historians who have attempted to focus attention on new explanations of decline in Europe. These scholars look for causes of decline other than those cited in the orthodox model: urbanisation, industrialisation, 'modernisation' (with its various meanings) and structural differentiation. Their implicit alternative master narrative points the way to a focus on (among other things) a comparative history of the institutions of European Christendom. Stark and Iannaccone, for instance, before they became distracted with an attempt to refute secularisation theory, called attention to the lack of competitiveness of European religious institutions. This lack of competitiveness was the theme of a path-breaking study of the churches in Reading by Stephen Yeo, whose influence has perhaps been limited by his choice of a colourless but none the less precisely accurate title: *Religion and Voluntary Organizations in Crisis*.[52] Subsequent work on New York, Berlin, the West Riding of Yorkshire and the much studied boroughs of South London, although different in many respects, continues the institutional focus found in Yeo, as does the work by Robin Gill on the mentality of Victorian architectural over-supply.[53]

Another line of inquiry, especially in the work of Hugh McLeod and Jim Obelkevich, concerns the peculiarities of social class in its relationship to religion.[54] European religious institutions have been seriously hampered by the class nature of the religious settlement of the early modern period, one that left elite class overtones to acts of voluntary participation that were very difficult to overcome in the nineteenth century, and generated a popular culture of indifference to institutional and therefore to religious claims in the twentieth century. I am using class in the imprecise sense that we find in nineteenth-century public discourse. Frank Turner's work is important in showing how the English professional classes were polarised along lines of religion by a specifically Victorian struggle for professional influence.[55]

Discussions of an alternative master narrative will revolve around these themes: (1) the emergence of the possibility of a decline in the social significance of religion; (2) the importance of the change in character of religion as it ceases to be imposed from above; (3) the relative competitiveness of European religious institutions, in terms of both social location and membership recruitment; (4) the distinctive imprint of social class on particular religious settlements. It is also important to treat modern religious history in the context of what Dipesh Chakrabarty has referred to as 'provincialization of Europe'.[56] The theory of secularisation represents a globalisation and universalisation of European experience, one that should be placed where it belongs, in the histories of particular places and times. The decline of Christendom in Europe may turn out to be a European experience, only some of which is replicated in the experiences of other parts of the world. The examples cited in this chapter have been for the most part from England, but they bring to mind the contrast with the United States, comparisons with other European countries that share in the decline of Christendom, and the story of large-scale overseas and imperial expansion of European Christendom in the nineteenth and twentieth centuries.

One of the most useful aspects of studying the missionary movement is the light it throws on the history of the churches in Europe and North America, since missionaries were forced openly to confront problems abroad which remained hidden at home. My own research comparing British and American Protestant missionaries in colonial Punjab demonstrates that missionaries with similar theological views, but different denominational and national backgrounds, behaved in very different ways.[57] The Victorian English missionary theorist, Henry Venn, speculated on this point as early as the 1860s:

the Missions of other denominations, supporting their own teachers and of their self-exertion for the extension of the Gospel:– as in the case of the American Baptist Mission among the Karens of Burmah, or the Independents among the Armenians of Asia Minor, and of the wonderful preservation and increase of Christianity in Madagascar after the expulsion of European Missionaries. The unfavourable contrast may be explained by the fact that other denominations are accustomed to take part in the elementary organization of their Churches at home, and therefore more readily carry out that organization in the Missions. Whereas in our Church the Clergy find everything relating to elementary organization settled by the Law of the Land:– as in the provision of tithes, of church-rates, of other customary payments, in the constitution of parishes, and in parish officers, our Clergy are not prepared for the question of Church organization; and therefore in the Missions they exercise the ministry of the Word without reference to the non-existence of the organization by which it is supported at home.[58]

At the time Venn wrote, the Church of England was in the midst of a lengthy and uneven transition from an early modern confessional church to a modern voluntary church. Venn recognised the unique problems faced by an established church, or by a denomination which shared the attitudes of an established church, under the new voluntarist religious settlement. Even missionaries often failed to realise that long-term success in a voluntarist environment rests upon a foundation of membership recruitment. The Church of England and other denominations were making choices about how to recruit members and maximise their influence at home as well as overseas, but like many European churches it confronted a contested and confusing definition of 'membership'. Among the strategies available to them were aggressive membership recruitment, the maintenance of social and political influence, a struggle to maintain or extend state funding, and the raising of private funds for the construction of religious institutions, including churches, schools and charities.

Recent scholarship has focused on the extent to which the British churches made decisions to defend and extend their social influence, and create new religious institutions to supply religious, educational and social welfare services to a general population. Examples include a very popular early twentieth-century British Sunday school programme that did not lead into church membership;[59] a Victorian church building programme that produced buildings designed more for the external effect on the pedestrian than for the convenience of the congregation;[60] a large-scale, decentralised commitment to maintaining social welfare services;[61] and a large investment in church-related schools, and later in religious broadcasting, that might have generated a vague 'diffusive Christianity' but failed to generate new members for the churches.[62]

These strategies were not 'mistakes'. To an historian, influence is as important as membership recruitment, and the churches have played important roles in education, politics, social welfare and the shaping of public values in nineteenth- and twentieth-century Europe. From an early twenty-first-century perspective, the nineteenth century appears a time of vigorous institutional revival.[63] What they have not produced is a body of individuals willing to make the sacrifices of time and money necessary to perpetuate these religious institutions from generation to generation. The large investment in the construction of institutions *for* the people, rather than *of* the people, has left many European churches with large, expensive, inflexible commitments. The struggle for influence nurtured a vague unaffiliated popular piety in modern European nations which is a substitute for active membership, and acts as a kind of inoculation which prevents new denominations from recruiting successfully in the general population.

The debilitating effects of a lengthy struggle for privilege and influence are not limited to Europe, but obviously affected the American Congregationalist and Episcopalian denominations in the period of the early Republic. American exceptionalism is taken much too far by many American church historians. A struggle for influence and privilege is a theme in American religious history as well as European, as is the declining social influence of the clergy. But in surveying the history of American religion one is struck with the sink-or-swim commitment to membership recruitment by nineteenth-century Baptists and Methodists, and twentieth-century Mormons and Pentecostalists. It may be the case that American institutional success has generated a popular culture that is more receptive to religious argument. Or as Simon Green has suggested of British religion: 'Conventional wisdom and common sense suggest that the people stopped going to church because they no longer believed what the churches taught them. Perhaps the causal mechanism was really closer to the opposite: they stopped believing because they stopped going.'[64] In the history of the success or failure of religious institutions in modern history, we may find the key to understanding the decline of Christendom in modern Europe.

At the heart of critical historical scholarship is a decision: which is the best story? The history of religion in modern Europe is impoverished by an absence of alternative stories. In recent scholarship, however, it is possible to see the outlines of an alternative master narrative, tentative and sketchy and relatively unpersuasive though it may be when compared to the master narrative of secularisation. As the discussion continues we may soon be able to ask: which is the best story to tell about the decline of Christendom in modern Europe?[65]

NOTES

1. See Steve Bruce (ed.), *Religion and Modernization: Sociologists and Historians Debate the Secularization Thesis* (Oxford, 1992).
2. For a summary see Hugh McLeod, *Religion and Society in England, 1850–1914* (New York, 1996), introduction, 1–10.
3. S. J. D. Green, *Religion in the Age of Decline: Organisation and Experience in Industrial Yorkshire, 1870–1920* (Cambridge, 1996), 17.
4. *Ibid.*, 16.
5. 'Religious change in an American city. A conversation with Jay Demerath', in *Religion and Values in Public Life: A Forum from Harvard Divinity School*, 1(4) (1993), 8.
6. David Martin, 'Towards eliminating the concept of secularization', in Julius Gould (ed.), *Penguin Survey of the Social Sciences* (Harmondsworth, 1965), reprinted in his *The Religious and the Secular: Studies in Secularization* (New York, 1969); Lucian Hölscher, 'Secularization and urbanization in the nineteenth century. An interpretive model', in Hugh McLeod (ed.), *European Religion in the Age of Great Cities 1830–1930* (London and New York, 1995), 263–88.
7. See Malise Ruthven, 'The fundamentalism project', *TLS*, 4700, 30 April 1993, 14.
8. *The New York Times*, Friday, 4 August 1989.
9. *The New York Times*, Thursday, 13 February 1997.
10. *The New York Times*, Thursday, 7 March 2002, A14, quoting an American major in Afghanistan: 'the local fundamentalists have called a jihad against the Americans . . . we've got confirmed kills in the hundreds'.
11. Kingsley Martin, *Critic's London Diary: From the New Statesman, 1931–1956* (London, 1960), 130.
12. *TLS*, 15 February 2002.
13. Bryan R. Wilson, 'Reflections on a many sided controversy', in Bruce (ed.), *Religion and Modernization*, 195–210, 209.
14. Peter Burke (ed.), *The New Cambridge Modern History*, vol. XIII, *Companion Volume* (Cambridge, 1979), 312, 316.
15. Demerath conversation, discussing his book, N. J. Demerath III and Rhys H. Williams, *Bridging of Faiths: Religion and Politics in a New England City* (Princeton, 1992).
16. Rodney Stark and William Sims Bainbridge, *A Theory of Religion* (New York, 1987), especially chapter 9.

17. Emile Durkheim, *The Elementary Forms of the Religious Life*, trans. from the French by Joseph Ward Swain (New York, 1915).
18. Rodney Stark and Laurence R. Iannaccone, 'A supply-side reinterpretation of the "secularization" of Europe', *Journal for the Scientific Study of Religion*, 33(3) (1994), 230–52, at 231.
19. *Ibid.*, 231.
20. See Paul Tillich, *What Is Religion?* (New York, 1969).
21. *The Des Moines Register*, 11 January 1992.
22. *The Baptist Standard*, 28 October 1992. Half of those who believe in the devil believe that he/she is an impersonal force.
23. Wilson, 'Reflections', 203.
24. Bryan Wilson, *Religion in a Secular Society* (Baltimore, 1966), chapter 6.
25. *Ibid.*, 122.
26. Roy Wallis and Steve Bruce, 'Secularization: the orthodox model', in Bruce (ed.), *Religion and Modernization*, 21.
27. Wilson, 'Reflections', 206.
28. Daniel Bell, 'The return of the sacred?', *British Journal of Sociology*, 28 (1977), 419–90; Bryan Wilson, 'The return of the sacred', *Journal for the Scientific Study of Religion*, 18 (1979), 268–80.
29. Callum Brown, 'Did urbanization secularize Britain?', *Urban History Yearbook* (1988), 1–14; and 'The mechanism of religious growth in urban societies: British cities since the eighteenth century', in McLeod (ed.), *European Religion in the Age of Great Cities*, 239–61; Alan D. Gilbert, *Religion and Society in Industrial England: Church, Chapel and Social Change, 1740–1914* (London, 1976), viii, 205.
30. Karel Dobbelaere, 'Church involvement and secularization: making sense of the European case', in Eileen Barker, James A. Beckford and Karel Dobbelaere (eds.), *Secularization, Rationalism, and Sectarianism: Essays in Honour of Bryan R. Wilson* (Oxford, 1993), 31.
31. See for example Phillip E. Hammond and Mark A. Shibley, 'When the sacred returns: an empirical test', in Barker *et al.* (eds.), *Secularization*, 37–46.
32. Steve Bruce, 'The truth about religion in Britain', *Journal for the Scientific Study of Religion*, 34(4) (1995), 417–30; with comment, 'Truth? A reply to Bruce', *Journal for the Scientific Study of Religion*, 34(4) 1995, 516–19.
33. Wilson, 'Reflections', 198.
34. *Ibid.*, 209.
35. Unless one takes description in a broad, analytical sense that encompasses explanation, but that is not the way Wilson appears to be invoking the word.
36. Wallis and Bruce, 'Secularization: the orthodox model', 9.
37. See Allan Megill, 'Recounting the past: "Description", explanation, and narrative in historiography', *The American Historical Review*, 94(3) (1989), 627–53.
38. Allan Megill, '"Grand narrative" and the discipline of history', in Frank Ankersmit and Hans Kellner (eds.), *A New Philosophy of History* (Chicago, 1995), 151–73.
39. Dorothy Ross uses the phrase 'grand narrative' to mean roughly what Megill means by 'master narrative'. Dorothy Ross, 'Grand narrative in American historical writing: from romance to uncertainty', *American Historical Review*, 100(3) (1995), 651–77. Others use the phrase 'meta-narrative', which takes us beyond narrative altogether.

Megill's distinctions are imprecise but none the less useful, especially perhaps to historians.

40. Owen Chadwick, *The Secularization of the European Mind in the Nineteenth Century* (Cambridge, 1975), 2 (emphasis mine).
41. Wilson, 'Reflections', 210.
42. *Ibid.*
43. Frank M. Turner, *Contesting Cultural Authority: Essays in Victorian Intellectual Life* (Cambridge, 1993).
44. Martin, 'Toward eliminating the concept of secularization'.
45. See for instance Lamin O. Sanneh, *Encountering the West: Christianity and the Global Cultural Process: the African Dimension* (Maryknoll, NY, 1993).
46. See for instance Os Guinness, *The Gravedigger File* (London, 1983).
47. Edward W. Said, *Orientalism* (New York, 1978), 204.
48. Alan Gilbert, 'Secularization and the future', in Sheridan Gilley and W. J. Shiels (eds.), *A History of Religion in Britain: Practice and Belief from Pre-Roman Times to the Present* (Oxford, 1994), 503–21, at 520.
49. Brown, 'A revisionist approach to religious change', 31–58, 55–6.
50. On the British and American clerical response to the challenge of 'positivism', see Charles D. Cashdollar, *The Transformation of Theology, 1830–1890: Positivism and Protestant Thought in Britain and America* (Princeton, 1989); on evangelical Protestant adaptations to Darwinism see James R. Moore, *The Post-Darwinian Controversies: A Study of the Protestant Struggle to Come to Terms with Darwin in Great Britain and America, 1870–1900* (Cambridge, 1979).
51. For the large literature on 'confessionalism', see the summary in Benjamin J. Kaplan, *Calvinists and Libertines: Confession and Community in Utrecht 1578–1620* (Oxford, 1995), Introduction. I am using the word 'voluntarist' in a different sense from the variant of the nineteenth-century term 'voluntaryist', implying simply a commitment to the separation of church and state. For this use of the term see J. P. Ellens, *Religious Routes to Gladstonian Liberalism* (Pennsylvania, 1994). I do not intend here to invoke the misleading metaphor of a 'free market' in religion, which I discuss in Jeffrey Cox, 'Religion and imperial power in nineteenth-century Britain', in R. W. Davis and Richard Helmstadter (eds.), *Freedom and Religion in the Nineteenth Century* (Stanford, forthcoming), 339–428, 340–1.
52. Stephen Yeo, *Religion and Voluntary Organizations in Crisis* (London, 1976).
53. Hugh McLeod, *Piety and Poverty: Working-Class Religion in Berlin, London, and New York, 1870–1914* (New York, 1996); Jeffrey Cox, *The English Churches in a Secular Society: Lambeth, 1870–1930* (New York, 1982); J. N. Morris, *Religion and Urban Change: Croydon, 1840–1914* (Woodbridge, Suffolk, 1992); Robin Gill, *The Myth of the Empty Church* (London, 1993); S. C. Williams, *Religious Belief and Popular Culture in Southwark, c.1880–1939* (Oxford and New York, 1999).
54. Hugh McLeod, *Class and Religion in the Late Victorian City* (London, 1974); McLeod, *Religion and the Working Class in Nineteenth-Century Britain* (London, 1984); McLeod, *Religion and the People of Western Europe, 1789–1970* (Oxford, 1981); James Obelkevich, *Religion and Rural Society: South Lindsey 1825–1875* (Oxford, 1976).
55. Turner, *Contesting Cultural Authority*; see also James R. Moore, 'Theodicy and society: the crisis of the intelligentsia', in R. Helmstadter and B. Lightman (eds.),

Victorian Faith in Crisis: Essays on Continuity and Change in Nineteenth Century Religious Belief (Stanford, 1990), 153–86.

56. Dipesh Chakrabarty, 'Post-coloniality and the artifice of history: who speaks for "Indian" pasts?', *Representations*, 37 (1992), 1–26.

57. See Jeffrey Cox, *Imperial Fault Lines: Christianity and Colonial Power in India, 1818–1940* (Stanford, CA, 2002).

58. Church Missionary Society Minute of 1861 on the Organization of Native Churches, cited in Max Warren (ed.), *To Apply the Gospel: Selections from the Writing of Henry Venn* (Grand Rapids, MI, 1971), 66–8.

59. Green, *Religion in an Age of Decline*, chapter 5.

60. Gill, *The Myth of the Empty Church*.

61. Cox, *English Churches, passim*.

62. Asa Briggs, 'Christ and the media: secularization, rationalism, and sectarianism in the history of British broadcasting, 1922–1976', in Barker *et al.* (eds.), *Secularization*, 267–86, at 282.

63. Callum G. Brown, *The Death of Christian Britain: Understanding Secularisation, 1800–2000* (London and New York, 2001).

64. Green, *Religion in an Age of Decline*, 390–1.

65. A conference on 'Alternative master narratives of religion in the modern world' was convened at the Research Center Religion and Society, University of Amsterdam, in April 2002.

13   A missiological postscript

Werner Ustorf

The Missiology of Western Culture's History Group had the intuition that Christendom might be a useful lens through which to gain a missiological perspective on the history of Christianity in the West. When twenty-two scholars from eight countries gathered in the Maison Nicolas Barré, Paris, in April 1997 for the group's third colloquium and to discuss the decline of Christendom in western Europe in the last two or so centuries, there was already a sense of unease about the future and, more importantly, the nature of Christianity. In our brief to the participants, the History Group had defined Christendom rather broadly, but in distinction to Christianity: Christendom is a civilisation in which (a) Christianity is the dominant religion and (b) this dominance has been backed up by social or legal compulsions. For discussion we offered the following working hypothesis: the coercion, control and domination that were part of the Christendom model of church and mission carry within themselves the seeds of the modern repudiation of Christianity in Europe.[1] (In focusing on western Europe, we did not consider how far our definitions might apply to other Christendoms, such as Ethiopia.)

The participants, representing different national, cultural, political, historical and often denominational traditions and each being an expert in his or her field, quickly detected the dissenters' voice or the radical Reformation bias in all of this and demonstrated that the matter was much more complex and the overall picture more diverse and even ambiguous than this (see Hugh McLeod's Introduction). Since understandings of religion are continually changing, and since there has been no consensus even at any one point as to what religion (and Christianity) is, there can be no objective criteria that would justify the language of decline. Nor has any new grand narrative been found that would cover the multifarious historical evidence. It seems that, by Christianity, different cultural and social groups, different periods of history, and different contexts have understood rather different things.

A missiological interpretation of Christianity's history in the West will gain in credibility and reliability if it is informed by the wealth of material and readings historians have to offer. So far, this is a task still to be accomplished. On the other hand, it must be said that historians – even church historians – do not really read missiological literature. Crossing the boundaries of the disciplines and looking at the interplay between gospel and culture within the lands of the West is a promising approach – and one that gave the Paris Colloquium a sense of a new venture.[2] How do this venture and its in many ways inconclusive results then fit into the wider missiological discussion?

In the first century of its academic existence missiology was very much a domain of the West. It had often been applying a practical form of missiological materialism: unable to demonstrate rationally or philosophically the non-truth of other religions, ways of life and convictions, or the certainty of the victory of Christianity over its rivals, it resorted to resolving the question of truth through practical means by claiming that, ultimately, numbers and 'spiritual experience' would endorse and vindicate the superiority of Christianity. This position is intellectually untenable and historically a high-risk strategy to say the least. It still has its defenders. Much celebrated among missiologists today is the metamorphosis of Christianity into a non-Western religion. The church, indeed since 1492, has experienced a double process, namely a large numerical increase, or accession (in the Americas, Africa, Asia and the Pacific), and a substantial decrease, or recession (mainly in Europe). The alternation of periods of accession and recession in the history of Christianity was made an organising principle by Kenneth Scott Latourette (1884–1968), Yale's prominent mission historian, in his *A History of the Expansion of Christianity*.[3] Statistically, these developments have always been carefully monitored. The leading authority in this field is currently David B. Barrett, professor of missiometrics (in the US, not surprisingly) and one of the authors of the *World Christian Encyclopedia*.[4] This encyclopedia supplies us with data such as these: the Christian share of the world's population has been static (around 33 per cent) for the last hundred years, and will very likely remain so for the foreseeable future – despite the increasing number of Christian missionaries working in countries other than their own (at present around 420,000) and despite sophisticated plans for global evangelisation (770 such projects are currently underway).

After all, the making of Christians is expensive: 46 billion dollars per year are currently spent on home and foreign missions. Statistically, however, mission is a lot cheaper in the Third World than in the West: the 'cost-effectiveness' of baptism in the Third World, i.e. of getting one person baptised in the Congo (Zaire) for example compares to that of the UK at a ratio of about 1 to 693. The meteoric rise of the Pentecostal, Charismatic and neo-Charismatic renewal (at present 27.7 per cent of organised global Christianity) is in its majority (more than two thirds) a non-white and non-Western phenomenon. The West is indeed a problem for those who apply the inherited (sometimes rather Victorian) images of church and mission to world Christianity, and not only in terms of money: despite what Barrett describes as the 'massive gains' of Christianity in the Third World, particularly in Africa (23,000 new Christians per day), the total numbers are kept down by 'the massive defections' in the West (7600 per day), mainly in Europe and in North America. Where do these western defectors go? According to the Encyclopedia, they join the 'secular quasireligions', a term that lumps together agnosticism, atheism, materialism, secularism, communism, nazism, humanism and 'constructed or fabricated pseudo-religions'. As said before, the inclusion of the materials and readings historians have to offer can only improve the reliability of this kind of missiometrics. In one regard, however, all missiologists, whatever their particular point of view, would agree: the topography of world Christianity has changed beyond recognition. Christianity today is split into approximately 34,000 separate denominations (a number that includes the African Independent Churches) – it is a 'massive Babel of diversity' (Barrett) or, in the words of the late Adrian Hastings, a 'chameleon' and 'many-faced monster'.[5] How does one describe the shape of this monster without imprisoning it in one's own views and tradition, likes and dislikes?

Two examples, taken from the missionary movement, will show that the idea of Christianity as a shape-shifter outside the West has a tradition and that, therefore, the transformations of the European shape of Christianity discussed in this volume are actually endorsing a wider perception of the realities of the faith. A first attempt at what was later called a 'new style of missionary historiography'[6] goes back already to the 1950s. In 1954 the International Missionary Council commissioned a series of depth studies of churches in the non-Western world, and in the sixties these were published by the Division of World Mission and Evangelism of the World Council of Churches (WCC) under the title *World Studies of Churches in Mission*.[7] The novelty of these studies lay in their approach, since they were written not from the point of view of mission boards or of mission historians from the West, but from the indigenous churches' own understanding of what it meant to be Christian in their specific contexts. This approach reflected on the one hand the process of decolonisation, on the other a shift in missiological methods: instead of coming with pre-established biblical criteria against which to measure these churches, the process was reversed, with the hope being that the life of these churches would in turn generate a new interpretation of scripture.

When, in the sixties, following the slogan of the world mission conference of 1963 in Mexico City, 'mission in six continents', a couple of Western church contexts were added to the study series (Hamburg and Birmingham), it was made sure that non-Western scholars authored or at least co-authored these volumes.[8] The purpose of these studies was to take account of the variety of church contexts and of the diversity of Christian responses to different cultural and social situations. The great surprise, however, was that the variety and the diversity were far greater than had been anticipated. In fact, the research was, as the evaluation study put it, 'gloriously disappointing'.[9] It is quite ironic to note that one of the proposals of the WCC conference at Uppsala in 1968 had been to examine the worldwide church through field studies and decide 'whether any general principles emerge from them',[10] and here was such a field study which found no such principles, unless diversity as such is seen as a general principle. A simple and general pattern in church development could not be established, and none of the many possible definitions of church seemed to describe a single one of the churches analysed in the study. The differences ran much deeper than surface level, and every church situation was different: its history, the cultural patterns, the self-definition, and the ways in which the boundaries to its environment were drawn; even biblical interpretation differed from context to context. The tighter the description was, the more contradictions surfaced, and the more elusive became the notion of 'the' church. Apart from the fact that they all related to the story of Jesus Christ and, hence, to the New Testament, there was no discernible unifying principle. At the end of the day, the church was regarded as beyond empirical or historical research, a comparison of churches did not lead to a safe knowledge about the church and Christianity, and the whole evaluation ended in a cheerful but 'very humble agnosticism'.[11]

The other example relates to the scholarly œuvre of the African missiologist Lamin Sanneh, one of the successors to the chair once held by Latourette at Yale Divinity School. Sanneh offers a rereading of colonial and mission history (just as the present volume does in relation to the recent Christian history of Europe) and presents a challenge to what he calls the received academic orthodoxy or the 'standard historiography' of Christianity.[12] Early on, Sanneh decided that the discipline of missiology ought to be liberated from its captivity to 'Western ethnocentrism',[13] and focus on the central aspect of religious transformation in the recipient local culture. This had two immediate consequences for the further direction of his scholarly work: one is the rehabilitation – in this case – of the African agency, or 'the African factor', in the process of religious change. The other is the question of the relationship between culture and religion, because one can only single out the religious nature of the transformation if one makes the distinction between what is, and what is not, religious.

Focusing on the African factor led to a reinterpretation of mission history and to the twin result (1) that Africa actively 'captured' Christianity (and Islam) for herself, and therefore changed their interpretation, and (2) that 'Western charts' and interpretations are no longer to be regarded as the universal yardstick in world Christianity.[14] The implication of this is not only that African cultures had a substantial import in reinterpreting the Christian message, that the colonialist verdict of inferiority was untrue, but that Christianity and mission, in so far as the message is 'captured' through a process of translation and vernacularisation, are not the destroyers of local cultures, but their allies and preservers. Embracing Christianity therefore actually meant to embrace African culture.[15] In other words, operating here is implicitly a modified theory of fulfilment (the Christian message as fulfilling the aspirations of the previous religion). That leads to the second aspect.

The relationship between culture and religion is seen as a dialectical process oscillating between the destigmatisation and the relativisation of culture. This is based on the familiar paradox of their essential disparity and formal unity. Christianity is at the same time in 'profound continuity' with, and thus the 'fulfilment' of, African traditional religions, and 'a radical force' in their critique and transformation – because culture, including cultural expressions of the faith, is always 'non-divine', 'earthly' and 'non-absolute'.[16] God remains different from any cultural presupposition, and the gospel keeps its culture-critical stance. However, without cultural life-images of God the Christian message becomes fossilised. We are touching here a cornerstone of Sanneh's interpretation: just like Greschat in this volume, he makes the struggle between using culture as a trajectory of the search for God and as the deification of cultural images of God an implicit principle,[17] even a universal law, of Christian and cultural history as such.[18] The regulative statement is anti-perfectionist, and claims that neither 'pure faith', i.e. a universal and transcultural standard of the faith, nor 'cultural purity' do exist.[19] On the other hand, the vernacular definition of the Christian message is highly profitable because this expands the general scope for understanding the message. When Christianity went through 'the crucible' of African traditional religions this new host-environment contributed the interpretation of hope, reconciliation, tolerance of diversity and the inclusiveness of human community as central issues of Christianity.[20] This still is culturally limited, but represents a new set of 'interpersonal ethics', a new model of 'normative principles' of what 'God might be saying to us'.[21]

What made Sanneh go against the Western concept of Christendom certainly is the root experience of God's inclusiveness, which he puts as 'God's faithfulness toward all peoples'.[22] If he is right about the nature of Christianity as a pluralist religion, and there is no transcultural concept of truth, we are actually facing a built-in structural vulnerability or disadvantage at the heart of the Christian religion. It is indeed rooted in the idea of the incarnation itself.[23] The only way for us to see the 'face' of God or, more theologically correctly, to be met by the 'divine self-disclosure',[24] is by using our respective cultural glasses or spectacles, without, however, sacralising or absolutising these tools. This struggle for the authenticity of the faith with, in and through culture then generates the space for human development, including the development of the faith, human freedom and the acceptance of our limitations, intercultural communication and intellectual inquiry, in brief the arena of history.[25] Sanneh does not deny the existence of exclusive norms of truth or an essence of Christianity, but it is affirmed that this is not at our disposal.[26] What is within our reach, and indeed of utter necessity, is what he calls a critical comparative perspective. This is the organising principle of *Translating the Message*, and it has a negative tendency: the comparison of one cultural expression of the faith in the light of another expression does not lead necessarily to 'truth', but it is the 'antidote' to the 'monolithic tyranny' of a particular inculturation of the faith, and therefore works against the forces of uniformity and centralisation.[27]

Missiologically, then, the big picture is like this: terms such as mission and Christian are holding precariously together what is in fact an enormous variety of experiences and expressions. Churches and theologies, on the one hand, are individual manifestations of Christian identity and history and, on the other, are improvisations, transition stages or transit camps of a much larger continuing and unfinished intercultural communication. Each of the new beginnings in Christian identity (that is the formation of new knowledge as to what it means to be Christian) is subjective and starts its rereading of all other Christian identities from its own specific contextual location. In this regard, each variation of Christian identity has its own centre, as every sphere its own centre of gravity. Differently perhaps from other great religions, Christianity does not insist on a specific cultural and linguistic shape – however, the necessary translation and appropriation of the message and the meaning of faith into the local context almost amounts to a kind of reinvention of the faith. This reinvention sketches a new vision of humanity, a new language of the sacred, and therefore constitutes a widening of the Christian vision. The Christian story is characterised by a high degree of malleability and a permanent trend towards the revision of its previous shapes (*fides semper inculturanda*). If Christianity, seen from an historical point of view, appears to be a chameleon it is clear that historians cannot claim to find the universally valid measure for all things Christian *within* the historical process. Domesticating the chameleon (that is: making a particular shape of Christian identity the yardstick of all others) is not their job.

If missiologists were to emancipate themselves from the point of view of mission boards or from the standard historiographies and look at the post-Christian (in Callum Brown's view) context of Britain or, perhaps, Europe, in the way the WCC study of the 1960s looks at the world church, or Lamin Sanneh at African Christian history, a new picture and interpretation of the transformations within European Christianity may emerge. This volume has produced some of the data that are useful for creating this new picture. The important methodological decision is to start not with the inherited and now often rejected doctrinal or institutional images Christianity in Europe has generated (this would represent a 'shrivelling of the spirit', to apply a phrase by Isaiah Berlin),[28] but with people's own understandings and the interpretations generated by the local European cultures in action and reaction to what they understand to be the gospel. This would require missiologists to pay attention to the European factor in the appropriation of Christian memory and to ask how far a European intepretation of Christianity, which has gone through the crucible of modernity, might enlarge the Christian vision.

Christian faith is in a constant conversation with the realities of the past. The European past is that of the Enlightenment and its secular trends. We can only work in the culture we have got. This culture may be, as Grace Davie argues, exceptional on a global scale, but it has produced a new agenda and a new set of questions that, at the end of the day, end up as questions about Jesus Christ. Christianity, in this cultural context, cannot avoid answering the questions the Enlightenment and, then, the post-Enlightenment have asked, in particular those they themselves could not answer. Other forms of Christianity, in Africa for example, have indeed demonstrated their strength to flourish largely outside the Enlightenment world-view. It would even be fair to say that the questions posed by the Enlightenment and postmodernity are not at the top of the priority list of most of the other varieties of Christianity. There, issues of poverty, war, marginalisation and environmental degradation are much more in the centre. The Christian discourses in our days just are very diverse. They are certainly not mutually exclusive. They even help, as Sanneh pointed out, to critique and correct one another. But the Enlightenment provided a new intellectual framework for the understanding of Christ in the west. The Christian appropriation of this culture is not, as Andrew F. Walls emphasises, a 'betrayal of Christian faith', but 'an indigenization of Christianity in Western terms'.[29] It has introduced new cultural and religious materials into the Christian story and is therefore, just like any other variety of Christianity, syncretistic. What matters, to continue the position of Walls, is not the religious and cultural content of the faith, but its direction towards Christ. A missiological perspective on the West does not mean to replace something old by something new, but to reorder the elements that are already there in such a way that they face towards Christ. God calls us into the future and to Himself, not necessarily into religion, Christianity or church. Viewing the Western context missiologically also means that there are no safe ways and that there is no predetermined pattern of Christian life and thought. All these are not to be prescribed by those who repeat what they always used to say, but by the new converts of the faith.

NOTES

1. The working methods of the History Group are described by Alan Kreider, *The Origins of Christendom in the West* (Edinburgh, 2001).
2. It is not really new; at least there are precursors; compare, for example, the succinct title of the German project to describe *Kirchengeschichte als Missionsgeschichte* in the 1970s. Two volumes only were eventually published; the first one contains the historiographical rationale of the project and was edited by H. Frohnes and U. Knorr (on the Ancient Church) (Munich, 1974).
3. Seven vols., New York and London, 1937–45.
4. David B. Barrett, George T. Kurian and Todd M. Johnson, *World Christian Encyclopedia: A Comparative Survey of Churches and Religions in the Modern World*,

vol. I, *The World by Countries: Religions, Churches, Ministries*; vol. II, *The World by Segments: Religions, Peoples, Languages, Cities, Topics*, 2nd edition (New York, 2001).

5. A. Hastings (ed.), *A World History of Christianity* (London, 1999), Introduction.

6. Thus the Dutch missiologist (then teaching at Union Theological Seminary, New York) Johannes Christian Hoekendijk in 1969.

7. Up to 1970 thirteen volumes had been published. An overall assessment of the study process is contained in Steven G. Mackie (ed.), *Can Churches Be Compared? Reflections on Fifteen Study Projects*, Research Pamphlet 17 (Geneva, 1970).

8. The church study on Birmingham, UK, for example, was done by K. A. Busia, a theologian and sociologist from Ghana, cf. *Urban Churches in Britain: A Question of Relevance* (London, 1966).

9. Mackie, *Can Churches Be Compared?*, 99.

10. Norman Goodall (ed.), *The Uppsala Report* (Geneva, 1968), 202.

11. Mackie, *Can Churches Be Compared?*, 101.

12. The following of Sanneh's publications have been looked at: *West African Christianity: The Religious Impact* (Maryknoll, NY, 1983); *Translating the Message: The Missionary Impact on Culture* (Maryknoll, NY, 1989); *Encountering the West: Christianity and the Global Cultural Process: The African Dimension* (Maryknoll, NY, 1993).

13. This impulse is to be found throughout his work, and within the here analysed materials first and strongly expressed in *West African Christianity*, xvii.

14. Cf. *West African Christianity*, xiv, 249.

15. *Encountering the West*, 16, 24.

16. *West African Christianity*, 227; *Translating the Message*, 1, 15, 53, 229.

17. This is the methodology of *Translating the Message*, enlarged in scope in *Encountering the West*.

18. He even extends this model to the interpretation of the presence of Islam in Africa. In this perspective Islam, rejecting African religions as a matter of principle (not always of praxis though), and unwilling to have the Qur'an translated into the vernacular, can be seen as guilty of the deification and then universalisation of the Arabic cultural expression of the faith. *Translating the Message*, 222–7.

19. *West African Christianity*, xvi, 215; *Encountering the West*, particularly 25.

20. *West African Christianity*, 244.

21. *Encountering the West*, 26, 31, 235.

22. *Translating the Message*, 233, also 31. In *Encountering the West* (141) the formula is 'the precious jewel of God's impartiality towards all peoples and cultures'.

23. *Translating the Message*, 83.

24. *Ibid.*, 32.

25. Cf. *Ibid.*, Introduction.

26. The definition of Jesus Christ given in *Translating the Message* (158) is accordingly 'soft': 'the historical and personal manifestation of God's power'.

27. *Translating the Message*, 30, 48, 51, 83.

28. I. Berlin, *Vico and Herder: Two Studies in the History of Ideas* (London, 1980), 215.

29. 'Enlightenment, postmodernity and mission', in T. Foust, G. Hunsberger, A. Kirk and W. Ustorf (eds.), *A Scandalous Prophet: The Way of Mission after Newbigin* (Grand Rapids, MI, 2002), 145–52, here 150.

Index of people and places

Aaron 166
Abélard (and Héloise) 146
Africa 10, 219, 220, 223, 224
    African factor in Christian history 221
    compared to the west 220, Europe 220,
        North America 220
Agulhon, Maurice 151
Ambrose, church father 175
America, the Americas 1, 219
America, North 6, 34, 39, 50, 101, 107, 109,
    169, 178
    compared to Africa 220
    Piety 204
    and urban religion 203
America, South 34, 105
Amsterdam 203
Angers 150
Anglo-Saxon countries 171
Anjou 149
Antoine l'Empereur 113
Antwerp 113
Aquinas, Thomas 176
Ariès, Philippe 147, 158
Aristotle 176
Armagh 101, 108
Asia 10, 219
Asia, East 16
Asmussen, Hans 136
Assisi, St Francis of 157
Augsburg 5
Augustine, church father 115, 176
Australasia 101, 107
Austria 6, 69, 116, 193

Babel 220
Bad Boll 133
Badone, Ellen 156
Bainbridge, W. S. 203
Baltimore 173
Bamford, Samuel 86
Barbey d'Aurevilly 169
Barmen Theological Declaration 133, 134

Barret, David B. 219, 220
Barth, Karl 131, 132, 133, 139, 188
Basque Country 3, 107
Bavaria 131
Beccaria, Cesare 7
Becker, Annette 155
Beckford, Jim 77
Belgium 4, 9, 116, 117, 163
Bell, Daniel 205
Bellah, Robert 66, 73
Bentham, Jeremy 7
Berger, Peter 14
Bergey, abbé 155
Bergson, Henri 163
Berlin 7, 12, 30, 131, 203, 211
Berlin, Isaiah 81, 223
Birmingham (UK) 220
Bismarck, Otto von 138
Blaschke, Olaf 18
Bloy 177
Boers (and Protestantism) 121
Bonaventure 176
Bontoux, P. B. F. 149
Bossy, John 103
Boullée, Etienne-Louis 148
Bowen, Desmond 104
Branly 165
Britain 2, 4, 5, 12, 13, 19, 20, 29, 37, 82, 89,
    103, 108, 109, 121, 131, 163, 223
    mission work, compared to that of the US
        212
    compared to the Netherlands 124
    and religions 30, 31, 34
    religious authority, compared to the US 207
    and religious knowledge 86
    and secularisation 37, 38
    social influence of churches 212, compared
        to the US 213
    and statistics 43
British Empire 10, 107
Brittany 3, 74, 107, 156, 165, 171
    and its changing culture 156

Subject index

abortion 4, 108–9, 113
'alternative' spiritualities 17, 18, 25, 30, 33, 35, 49, 63, 67
Anglicans 4, 5–6, 32, 33, 81–93, 112, 212–13
animals 53
anti-clericalism 9, 13, 17, 99, 103, 107, 151, 153, 154, 172
anti-Communism 130–1, 135, 138
anti-Semitism 121
anti-Socialism 136–7
aristocracy 5, 7, 8, 13, 16
atheists 7, 16, 40, 67, 70, 150, 194–5, 204
auto-spirituality 67, 72, 75
axial age 64, 65, 66, 76

baptism 2–3, 4, 11, 12, 31–2, 33, 34, 114, 151
Baptists 6, 33
Bible 13, 47, 70, 86, 87, 166, 175, 220, 221
books 7, 86–7, 165
bourgeoisie, see middle class

catechisms 85, 87, 103, 124
Catholics 2, 3, 5–6, 8, 11, 34, 185, 188
  in Britain 4, 34, 82, 83
  Catholic Association 99
  First Vatican Council 102
  in France 9–10, 11–12, 19, 25, 145, 163
  Gallican 102, 165
  in Germany 9–10, 131, 191, 193
  in Ireland 91, 99–110
  in Italy 4
  Jansenist 102, 148
  Liberal 172
  in Netherlands 114–25
  in Poland 193
  Second Vatican Council 19, 68, 75, 109
  in Spain 9–10
  in Sweden 49
  Ultramontane 102, 103, 165, 172, 174
censorship 4, 6, 7

charity, see welfare
childhood 34
Christendom 1–2, 4–21, 113, 131, 132–41, 218
Christian belief 3, 13, 17, 41, 47–9, 52, 53–4, 76
Christian culture 29–30, 35–6
Christian Democratic Union (Germany) 131
Christian identity 2, 3, 10, 50, 51, 223
Christianity and culture 130, 140–1, 221–4
church architecture 167
church building 17, 104, 105, 211, 213
church courts 82, 85
Church Fathers 175–6
church-going 3, 12–13, 18, 31, 34, 35, 41, 42, 47–8, 52, 56–9, 69, 76, 82, 83, 87, 99, 100, 102, 114, 123, 125, 204
church history 36, 119
church lighting 167–9
church membership 33–4, 41, 42, 49–51, 56
Church of Ireland 108
Church of Scotland 32, 33, 87, 90
Church of Sweden 49–51, 56–9
church–state relations 4, 5, 107–9, 114
  separation of church and state 5, 8–11, 57, 104, 116, 119
  union of church and state 8–11
civil registration 11
civil religion 50, 115–16, 120, 149, 158
clergy 9, 10, 12, 13, 16, 40, 65
  in Britain 18, 43, 81, 82
  chaplains 10–11, 137
  in France 7, 8, 145, 148, 149, 150–8, 163, 164, 165, 177
  in Germany 191
  in Ireland 99, 100, 101, 103, 107, 109
  in Netherlands 113, 115, 116, 117, 119, 120
  in Spain 9
coercion, religious 57, 82–3, 209–10, 218
communion 7, 11, 33, 57, 75, 83
Communists 5, 11–12, 68, 139, 156–7